Prodigals

CRUX
THE GEORGIA SERIES IN LITERARY NONFICTION

Prodigals

A Sister's Memoir of Appalachia and Loss

Sarah Beth Childers

The University of Georgia Press
Athens

Published by the University of Georgia Press
Athens, Georgia 30602
www.ugapress.org

Designed by Mary McKeon
Printed and bound by Sheridan Books

The paper in this book meets the guidelines for permanence and durability of the Committee on Production Guidelines for Book Longevity of the Council on Library Resources.

Most University of Georgia Press titles are available from popular e-book vendors.

Printed in the United States of America

27 26 25 24 23 P 5 4 3 2 1

Library of Congress Control Number: 2023940465
ISBN 9780820364636 (paperback)
ISBN 9780820364643 (ebook: epub)
ISBN 9780820364650 (ebook: pdf)

For my Smoo

CONTENTS

ACKNOWLEDGMENTS

Thank you to the Jentel Artist Residency, the Wildacres Residency, and the Hargis Fellowship through Oklahoma State University's Doel Reed Center for the Arts. I am grateful for the time, space, and financial support you gave me to write this book. Thank you also to Colgate University for the Olive B. O'Connor Fellowship and a travel grant for my first trip to Brontë Country. Thank you to Oklahoma State University's College of Arts and Sciences and Department of English for the grants and leave I needed to go back to the UK and to finish writing.

Thank you to my sister Rebecca, who reads everything, again and again, with a kind and critical eye. I'm not sure what writing would look like without you. Thank you also to the rest of my family—especially my parents, my sister Jennifer, and my grandpa for your love and support. Grandpa, when you said you didn't agree with everything I wrote, but you knew why I wrote it for the feeling it gave me, I knew you understood.

Thank you to Kevin Oderman and Sara Pritchard for years of friendship and support for my writing and teaching, and for being what feels like writing family.

Thank you to Jennifer Brice, who has influenced both of my essay collections with her astute comments and titling advice.

Thank you to the editors and reviewers at Crux for believing in this project and pushing me to tighten. Thank you to Ann Marlowe for allowing me to see this project through your fresh, meticulous eyes. This project wouldn't have been the same book without any of you, and I'm grateful.

Thank you to my writer friends, including Tyler Mills, who read, listened, and talked me through a horrible writing patch, and Hannah

Saltmarsh, Christina Turner, Janine Joseph, Ann Claycomb, Lori D'Angelo, Charity Gingerich, and Jessie Van Eerden.

Thank you to my students and colleagues at OSU, especially the creative writing program, Kate Hallemeier, and Lindsey Smith.

Thank you to Kashion Livsey for your mom friendship and love of words.

Thank you to Robert for reading, for coparenting so well that I could continue writing seriously after becoming a mama, for supporting me when I need to leave you for a while to write. Thank you to the rest of the Denyer-Hadaway-Copens family for letting me write at the Pawnee farm. Thank you to Ann for Lydia help and food.

Thank you to my daughter Lydia, my little girl with golden hair. Your fervent joy in riding in wagons, petting goats, and eating green ice cream reminds me of why I write. Thank you to my baby Miriam. In our three months together, you've brightened my life with your smiles, your "agoo," and the way you wrap your arm around my back when I hold you. The news that you were coming gave me the writing push I needed.

Thank you most of all to my brother Joshua, for your generous gift to Rebecca and me, telling us that we could write about you as long as you never had to see it. I love you even more than when I lost you, and I am looking forward to seeing you again.

The following essays previously appeared in literary journals or anthologies: "Smoo: An *Oxford English Dictionary* Definition" in *Blue Earth Review*, "Beagle in the Road" in *Superstition Review*, "A Hobo Like Me" in *Quiddity*, "Candy Crane" in *Sweet: A Literary Confection*, "Beaver Pond" in the collection *Mountains Piled Upon Mountains: Appalachian Nature Writing in the Anthropocene* edited by Jessica Cory (West Virginia University Press, 2019), "Things Sad People Shouldn't Have" in *PANK*, "Chariot's Comin'" in *Gravel*, "What Happens When You Drown" in *Brevity*, and "An Infestation" in *Colorado Review*. The "Lost Photographs" section in part 6 appeared in a slightly different form as "Portraits Within Portraits" in *Guernica Daily*. A substantial portion of the piece titled "Returning Cats," and various tiny fragments throughout the book, appeared in my essay "A Haunting" in *Shenandoah*.

Prodigals

Smoo: An *Oxford English Dictionary* Definition

Smoo, *n.*
Pronunciation: /smu/
Etymology: English SMALL, *adj*, via Germanic. Of limited size; of comparatively restricted dimensions; not large in comparison with other things. Origin when Joshua David Childers (1990–2012) weighed nine pounds, nine ounces, and his parents boasted about his size on the hospital phone. Eight-year-old Sarah Beth Childers worried on the ride to the hospital that her brother would be monstrous compared with Jennifer and Rebecca, her previous baby siblings, but she found an ordinary newborn who fit in her lap and arms. To correct her parents' idiocy, she called him SMALL. Change in form from SMALL to SMOO when Joshua David Childers lost the toddler's wobble in his walk and his hair transformed from blond curls to brown waves.
U.S. Regional (Huntington, West Virginia).

1. A charmer of diminutive size; a youngest brother beloved by his older sisters.
   - 1990 S. Childers *A finger in dust on a bookshelf.* Small is cute.
   - 1992 S. Childers *Birthday poem.* Small's not tall / he's the best of all!
   - 1995 Jen. Childers *Song, belted for hours on road trips.* How ya doing, Smoo? How are you? Are you feeling fine? Are you on the dime? How are you, Smoo? How are you?
   - 1996 S. Childers *Gel ink letter to a friend.* My Smoo just came in here with his underwear on his head.
   - 2009 S. Childers and Jos. Childers *Conversation.* S. Childers: Hey Smoo, can you hear the difference if we call you "Joshua" or "Smoo"? Jos. Childers: I can't even tell you which one you said.
2. A lazy, messy person whose laziness and messiness are charming.
   - 1997 Jos. Childers *Letter to Mrs. Kern, his first-grade teacher, on the topic*

"What do you do to help your mother around the house?" Dear Mr. Kenrn, I just be lazy. Love, Joshua. [Note: Here Joshua David Childers wrote *Joshua* because of school requirements, and here *Joshua* means *Smoo.*]

2010 S. Childers *Conversation with M. Childers, her mother.* Smoo's room is just full of smelly laundry, and I told him I'd wash anything he gave me. He threw a pair of Tasmanian Devil boxers into the hall.

3. A person who makes guilt-inducing requests through insinuation.

1996 Jos. Childers and S. Childers *Conversation.* Jos. Childers: Hey Sarbef, I have a great idea. Why don't I sing, and my sisters can record it on a tape? S. Childers: Okay, Smoo!

2011 Jos. Childers and S. Childers *Conversation.* Jos. Childers: Hey Sarbef, I've been watching movies by myself all month. I'd like to watch one with somebody so I could watch their reaction and, you know, have a fresh experience. S. Childers: Okay, Smoo.

4. A pompous artist and aficionado.

1998 Jos. Childers and Jen. Childers *Orders during a choral sibling recording of a song he wrote and sister response.* Jos. Childers: Jennifer, you sounded bad again! Rebecca will do the solo. Go do something else while we sing it right. Jen. Childers: Gosh! Smoo!

2010 S. Childers *Gchat conversation with R. Childers.* Smoo said he listens to all sorts of music to "keep his palate" something.

2011 Jos. Childers and S. Childers *Conversation.* S. Childers: Hey Smoo, you have to read *Hamlet*? Where are you in the play? Jos. Childers: Shakespeare is overrated.

5. An irresponsible person whose family enables his irresponsibility until the enabling becomes exhausting and difficult to escape.

2001 S. Childers *Spoken directions for fourth grade social studies report, after Joshua David Childers has sat at the kitchen table for an hour and drawn a stick man on the page.* Smoo, I'm going to go eat lunch. When I come back, you need to have two sentences.

2001 S. Childers *Spoken directions for fourth grade assignment, after she returns to find a hat and mustache on the stick man.* You are such a Smoo. All right, I'll sit over here and tell you what to say, and you have to be the one to write it down.

2004 M. Childers *Conversation with S. Childers.* This morning, I was dropping Smoo off at school, and he told Rebecca, "Get out faster and hand me my book bag. You're making me late for prayer!" I said, Lord forgive me, I've raised a brat.

2012 S. Childers *"Smoo's Schedule," Aug. 8 email to M. Childers, in which she discusses impersonating Joshua David Childers in email conversations with his community college professor.* That will show that Smoo actually respects his opinion (or our imaginary Smoo who is mature enough to write these emails).

6. A person who habitually goes astray.

   2011 S. Childers *"Re: (no subject)," Feb. 14 email to M. Childers, after Joshua David Childers has disappeared, yet again, from his parents' house for three days.* I hope Smoo came home.

7. Joshua David Childers (1990–2012), after he left his blackening body in his closet for his mother to find it.

   2012 S. Childers *Accidentally rude statement to her grandmother at Christmas.* Now that Smoo's dead you don't need to make all that fudge.

Smoo, *n.*

Pronunciation: /smu:/

Etymology: Old Norse SMUGA, *n.*, a hiding place; a narrow cleft to creep through; a hole.

Sea and freshwater cave in northwest Scotland, site of 18th-century murders. Ancient Norse entrance to the underworld.

c. 2010 *Smoo Cave official website.* Drive about half a mile out of Durness on the road to Tongue, until you see a sign for Smoo Cave.

2017 S. Childers *Notes for an essay.* When I walked into Smoo Cave alone at 10 p.m., I felt the joy of when I was little and Smoo was new.

smoo, *v.*

Pronunciation: /smu/

Etymology: English SMOO, *n*, sense 3.

intransitive. To make an insinuated, guilt-inducing request resembling such requests made by Joshua David Childers.

1999 S. Childers *Conversation with R. Childers and Jos. Childers.* I smooed and smooed that we wanted pizza for dinner, then I smelled that weird spice Daddy puts on the chicken.

2020 Jen. Childers *Conversation with S. Childers.* My cat smooed all night for me to let him out.

PART 1
THE PRODIGAL AT HOME

There's a photograph of me at three years old, hugging Scruffy, a twenty-pound mutt with fur that matched his name. One of my parents took the photo during the odd, brief time I was an only child: one month before the first of my two sisters was born, five years before the beginning of the twenty-two years, two months, and two weeks I'd have a brother named Joshua. The yard slopes up behind Scruffy and me, dead grass patched with snow, and my faux fur coat mixes with dog fur. Scruffy's tethered to a stainless steel stakeout, next to a blue plastic doghouse.

I only had Scruffy for a few months. I mention him now because I thought of him eighteen years later, during the spring and summer when my thirteen-year-old brother often disappeared from the house, from the neighborhood, walking for miles along the garbage-strewn roads outside of Huntington, West Virginia, up and down the Appalachian foothills. I thought of Scruffy again when my brother died.

In the Gospel of Luke, Jesus tells the parable of the Prodigal Son, the guy who asks his wealthy father to give him his inheritance now. His father hands it over. The Prodigal journeys to a "far country," blows everything on "riotous living," takes a job feeding pigs, nearly starves. The Prodigal "comes to himself," remembers his father's "hired servants" have plenty to eat. The Prodigal crawls home, ready to beg for a job, finds out his father has been watching the road. His father hugs him, slaughters the "fatted calf." The Prodigal's older brother whines. He's never left home, never wasted a cent, and no one has ever given him a party. Now they're celebrating this loser who "devoured" his father's life savings "with harlots." The father shames the whiny older son: "Thy brother was dead, and is alive again."

The quoted phrases in my parable retelling come from the King James Version of the Bible, completed in 1611. I adore its vocabulary and rhythms. But really I'm using that version because I grew up in a fundamentalist Christian home, attending at least three services a week at fundamentalist churches. I read to tatters a giant-print KJV, its blue leather cover etched with my name.

Joshua shouted, "Boy, we're poor!" at our parents from the time he was five, stamping our child-matted shag carpet, disappointed our parents couldn't hit the mall that evening for a new computer, a DVD player, new video games. Still, when Joshua was a child, he was happy to live in our house, with our family. There is a photograph of Joshua at six years old, standing with his three older sisters in our snowy backyard. Eight windburned cheeks, four running noses, the blue four-child sled our dad crafted from an iodine barrel he'd brought home from the pharmaceutical plant. The same material he used for Scruffy's doghouse.

My current dog, Peggotty, sleeps under my bedsheets, stretched next to my leg, but when I look at Scruffy's picture, I don't pity him. In all my memories of Scruffy, he's slipped his collar or broken his chain.

Like Scruffy, Joshua left us and left us, until he left us for good.

But let's start at the beginning, when the Prodigal lives in his father's house, twitchy and restless. His father has the money to travel the world, but he stays home, watching calves drop damp from their mothers, watching hired servants magic sheep's milk into cheese. The Prodigal stands to inherit part of that growing horde, but his joints will ache, his neck will hang loose under a gray beard by the time that healthy old man dies. The Prodigal wants to meet women, to use his young body. He wants to have city friends and glug wine like a king.

PaPa's Bed

When I was eight years old, PaPa, my mom's father, bought a new bed. Queen-size, with a control attached to a cord. One button raised the top half when his children and grandchildren came to visit, and another button lifted the bottom when he felt an ache in his phantom limb.

Eleven years before, PaPa had lost his left leg to a botched congestive heart failure procedure, and the surgeons had sent him home to die. But he hadn't died. He'd strapped on a prosthesis and walked his daughter down the aisle. He'd picked me up from kindergarten with a bucket of spaghetti and a package of Oreos. He'd bought a VHS camcorder the first day they were available and videotaped his granddaughters in the backyard.

"Play hide and seek with us!" I wheedle to PaPa on the tape.

"Oh, darlin'," he says from behind the camera, "I can't run anymore." He throws tears into his West Virginia accent for drama, but it's obvious he's happy. The camera follows me as I cavort across the lawn in my pink shorts, three-year-old Jennifer as she hugs the beagle.

Two years after that video, PaPa put away his camcorder, unstrapped his prosthesis, and settled into his new electric bed. His final grandchild was on the way, a boy at long last. He felt strong enough to live until that baby was born, and then he'd be ready to go.

Those months of waiting for my baby brother were hard on eight-year-old me. My mom grew larger, and more tired, than in her pregnancies with Jennifer and Rebecca, and PaPa grew smaller every day. During my short life, PaPa had never resembled the fried-chicken-loving father in my mom's childhood albums, but now his body seemed to be journeying to heaven a pound at a time, leaving his spirit on earth.

Once, on a PaPa visit, I bounced ahead up the stairs. "We're here to see you, PaPa!" I announced as I burst into his bedroom. I figured I'd have him to myself for a minute.

I didn't. Anita, PaPa's sister who nursed him, was in there already, and I'd interrupted PaPa's bath. He sat on his bed, white T-shirt off, his white briefs loose around his hairless stump, arms lifted so Anita could scrub him with a rag. Anita had told my mother, "Ralph's armpits look like caverns," and now I saw them for myself. I was afraid I'd peer into a hollow armpit and see PaPa's congested heart. I cried alone in the hall until my mom and sisters made it up the stairs.

When PaPa had his shirt on and a bedspread over his stump, Anita called us into the room. I sat next to my grandfather, on top of his rumpled bedspread, and leaned against the bed's raised head.

"I love you, PaPa," I told him.

"I love *you*, doll," he said, gripping my hand.

"I *love* you, PaPa."

My love was the only medicine I had.

⁂

Joshua was born on Father's Day, and my mother called her father on the birthing room phone the first moment she was able. "It's a boy," she breathed, stroking her baby's bald scalp. During the phone call, my dad napped in a nearby chair. I sat on the edge of the bed with my sisters, inches from newborn skin. "Nine pounds, nine ounces," my mom said. "My Joshua David."

PaPa chuckled into his phone, an impossible seven-minute drive away. "Nine-nine," he gloated. "What do you know about that?" The last time my mom had given birth, just two and a half years earlier, PaPa had shown up with his camcorder, and he'd lined up a date with a new grandmother in the windowed hallway outside the neonatal ward. Now PaPa's sister helped him crawl to his potty chair, but his grandson was born, and PaPa was still alive.

"Joshua David, huh?" he continued. "That's a prissy name. You'll call *that* boy J.D." PaPa had taken the sex and weight and conjured up a whole life for this grandson he'd only see as a baby. Peewee football helmets, high school football helmets. A sexy prom date, a powerful job, a pregnant wife.

"J.D. my foot," my mom said, smiling. She took Joshua to visit PaPa two days later.

As we tromped up the stairs with our baby, I heard Anita through PaPa's open door. "Ralph, we've got to sit you up, honey. Somebody new is here to see you." I heard the buzz of the electric bed.

Because of the bathing incident, I knocked on the doorframe and waited for Anita's "Come on in, sweetie." But that didn't stop PaPa from vomiting into a plastic cup as I crept into the room.

"It's just clear fluid," PaPa soothed me when I cringed. My mom plopped Joshua next to her father and stood by the bed, asking Aunt Anita worried questions about the vomiting. I sat on the bed by PaPa and played with my brother's toes.

"Well, hello," PaPa cooed, wrapping an emaciated arm around his grandson. He straightened Joshua's embroidered yellow shirt, then he unpinned the cloth diaper and peered inside. I was mystified, but my mom knew what her father was doing. He needed to know if Joshua had been circumcised. PaPa's masculinity had gotten chipped away by overseas combat, two divorces, and heart failure. His grandson needed to start off his life with every centimeter of manhood he could get.

Joshua's tiny foreskin was still where God put it, and PaPa sighed with pride and relief. "That's my J.D.," he said.

I stood up and balled my fists. I yelled, "J.D. my foot!"

PaPa buzzed the head of his bed higher and grinned.

❦

Three months later, Anita called my mother in the morning. "Marcy? I just went up to check on Ralph, and I think he's dead."

"You *think* he's dead?" My mom wasn't buying it. I huddled closer to her shoulder in the kitchen.

"Oh, Marcy, he's dead."

PaPa had woken in the night, pulled his white T-shirt halfway off, and ridden that bed into the sky.

My grandfather's body went under a veteran's headstone at Ridgelawn Memorial Park, and his bed found a new home in the room I shared with Jennifer. Previously the two of us had slept together in a decades-old full-size that spouted orange spores when we jumped. I felt ecstatic when my dad and uncle dragged that old mattress and frame out of the house, on their way to the dump.

After the new bed was in the old bed's place, bare of sheets, empty of PaPa, my sisters and I stared at it reverently for a few minutes. Then I remembered the bed had an electrical cord. I plugged it in next to my reading lamp, and the three of us rode either end up and down, put both ends up and squished ourselves together in the middle, turned on the vibrate function and belted hymns. Eventually our mother appeared with sheets and shooed us into the hallway.

Sleeping in that bed, I sometimes dreamed of PaPa. The doorbell rang, and PaPa stood on the porch. He wore a hat with a red and brown feather, and he'd concealed his prosthesis with loafers and tweed. "I'm back, doll," PaPa said. After those dreams I woke up sobbing, crying harder than I had when he died. My mom had me sit in the blue recliner, another inheritance from PaPa's bedroom, and handed me baby Joshua. I stared at my brother and kissed his cheeks until my grief pains melted away.

A year after PaPa died, my best friend spent the night at our house. Carrie was a skinny girl with a poodle perm, marbles with names, a plan for her wedding, and a home life I couldn't understand. Jennifer joined Rebecca in her twin bed down the hall, so Carrie could sleep next to me.

Carrie and I read a chapter or two of our chapter books, then I rolled toward her and raised my eyebrows. "I've got a secret," I whispered, and she put down her book and tucked the sheets under her chin.

"Okay, you've got to tell me." From the look on her face, I could tell Carrie was expecting a story about her crush, or perhaps the boy I'd hurled a pencil at in daycare.

I lowered my voice still further. "My PaPa died in this bed."

Carrie jumped out of the bed like she'd seen a rattlesnake, gripping the top sheet in her hands. She looked frantically around the room, like she expected an appearance from a one-legged, elderly ghost. I laughed and laughed, flopping around in the empty space Carrie had left behind.

With a nine-year-old's egotism, I felt I knew something Carrie didn't: joy and heartbreak can strike together. A new baby brother and a dying PaPa. A dead PaPa and a nearly new queen-size bed. A creepy joke I could tell at sleepovers and visits from PaPa in my dreams.

Herbie

THE LOVE BUG

At two, Joshua watched and rewatched a VHS of *The Love Bug*, the 1968 Disney comedy about a sentient Volkswagen Beetle. Herbie wins the hearts of his drivers and a race by bouncing across ponds and zooming down mountain roads.

The movie created a loneliness in Joshua, a need for a friend who honked and flapped his wipers when he got angry, who squirted oil on a bad guy's boot. And the movie gave him an urge to cruise on winding asphalt. He'd seen a shelf of Herbies in Kmart: Little Tikes Cozy Coupes with rounded Beetle-like tops and plastic headlights that looked like they could wink at him.

Early one summer morning, when my sisters and I were still asleep, my mom looked away from Joshua for a moment, and he disappeared. My mom ran first to the stove—once before, she'd found him with his diaper on a burner, playing with the knobs—then she checked the bathroom, since parenting books advised that out-of-sight children were likely face down in the toilet. She checked the closets, the cabinets, under the beds; she shooed Kassie out of her doghouse so she could peer inside. Frantic, about to call her husband and the police, my mom took a walk down the road. She spotted a Cozy Coupe meandering around a neighbor's house. Joshua was at the wheel, powering the car like Fred Flintstone with his feet.

Joshua must have spotted the toy car on a walk around Twin Valley, our neighborhood, and waited for an opportunity like this. He screeched when his mother tugged him out of the driver's seat. "Me drive the Herbie!" He'd felt the wind rush past the glassless windows. He'd driven a car that was alive. My parents knew they'd lose their toddler to the neighbor's yard, so they scraped up the money and went to Kmart. My sisters and I had whimpered for battery-powered Barbie Jeeps to no avail, but we didn't begrudge our brother his Herbie.

Over the next few years, Herbie's black wheels turned a dusty gray, and Joshua built calluses on his toes. Joshua zoomed up and down the hall, rattled across the wooden deck, hurtled down the backyard hill and slammed into the house. He reached fifteen miles per hour downhill on the steep Twin Valley roads when he could get his sisters to push him. I grabbed the back, Jennifer and Rebecca each clung to a side, and we flew in a crumbled asphalt cloud.

Years later, after my share of an insurance settlement from a family car wreck allowed me to purchase a car for college, I chose a Volkswagen New Beetle, imagining I'd someday see Joshua back behind the wheel of a Herbie. But he never showed any interest in driving. When Joshua was a teen and young adult, his friends drove themselves to school, to music festivals, to Mexico in their parents' cast-off sedans. Joshua caught a ride, or, more often, stuck with destinations he could reach on foot. I wonder if he expended a lifetime of driving passion coasting in his Cozy Coupe, with no window glass between himself and the sun.

HERBIE RIDES AGAIN

After my dad's rusty work car got towed away, my mom had to drive him to work and pick him up. Some evenings, we all wove through the farmland and trailer parks to Prichard, West Virginia, but often my sisters and I stayed at home, pretending our inflatable pool was a Barbie-sized lake or reenacting the book of Genesis with paper dolls. Four-year-old Joshua rode along to Prichard every day, hoping the car would need gas and he'd get a candy bar, or our dad would emerge from the pharmaceutical plant with a can of grape pop.

One day when my mom left for Prichard, Joshua lay asleep on the couch, its cushions turned cracked-vinyl side down, cheap-cloth underside up, so it wouldn't be too sweaty to use. Every time my mom left the house, she had to wrangle Joshua into his tennis shoes and car seat, and she was running late already. She put me in charge of my brother and backed down the gravel driveway as quietly as she could.

It took forty-five minutes to get to Prichard and back, and Joshua snoozed on the couch for thirty-five. But those final minutes were desolate. Joshua buried his face in the carpet, flailed his limbs, and sobbed.

How could Mama forget him? He went with her every day. How could Mama forget her own son?

With three minutes to wait, Joshua stopped crying. He got up and wiped his nose. He found his *own shoes*—maybe he'd done this once, when he wanted to go sledding—and shoved them, still tied, on his feet. With the face of a man who'd decided to walk across the United States, he declared, "I'm going wif Mama."

My sisters and I quivered with excitement. We wondered how far he would take this. We followed him out to the deck, where he pushed his car down the wooden steps with a thunderous grunt, showing us how hard he was working. Normally I carried Herbie down those steps, but I could tell that this time only, Joshua would be offended if I didn't let him move the car on his own.

The steps conquered, Joshua pushed Herbie to the top of our steep driveway and aimed him toward the road. Surely our brother would push the car down the driveway. Surely Joshua had learned from the time Herbie had attempted a somersault halfway down the forty-five-degree hill, giving his driver a cheek full of gravel. But no, Joshua opened the red plastic door at the top of the driveway and settled himself in the seat. I ran, barefoot, and caught Herbie without speaking. I held on to Herbie's top and steered my brother down the driveway, ignoring the rocks that bit into my feet. Then I ran inside and watched with my sisters at the living room window.

A red and yellow spot down on the pavement, Herbie rolled away from the dead end, past our rusty brown mailbox, past the front yard the neighbors used as a parking lot, past another neighbor's wooden fence, past a litter of Chihuahua mix puppies. Herbie stuttered up a low hill, and we couldn't see our brother from the window.

With Joshua out of sight, I imagined him making the blind left turn out of the subdivision and down the hill, past Clay's, the gas station store where we bought bananas and milk. He turned right, toward Prichard, onto Docks Creek Road. On the Tolsia Highway, he hit sixty miles per hour, so fast the coal trucks didn't tailgate him. I imagined my out-of-sight brother then the way I sometimes imagine him now. He curses in Manhattan and Chicago traffic, cruises over the Rockies and down the Pacific coast in a 1960s Beetle he bought for a song.

I let Joshua drive unsupervised for thirty seconds, long enough to pass one mailbox at Herbie's uphill pace. Then I tugged on my shoes, ready to turn my brother around before the situation got dangerous. As I jogged outside, my sisters following behind me, the family minivan pulled up the driveway. My dad was at the wheel, like always on the trip home, and Joshua was crunching M&Ms in his booster seat. My mom must have bought them for Joshua on the way home as an apology for leaving him behind.

My dad lifted Joshua from his booster seat, then Herbie from the trunk. "I did it, my sisters!" Joshua yelled. "I went wif Mama!"

"Joshua drove all the way to Prichard," my dad said, his voice grand. It really seemed like he'd done it. He was so happy, my parents didn't mention my horrible babysitting. After my dad set Joshua down on the deck, next to his car, Joshua patted Herbie's roof. He screwed open the plastic fuel cap and used a forgotten Styrofoam cup to pour in water from the pool, replacing the gas he'd expended on the drive.

Beagle in the Road

I'm thirteen years old in the West Virginia summer and my beagle has bolted out the kitchen door. Kassie's fat but young, nearly impossible to catch: she runs faster at the sound of her name. Barefoot on the concrete steps, I yell anyway—"Kassie!"—and watch her speckled white legs pump harder under her lozenge-shaped body, skidding on the left turn from our driveway onto the one-lane asphalt.

Kassie always turns left out of the driveway when she escapes, even when she ends up to the right of our house, in the woods at the end of our dead-end street, or in the cow pasture that lies straight ahead beyond a few dozen three-bedroom houses, or straight back, behind our backyard, down a ravine to Twelve Pole Creek. She follows the path our family car takes when we load up and disappear for hours or a whole day, leaving her to watch from her backyard tether. Left leads out of Twin Valley to my piano teacher's studio, to my grandparents' pool, to the Cincinnati Zoo. With a left turn, Kassie could go anywhere.

Normally I let Kassie explore on her own when she escapes, settling on the child-stained couch with a book while my mom calls down the driveway, "Have a good one, honey," and slams the door. But this time I put on my flip-flops and run. This time it's my fault—Kassie burst out when I came in with the mail—and I need a break from Nancy Drew. I might as well witness a day in the life of a loose beagle.

Kassie trots ahead of me, copper nose on the ground, white-tipped tail up like a flag. Now that she's made her customary left turn, she prefers a path across our neighbors' hilly front yards. Every few feet, she stops and looks down at me over her shoulder, my tangled blond hair and my flip-flops flapping across the asphalt. She's making sure I'm too far back to grab her collar, and she's making sure I'm still there. Satisfied, she puts her nose back on the trail: a raccoon, an opossum, a neighbor dog, a kid with an interesting sandwich. She reaches an unmown vacant lot and trots with the confidence of her British beagle ancestors, tail tip bouncing above the weeds.

I'm happy too. Today I'm Kassie's chosen companion instead of a weight on the other end of a leash, restraining her movements most painfully on garbage day. I don't normally feel close to this dog. For Kassie, I'm the girl who buries her mother's under-seasoned chicken dinners in the dog food bowl, who closes the door too slowly when she gets the mail. I'm jealous of my cousins' genuine friendship with their golden retriever. But today I understand why my dad stopped the car at a hand-painted road sign that advertised baby Kassie: "Beagle—gun dog for sale." I understand what he felt as a child when he spent afternoons with Bud, his thirty-years-ago beagle, along the Ohio River. My dad caught dragonflies and fished for bluegill, and Bud disappeared into the woods along the riverbank, reappearing when the scent trail led out of the woods, when he needed to make sure his boy was still there.

Kassie emerges from the other side of the vacant lot, and she has a choice to make. She can turn left, over the neighbor-yard hill into woods and, later, a horse pasture; she can turn right, down a quiet neighborhood road with a dozen more houses, trash cans, neighbor dogs, and cars with dog-pee-scented tires; or she can head straight, toward the blind turn onto Walker's Branch, the winding road drivers take at fifty miles per hour despite blind spots every fifteen hundred feet. People only walk Walker's Branch when their cars break down, and they pray every moment they're walking. Kassie heads straight, faster now, the trail's getting fresher. Five hundred feet from Walker's Branch. I follow, screaming her name, scuffing my toes on the road.

As I run at my top P.E.-class speed, chasing after this twenty-five-pound hound that's trotting merrily toward an intersection, I've forgotten the happy Bud stories my dad tells me when we walk Kassie by the Ohio River. Now I'm imagining Bud's awful end. When my dad was thirteen, exactly my age, his family moved away from the river to a house with a fenced-in backyard. Never again would Bud mope in a concrete-lined, roofed pen until my dad came home from school. He'd bark at cottontails, dig up flowerbeds, nap in the sun. But the day after the move, Bud escaped. Maybe someone left the gate open, or maybe Bud dug under the fence. This much is sure: Bud nosed a trail out of the neighborhood onto a busy road, under the wheels of a delivery truck. I think of my dad's grimace as he tells the story. I imagine him running to his broken dog. I imagine him sitting with Bud during the final minutes he could breathe.

I keep hoping Kassie will turn around, back into our land of tricycles and parked cars, hoping whatever she's tracking turned back into Twin Valley hours before. But she trots on, past the penultimate house, the last house, the Twin Valley sign, to the end of her trail. Kassie sees her quarry before I do, and she smells it before she sees it. Early this morning, an opossum must have moseyed across our neighborhood and met his maker on Walker's Branch. Kassie claims a tracker's prize: a roll in opossum innards, belly up, in front of the worst blind spot on the road.

No cars are coming right now, but I know this could change any second. To the right of the Twin Valley entrance, Walker's Branch is relatively flat, and I can see for a few hundred feet. To the left, Walker's Branch disappears down a steep hill, plunging to Clay's. Cars appear out of nowhere at the top of that hill, hitting the gas at the flat spot at the top instead of slowing to check for animals or left-turning minivans. At fifteen, when I'm learning to drive, I'll scream on that turn for weeks. Today, my beagle lies in the path of those magically appearing cars, and I've made a decision. This is NOT the place or time she's going to die.

My dad will not come home from the pharmaceutical plant and bury a squashed beagle under the oak tree. My dad and I will put Kassie on a leash for years and years and walk her around Twin Valley, through state parks, and along the Ohio River. She will die as an old dog in a sunny patch in the backyard. I yell "Kassie!" one more useless time, then I follow her onto Walker's Branch.

No cars are coming right now. I feel like everything except Kassie and me has frozen, that the dragonflies have stopped midair. I crouch and tug on Kassie's grimy blue collar, and she refuses to get up. All four paws in the air, eyes closed in ecstasy, body wriggling in intestines and blood. I stand upright for a couple seconds, so a driver could see me if they happened to appear, then I reach down and drag my beagle by the collar off the opossum, off of Walker's Branch, back into Twin Valley. When we leave the road, time unfreezes, and I hear traffic again on Walker's Branch. Since I have no leash, I have to bend down and walk a quarter mile with my hand on Kassie's collar, until we reach our kitchen. I wet bath towels and wipe her until the intestine smell dies down.

Later that evening, after my dad turns into our intersection, passing only a dead opossum, and after my chicken breast is inside Kassie's stomach, my dad stands up from the kitchen table and asks me to get the leash. "That beagle looks like she could use a walk," he says, and she does. Kassie jumps out of her dog bed and wriggles all over, wagging her bum and belly along with her tail. I'm sure she knows the word *walk*, but she doesn't need that word to know a walk is coming. Something in our movements—in the way I put on my flip-flops, in the way my dad stomps around searching for his ballcap—causes her to bounce and cry until she's leashed and sniffing down the road.

My dad takes the leash, I carry the empty paper lunch sack, and we keep to the roads inside the neighborhood. As I chatter about the books I'm reading, the guppies in the backyard pond, my fears for the first day of school, I stare at Kassie and smile a secret smile. This dog is alive because of me. I'm proud of her wholeness: her unbroken legs that trot next to my daddy, her unburst belly that jiggles with each step, her unbloodied ears that graze the ground as she explores the neighborhood with her nose.

Somehow, though, I keep my pride to myself. As my dad walks down the road, chuckling at my jokes, pointing out bluebirds and chickadees, I can't bring myself to boast about the fact that I boldly risked my life to save the family beagle. I have a feeling he'll miss the story's happy point and get stuck on an image of horrible possibility: his Sarah Beth in the intersection, flip-flops gone, blood on her cotton shorts and blond hair. In my thirteen-year-old mind, dying for a dog feels heroic, but I can't trouble my dad with the idea that he might have had to live on without me. Replacing utterly that memory of smashed Bud with a memory of his smashed little girl.

A Mountain Dry and Good

When Joshua turned six, he decided to become a singer, putting on hold his previous plans to become a magician. Uncle Mark, my dad's younger brother, had given Rebecca a hot pink cassette recorder the previous Christmas, and Joshua commandeered it to record his original songs.

When I got baptized, I got slung like a top. When I got baptized, I got slung like a slingshot.

We a-cided to go to the moon in a homemade rocket.

My job was to push Record and announce the song's title like a radio DJ while Joshua took a deep breath. But occasionally he required backup singing. He stopped before the chorus and yelled, "Now, my sisters, let's sing, all of us!" And we sang.

It couldn't have been hotter! The baptism water!

In a homemade rocket! In a homemade rocket! We went up to the moon in a homemade rocket.

I resurrected a tradition I'd begun when I was a singing six-year-old: I announced a meeting of the arts appreciation group called the Indian Feather Club, in culturally appropriated honor of our distant indigenous roots. Each invited guest received a slip of paper cut from my grandmother's memo pad, inscribed with a hand-drawn feather and the precise time everyone had to be sitting in our grandparents' upstairs living room.

For the main performance I remember, Mark was in town. Thirty-six years old, unmarried, and childless, Mark seemed to have forgotten he was once a little brother himself. He bought Joshua piles of toys, but he had trouble tolerating his company. "Is he always like that?" Mark asked my dad when Joshua whooped and bounced by. I loved Mark but was astounded that anyone could feel anything but ecstatic at the chance to spend time with my Smoo.

Mark was the only adult at the performance. Our parents were out shopping. MaMa, our grandmother, refused to take a ticket because she was making vegetable soup. "Do you all want to eat, or don't you?" she asked. I knew better than to disturb Grandpa while he was mowing the lawn and covertly smoking. But Mark took it easy when he was at his parents' house for the weekend, and he had no excuse. He plopped down in a pink wingback, gray sweat socks stretched in front of him, and Jennifer and Rebecca lounged on the couch, expectant.

I stood next to the coffee table and called the meeting to order. "Tonight at the Indian Feather Club, we have a special treat," I announced, as if there could ever be a different star performer. My sisters and I had hung up our microphones the day Joshua grew old enough to sing. "Let's give a big round of applause to *Joshua Childers*!"

Joshua leaned over and whispered in my ear.

"He'll be singing 'There Was a Mountain Dry and Good'!"

When the applause died down, Joshua sang. In an unnaturally deep voice, styled to imitate Rossano Brazzi's performance of "Some Enchanted Evening," he described the goodness and dryness of the mountain. The grass, the flowers, the perpetual joy of the people who lived there. Then his voice slowed and deepened further. *There was a mountain . . . WET! and BAD!*

A second verse was more than Mark could handle. A six-year-old singing for three full minutes about a dry and good mountain was one thing, but three additional minutes about a wet and bad mountain was clearly another. Mark stood up and clapped his hands, yelling "Yay!" over Joshua's singing until Joshua was silent.

I stood up too, my eyes on Joshua's face. At that time I felt like my main life role was protector of my brother's happiness, encourager of his dreams. I could have blissfully listened to that song all the way through, then enjoyed it fifty more times on a cassette tape. I had no way of knowing that my role of happiness protector would eventually become so difficult, so thankless, that I'd give it up entirely. That I'd wonder if I'd given up the happiness-protecting sooner, encouraged him to learn instead how to deal with life's wetness and badness, he might not have died.

I also couldn't understand that Mark at thirty-six—my age when writing this—might have wished he had something better to do with his weekend than lounging in a chair at his parents' house, watching a performance from his nieces' and nephew's club with a racist name. I didn't know he wished to be married. Perhaps he already drank when he was depressed. Now that Mark and Joshua are buried inches apart—Mark at forty-nine, Joshua at twenty-two—I sometimes marvel that my dad's sad little brother managed to live so well for so long.

I only understood that I could keep my Smoo from crying, remove that distressed look from his face. So I stood up beside Mark, met Joshua's eyes and clapped, and my sisters stood up along with me. How could Joshua cry now? He had a standing ovation. Joshua bowed deeply, and Mark escaped down the stairs.

Curious

In the Appalachian foothills, in a too-small house, up one wooded hill from a cow pasture, a train track, and Twelve Pole Creek, my siblings and I sat on brown shag carpet, writing on a wooden coffee table with finish softened by spilled milk.

In a gray sandstone parsonage, with a front door that opened onto the West Yorkshire village of Haworth and a back door that opened to the windswept, treeless Pennine moors, four children—Charlotte, Branwell, Emily, and Anne Brontë—dipped their pens, bent over tables, beds, and sandstone floors.

Our writing began with play. *Our* meaning all of us. The little Brontës with wax-faced dolls and wooden soldiers, the little Childerses with Cabbage Patch Kids and limbless Little People from Fisher-Price. We played with our characters, became our characters, then wrote. Most of us wrote shamelessly about people and places we didn't understand, and we all shaped our stories from what we saw and read, from our real and imagined lives. Charlotte and Branwell wrote British cities in colonial Africa, based on their imagined version of London. Emily and Anne wrote genii and fairies on the moors outside their back door. I wrote the people who boarded Noah's Ark, and the people who drowned; I wrote teenage Jewish survivors of Nazi Germany. Jennifer wrote Pocahontas-inspired narratives of West Virginia's indigenous peoples and little bears who wouldn't sleep. Rebecca wrote about a fussy king who couldn't wait for holidays to open his wife's presents. Joshua invented hobos, river pirates, and princes, acting out his stories while I wrote them down. I transcribed his storytelling tics—"And, Sarbef?" "You know what?"—no matter how often he asked me to stop.

I bound our stories into books before we wrote them. Took a stack of looseleaf paper and scissors, removed the holes by cutting down the pink line. Folded ten sheets in half, top to bottom, a typing paper cover on the outside. Layered Elmer's glue in each crease, between each sheet. Inked the rising-sun logo of Sunshine Books, our Golden Books knock-off publishing company, on the front cover. Pressed the books between our dad's college chemistry textbooks to create a sturdy spine.

The little Brontës' handmade books were better than ours. In imagination, surely, but I mean in construction: hand-stitched bindings, wallpaper covers, watercolor illustrations, newsprint-like handwriting so minuscule it was illegible to their pastor father and aunt. When, at twenty-eight, I saw one of those one-by-two-inch books under a magnifying glass in the Brontë house, I remembered paper cuts, the way glue dried in dirty balls on my fingers. I felt the pride and insecurity of a fellow craftsman.

There's a persistent romantic image of the Brontës—crafted in the 1857 book *The Life of Charlotte Brontë* by Elizabeth Gaskell, Charlotte's friend after fame and the family's first biographer—that the four Brontë children were childhood geniuses, forged by trauma and isolation. The trauma was real enough: their mother died of cancer when they were little, and then their two older siblings, both girls, died of tuberculosis they caught at a charity school. And they did spend much of their youth at home together in a tiny village surrounded by moors. Patrick, their father, pulled his remaining daughters from the charity school when Charlotte was nine, the new oldest child, and he never intended to send Branwell to school at all. And Patrick didn't socialize. He was studious by nature, and his clerical position kept him poor but too upper-class to mingle with Haworth's millworkers and merchants. Branwell snuck out, Gaskell says, to play with the "lads of the village," but the girls walked the moors or helped with the housework, and all four of them lived deep in their imagined-together worlds, killing off and marrying off each other's characters. Gaskell quotes a letter she received from Charlotte's friend Mary, describing Charlotte at fourteen, when Charlotte was a new student at the school they attended together. "Shy and nervous," "dressed in old-fashioned clothes," speaking with a "strong Irish accent." Charlotte's voice was untouched by Yorkshire: she spoke the way she'd heard her Irish father talk at home.

Still, the young Brontës weren't closed off from the world. In her much more recent biography *The Brontës*, Juliet Barker points out the family's access to books; to art and language instructors; to women's magazines their aunt, who came to live with them, had carried in her suitcase; to lectures on history and science; to concerts in neighboring towns and at the Black Bull, a pub five hundred feet from their front door. Long before Branwell staggered home from the Black Bull after long nights of drinking, Barker believes he performed there on the flute.

There's a persistent romantic image of Appalachia: isolated, uneducated whites fiddling, cursing, hymn-singing, boiling herbs instead of calling a doctor, cooking meth on filthy stoves, roasting whole pigs, talking only to (and, as the joke goes, marrying) their blood relations in hollers tucked between mountains. Like many stereotypes, this image contains but obscures the truth. It erases Appalachian people of color. Like many stereotypes, it blends disgust and pandering admiration.

I fear feeding such stereotypes, and, conversely, I worry what happens to my Appalachian story if I don't fit neatly inside. But here is my story. My siblings and I were isolated as effectively as if we'd lived in a mountain holler, and we weren't cut off from the world. Like the Brontës, we had plenty to read—my mom took us to the library every Saturday—and, like the Brontës, we spent so much time at home. We didn't have friends in our neighborhood because the other kids put on shorts or jeans and cheerfully (as we then imagined) boarded the public school's yellow bus, while we put on knee-length skirts or, in my brother's case, khakis, and climbed into our parents' barely functioning car for a ride across town to a fundamentalist Christian school. The school isolated us intellectually—no evolution, no sex education, no information that compromised the sanctity of our country—and we didn't make many friends there. We were the wrong kind of fundamentalists. Our school was filled with staid, pew-sitting Baptists, and we were Pentecostal, dancing in front of our church's chairs and praying in tongues. The other students, and teachers, whispered that we handled snakes. So while Joshua mingled sometimes with the lads of the village, my sisters and I talked to each other. All four of us imagined ourselves into newspaper writers, farmers, and apartment-dwelling socialites, and we wrote. Once, a girl from my high school stayed on the phone after she called with a homework question, and I forgot to hang up the receiver. She confessed the next day and told me she was astonished. I rarely spoke at school, but at home I sang, joked, invented stories with my siblings. She'd looked through a portal into our world.

❦

Gaskell describes the young Brontës' writings as "curious." *Curious* as in *curiosities*, so weirdly fantastic as to make the young Brontës themselves worthy of exhibition under a magnifying glass. She describes a "curious packet . . . containing an immense amount of manuscript, in an inconceivably small space; tales, dramas, poems, romances." In the packet Gaskell discovered a list, titled "Catalog of my books," that Charlotte wrote at fourteen years old, something like the ever-growing list of Sunshine Books I wrote in the back of every new publication. Gaskell quotes the whole list in her biography—"The Search after Happiness, a Tale," "Interior of a Pot-house, a Poem"—giving readers a "curious proof" of "how early the rage for literary composition had seized upon" Charlotte and her siblings.

As Barker sees it, the Brontës' tiny books were not astonishing. Far from curious. Hardly the work, as previous biographers framed it, of "born novelists" with nothing to learn. The Brontës used little to no punctuation well into adulthood. Their characters were shallow, their plots all melodrama. After Charlotte left for school at fourteen, and she and Branwell continued collaborating by letter, Branwell asked her, unsuccessfully, to tone down the magic, to write about real people with real lives. What's more, Barker says such books weren't unusual. Without diminishing, she says, "the Brontës' achievement in producing such a volume of literature at so early an age," she describes other families of children with sufficient literacy and leisure who crafted books similar in appearance and content. "For whatever reason," she writes, "bright children at this period were drawn to writing little books and inventing fictitious kingdoms."

I know my childhood writing wasn't *curious*, and neither was my siblings'. Not shockingly good and not unusual, even for the late twentieth century, for children who wished to be writers. But when I dragged my suitcase up a mountain road in Yorkshire to a house where four children wrote books they bound themselves, I felt both captivated and curiously comfortable, like I was approaching my parents' home.

As a teen, I discovered the Brontës in the public library: Charlotte, Emily, Anne etched on hunter green binding, shelved together under *B*. Writing siblings. *Like us*, I thought, dreaming. My brain connected my family so deeply to those books on the shelf that I wasn't surprised, a decade later, to learn the Brontës wrote together as children. I wasn't surprised they had a brother. I wasn't surprised their father burned their aunt's women's magazines the children had been reading in secret, deeming them sinfully trashy, just the way our mother purged our film collection after our bad family car wreck, filling a black trash bag and slipping as she lugged it down our long, wet hill for the garbage truck to take it, believing we'd brought the evil on ourselves. Of course Charlotte was the bossy one. Of course Branwell was joyful and whiny, performative, social. Of course all four moved away and returned home, over and over. Of course Branwell grew up and wailed in the night.

A Hobo Like Me

I was fifteen, more than old enough to watch seven-year-old Joshua while our mother escaped to the grocery store. She'd be back in an hour, two at most if the lines were long or she stopped by The Potpourri to look at china dolls and dinner plates that hung on the wall.

And Joshua and I had a plan. We were going to spend the afternoon in my bedroom, a space we both found ideal for artistic production, writing a one-man play. After an intense lights-on/lights-off dispute, Jennifer had recently moved to a bunk bed in Rebecca and Joshua's room, and PaPa's bed had moved to the dump. I was now the proud owner of a brand-new twin bed and five square feet of empty floor space. I sat on that bed, holding looseleaf paper and a pencil, and Joshua paced that empty floor, preparing to use my blue carpet as a stage. My brother had been watching *The Red Skelton Show*, one of the only programs that fuzzed through our attic antenna, so he considered hobos the height of comedy.

"All right, Sarbef," he said, and he stopped in the center of the floor and heaved an enormous breath. "At the top, put 'The Hobo.'" I penciled the words at the top of the first sheet. Joshua tucked my long hair behind my ear so he could read over my shoulder, then he nodded with satisfaction. "You haven't seen a hobo like me in a while," he began.

Joshua collapsed into a seated position like a marionette, and I could see in his eyes that he'd transformed. His blue ringer T and khakis had become too-large pants with a patched knee, a shirt cut from a Depression-era flour sack, and a top hat someone had punched through the crown like Mr. Banks's hat in *Mary Poppins*.

Then something went wrong. Maybe it happened because we were out of hot dogs, Kool-Aid, and Nesquik, and he'd lunched on a peanut butter sandwich with white milk. Or maybe something in my bedroom—a brunette Barbie, a blue sock—reminded him of the girl he loved at school. Cindy had passed Joshua a note that said she liked him, then she'd spent naptime sneaking onto other boys' Kindermats.

Whatever the cause, Joshua stood up and stared at me, no longer a hobo, no longer my cute little brother. He grabbed my smiling Barbies from their shelves and hurled them against the wall. I hid the one-man show under my pillow so he couldn't crumple it, the pencil under my bed so he couldn't stab me. His life was awful, and he knew why: he was skinny. "If I was fat like Cody, Cindy would like me. Why can't I be fat? Girls only like boys if they're fat. Everybody in our family is skinny." He looked at my bony frame and snorted.

I knew what came next. It was *my* fault he was skinny. I picked up forty-five pounds of rage and tossed him onto my bed, then I dashed for the door. I had a few-second head start, just enough time to get into the hall and shut the door before my brother slammed his body against the hollow plywood. The door wouldn't lock from the outside, so I wrapped both hands around the gray metal knob, determined to keep it from turning. Since the knob wouldn't turn, he shook the door until I feared for my arms and the hinges. When that didn't work, he went back to screaming. "You *want* me to be skinny, Sarbef! It's your fault."

After a few minutes, the doorknob relaxed. Joshua kicked the door a few times, then he melted into a puddle of scream-cries, alone in the space that would one day be his bedroom. On a lonely night in that bedroom, he'd turn his anger on himself.

But that afternoon, Joshua quit crying and leaned against the door.

"Sarbef?" he said, his voice small. He sounded like my little brother.

"I love you, Smoo," I answered. "It's okay."

I kept my hand on the knob, but I sat down by the door, up against the place I felt him leaning. We comforted each other with the warmth of our bodies until our mother got back from the store.

Candy Crane

Joshua lost interest in Walmart's toy crane at eight, shortly after he gained enough hand-eye coordination to manipulate the metal claw. Too many times, he'd failed to grab a plush hedgehog or Game Boy until our parents ran out of quarters, then slid, despairing, onto the grimy concrete floor. But the candy machine's glass front bore a promise: *A win every time.* The candy claw moved with more precision than the one with the toys, and it stayed active until it had snagged enough candy to fill a child's fist. Fun-size M&Ms, lime Dum-Dums, butterscotch rounds.

My sisters and I took turns with Joshua at the candy crane during our family's shopping trips until the day my winnings caused me to vomit. A box of Junior Mints, the chocolate coating chewed and defecated into millimeter-wide pebbles, grubs wriggling in the minty center when I took a bite. After that day, we girls stood around waiting while Joshua manned the controls alone. It took more than beetle larvae to scare him away.

On one Walmart trip after the wormy Junior Mints, Joshua ran ahead to the candy crane while our parents selected a buggy. "Watch Joshua," my dad said, filling my palm with extra quarters. I moseyed to the arcade area, pausing over the fresh for-sale candy, the tabloid speculation about the murder of JonBenét Ramsey, with Jennifer and Rebecca ambling behind. I hid the quarters in my pocket, hoping Joshua would satisfy his stomach with whatever slid out of the metal chute before we arrived.

But when we reached the candy crane, another child was squeezing the controls. Joshua wasn't at the toy crane, wasn't anywhere. I'd always noticed a draft in that area, chilly in winter, sticky hot in summer. A cool breeze that day, early spring. For the first time, I really looked around. The bottom six feet of the exterior wall was made of transparent vinyl flaps, a wall created for blue-vested workers pushing buggy trains. "Is Smoo out there?" one of my sisters whispered. I split up our search party: one sister to find our parents, another to lap the inside of the store. I burst through the flaps, out into the last light of the sunset, screaming our brother's name.

A few minutes later my dad joined me outside, along with a frightened-looking manager and two cart boys. My mother, my dad told me, had requested a call for Joshua over the store intercom. He took a look at that vinyl wall, gasped, "Joshua's been kidnapped. Some pervert came in through there."

My dad merely echoed my fears, but when I heard those fears said out loud, I felt unable to stand. I collapsed, tearless, onto the curb by the pop machines. The intercom called again and again: *Joshua Childers, come to the front of the store.* The manager muttered into his walkie-talkie, and the cart boys pledged to look for a stray little boy along with the carts. My dad sprinted for the minivan to drive around: past the bus stop, past the colony that lived in their station wagons, past the unauthorized used car lot and vegetable stands, now closed for the night. Past rows and rows of shoppers' coupes, minivans, pickups, sedans. So many ways to disappear a child.

Finally, after another ten awful minutes, Joshua approached the entrance from the parking lot, humming to himself. He'd snuck off to the toy aisle and then, feeling unsure how to find us, decided to wait by the car. He'd gotten bored and returned by a circuitous route, barely missing our dad. I squeezed Joshua's skinny body, laughed and cried.

Years later, when I found out Joshua was actually dead, I remembered those minutes when I'd felt certain I'd never see him again. I remembered how silent the world had felt without him. How I had wondered who I'd be with him gone.

Jennifer and Rebecca both ran away repeatedly as children. Maybe they'd had a scolding from our parents or a horrible day in elementary school, but it was theater, based on the Prodigal Son and an image my sisters and I found thrilling in children's books and cartoons. A child, a Smurf, a pink-nosed mouse trudged from home, head bowed with heartbreak. Resting over one sad shoulder: the long wooden stick of a hobo's bindle. All that was left of the runaway's old life tied in a red handkerchief at the top.

My sisters and I drew our Prodigal Son inspiration from the *Read-n-Grow Picture Bible*, a glossy tome we called the Bible Storybook. Inside, there are six bright panels to a page, with dialogue and narration printed at the bottom of each panel. Each night, after baby Joshua fell asleep, my mother, Jennifer, Rebecca, and I read that book together in PaPa's bed, under a floral cotton sheet some relative gave away. My mom and I took turns reading the words aloud while my sisters poked at the pictures. On the book's glossy cover, a smiling Jesus wipes healing mud across the squeezed-shut eyes of a smiling, gap-toothed blind man. A little boy and a little girl watch, entranced.

When Jennifer or Rebecca ran away, I encouraged my sister to leave and helped her depart. I told my parents both girls were playing with me, so they'd confine their attention to Joshua. I was about ten, a kid they could (usually) trust. I considered fetching my dad's walking stick from the storage building, creating a real-life bindle, but decided my involvement would be too obvious. I settled for a frayed school-bag, tossed in a juice box, an apple, an individually wrapped slice of American cheese. I tied the runaway's little-girl tennis shoes, caught the screen door so it wouldn't slam on her way out.

The Christmas after Joshua was born, I tore bright paper and discovered a new copy of the Bible Storybook. We'd read the original until it had lost both covers, plus the beginning, where Adam meets Eve and Cain kills Abel, and the ending, where Jesus floats back to modern-day earth on a cloud. This copy still has its cover, with my mother's blue ink inscription: *To all our precious children who will read this book. December 25, 1990. Tuesday Morning.* On that Tuesday morning, my brother had twenty-one years, eight months, and six days left in his life.

I officially discovered my sister was missing five minutes after she left, but I kept the knowledge to myself. Control of information was key. If my parents found out too early, they might panic, or simply go pick her up in the family car. I wasn't aiming to cause trauma, only perform it, and I wanted to play the hero. I crept out the back door and rattled our red Radio Flyer wagon down the driveway.

My sisters' runaway years coincided with our beagle's daily escapes. As Kassie raced down the driveway, she tossed back an exultant look at whoever tried to chase her. A look that said, *I love you, but I'll come back when I'm good and ready*. I have no memory of Scruffy leaving the yard, but I can't believe he looked back.

I found my runaway sister, maybe two hundred yards down our quiet street, and she climbed into the wagon. When we got back to the house, I made a grand announcement. My sister ran away, but I brought her back. Everyone hugged her, then hugged me. Someone handed the runaway a cherry Popsicle. Our parents surely understood and joined in the performance, but my family's joy was real. We were experiencing the conclusion of a marvelous story. Our prodigal had come home.

When Joshua grew old enough to seriously play with us, I could have infused young blood into our runaway performances. I threw away the imaginary bindle instead. I was in my early teens, but I can't really blame (or credit) my age. I was up for imagining MaMa and Grandpa's hallway into a town, with Joshua as the mailman. I was up for riding the wagon down a flight of garden stairs.

The Prodigal Son looks thirty-five in the Bible Storybook, with pronounced nasolabial folds and a full brown beard. Still, surely as a child I noticed the slouchy, happy, shifty little-brother look he has about him in that first panel, before he leaves home. The Prodigal's eyes look like my little brother's when I placed a new Hot Wheels car in his hands.

I didn't stage runaways with Joshua because of my fierce love for my youngest sibling. I couldn't handle even pretending to lose him. And something about him always felt restless. I could encourage my sisters to run away because I was certain they'd plod down their usual route until I showed up with the wagon, and they'd sleep in their beds that night, predictable as our beagle's return to the yellowed pillow by the kitchen door. If I handed Joshua a schoolbag of snacks and sent him down the driveway, part of me feared he'd disappear.

PART 2
DEPARTURE

One morning, the Prodigal wakes up feeling the weight of his father's roof, the pressure of his father's walls. He saunters up to his father and asks, King James Version–style, "Father, give me the portion of goods that falleth to me." And the father divides his wealth in two. Half to the son with one foot out the door, half to the son who watches calves alongside him, steady as rock under desert sand.

On an audio cassette of an ordinary day when I was three, taped to preserve my toddler voice, I whine, "Daddy, Daddy, Scruffy's missin' again. Daddy, are we gonna look for Scruffy?" My West Virginia accent is startlingly strong, a trait I lost to my own wish to be somewhere else.

After the Prodigal's father divides his property, the Prodigal "gathers all together." I picture him ordering a servant to drive half the herds to market, negotiating a price on half of the family vineyards. Perhaps he orders a rough-handed woman to stitch him a new coat, to retool the cowhide on his sandals, to fill drinking horns with wine and water, to stuff a sack with dates and figs.

On the cassette tape, my mom says, "David," before my dad can answer me. Her voice is higher pitched and more plaintive than I can remember it. In my mom's voice, I can hear her pregnancy with Jennifer, in its final month. I can hear the brown softness of her hair. She lilts, "Sarah Beth's been asking all day." My dad sighs, clearly just home from work. He says, "All right, let's go look for him." The screen door creaks, and the kitchen door thumps shut behind us.

Jesus didn't reveal the Prodigal's method of travel to the far country. The Bible Storybook creators don't either. They show the Prodigal staring at his bulging animal-skin bag of coins and put his travel in a caption: "The younger son . . . set off for another country far away."

I imagine the Prodigal on camelback, patting his purse, bumping along with a merchant's caravan. Then he crosses the Mediterranean in one of those biblical ships that always seem to hit stormy seas. The Bible never leaves out a good storm story, so I'm betting the Prodigal's journey was peaceful. He stands on deck, a warm wind at his back, while the invisible ropes that bound him to his father's evening sighs, his fun-hating brother, snap and disappear under the waves.

The only photo I have of Scruffy is that one where I'm hugging him in the backyard. I wish I had a photo that captured that dog's spirit. Scruffy: mid-trot in summer on our one-lane road, scraggly tail angled up, neck fur indented from the slipped collar, his belly still full of that evening's bowl of Dog Chow.

I'd put that Scruffy picture in a two-photo frame, next to an imaginary shot of my thirteen-year-old brother on that spring afternoon when he gathered nothing together. When he strode down the driveway in a T-shirt and shorts, unencumbered as a collarless dog.

I was terrified when Joshua left, but now that he can't turn up alive again, I wish I had a photo of nearly everything, even the difficult moments of his life. Joshua: mid-stride down that same road as Scruffy, not yet sunburned, belly filled with an Angus beef hot dog wrapped in whole wheat bread. Determined green eyes, gray asphalt, blue sky.

The First Time

The first time my thirteen-year-old brother disappeared, walking out my parents' side door and down the driveway without a word, I drove around for hours, searching. That summer, my family would grow used to Joshua slinking down the road without warning, but that day I screamed with my sisters, our heads poked out of my Beetle's windows. Our dad was speeding home early from work, and our mom stayed home and prayed by the phone.

Not long after I graduated from our fundamentalist school, when Joshua was entering the fifth grade, my siblings had successfully begged our parents to let them change to public school and join Twin Valley's yellow-bus-riding crowd. But even with this new connection to our neighborhood community, Joshua didn't have any friends or crushes I knew of in walking distance. So I drove around at random. Joshua's middle school, a restaurant with a sewage reek and good pizza. Clay's, where my dad and I looked for Scruffy.

I remembered my three-year-old self shouting "Scruffy!" by Clay's dumpster, wondering if he could have scrambled inside. When Joshua disappeared, I checked the candy aisle. Perhaps he got hungry on the first half mile of his journey, stopped to ogle the gummy worms with empty pockets and self-pitying tears. Joshua wasn't there, and the cashier hadn't seen him. I bought him a king-size Tootsie Roll, feeding my hopes he'd come back home.

The first time Joshua disappeared, I had an important banquet that evening. It was just university catering, pasta primavera and watery iced tea, but I was going to be given a scholarship, the Marshall University history department's highest undergraduate honor. I knew Joshua didn't mean to ruin my evening; he just didn't have the energy to care about my life. And my parents weren't planning on going anyway.

My parents were proud of me, but they expected me to cover my tuition with scholarships, to be one of the best students at the local, low-ranked university. I was stable as the Prodigal's older brother. Who needs pasta primavera to celebrate that?

The first time Joshua disappeared, he was in the throes of puberty. Not long before he walked off, he sighed on his unmade bottom bunk, hands gripping his shoulder-length wavy hair at the roots.

As a live-at-home university student, I spent the bulk of my time at home typing up my barely legible history notes in my childhood bedroom. But I often popped across the hall to my siblings' room and sat on Rebecca's twin bed, one foot from my brother, for a chat.

"Sarbef," he said, "the awful thing about puberty is you have to think about girls all the time."

The thing was, Joshua had always thought about girls. He'd experienced passionate, unrequited crushes on his elementary school classmates, but the girls he'd thought about most had been his sisters. "Hey, my sisters!" he'd always begun, when he had something to say, something he wanted to do.

But now, when Joshua talked to me, he talked about the girls at his middle school. He liked them waifish, dark-haired, pale-skinned, and loud, with enormous brown eyes. I sat and listened, but I was jealous. I felt heartbroken over losing his love, and guilty for wishing I could keep him to myself.

The first time Joshua disappeared, he was in the throes of puberty, and something other than girl obsession had shifted in his brain.

He'd thrown tantrums as a child, but now, when he got angry, his eyes darkened. He possessed what seemed, for a scrawny thirteen-year-old, to be superhuman strength and determination. He could sit on the closed lid of our house's one toilet for six hours at a stretch, making our mother—and the rest of us—suffer. He could punch through a thin closet door.

When Joshua disappeared, I was afraid he might try to walk anywhere. Six hundred miles to New York City. Five hundred miles to the Atlantic coast.

❦

The first time Joshua disappeared, I decided to go to my banquet, and Rebecca came with me. We left my dad and Jennifer to keep searching, and my mom to keep praying away on the front porch, watching the driveway, clutching the cordless phone.

If Joshua had walked off two years before, I would have missed my banquet, missed the rest of the semester if necessary, let the scholarship go to someone else. Perhaps it was college—I'd learned to my shock that women had invented agriculture, and not Cain, the brother slayer in the book of Genesis—or maybe I was simply growing up, but I'd been changing along with Joshua. I felt less willing, even in a crisis, to give up every part of myself for my family. And, like the Prodigal's older brother, who worked steadily on, quietly resenting his father for never giving him a feast, I secretly craved my own celebrations.

Still, I wanted family with me when I went anywhere. Fifteen-year-old Rebecca, who was experiencing mental shifting similar to my own, was the only one willing to go. The two of us put on floral skirts and eyeliner, costumes of girls who weren't worried their brother had been abducted, drowned in Twelve Pole Creek, or squashed by a car. At the banquet, we spilled iced tea on the tablecloth, dropped forks on the floor, forced smiles when I accepted my award.

❦

The first time Joshua disappeared, no one in my family had a cell phone. So Rebecca and I had no clue, but right after we left for the banquet, my mom got a call.

"Lookin' for Josh?" a young female voice twanged.

Joshua hadn't drowned in the creek. He hadn't been visiting a waifish, dark-haired girl, and he hadn't, apparently, any intention of walking to the Atlantic coast. He'd followed his middle school bus route four miles to visit his friend Tyler. He'd watched TV shows our parents considered filthy and stuffed his belly with snacks our parents wouldn't purchase: Twinkies, frozen pizza, mini corndogs.

“Why don’t you let Josh stay here tonight?” Tyler’s stepmom said on the phone, her voice condescending and calm. “He’s just chillin’ out. He likes it over here at our house.”

“Thank you so much, but no,” my mom said firmly. My dad was already starting the car.

❦

When Rebecca and I got back from the banquet, Joshua lay with his face and hunched shoulders to the wall, on top of the rumpled sheets in his bottom bunk. The way he always looked after his superhuman energy melted into sadness.

My parents stood in the bedroom doorway, watching him sleep. I don’t think I showed my award certificate or check to my parents, and I don’t remember feeling slighted. I remember standing in the doorway with my parents and both sisters. He wouldn’t let us hug him, but we could stare. Scars on his calves from 4-H camp mosquitoes, long brown hair, a T-shirt I’d bought him at JCPenney. A sunburnt version of the boy who’d walked away.

Yet he wasn’t the same. Or maybe I wasn’t. Whatever the reason, after Joshua disappeared for the first time, I saw something different in that hair, in the slope of his shoulders, even his T-shirt. Weeks before, I’d laughed when he’d camped out all day on the toilet, striven to view the situation as a harmless joke from my darling Smoo. Now I saw someone with power. Someone uncontrollable as Scruffy had been after he’d decided to leave us. Perhaps Joshua would truly prefer to chill out somewhere else. Perhaps he’d decide to hurt us all.

But I must have stared for twenty minutes at his sunburnt hands, those shoulders. My brother was home.

Lost Photographs

Beech Fork State Park in Lavalette, WV. Summer 1993. Joshua jaunts over a hill with his sisters and Daddy. His first hike. He's wearing a blue-and-red toddler-sized ball cap and carrying the frayed red backpack I used for my first day of kindergarten. He insisted on bringing the bag, on packing only Elmo, a soft-bellied, not-ticklish version with chipped eyes. Joshua loves snuggling Elmo, loves the sound those eyes make when he grabs Elmo by his rope-thin legs and hurls him at hard furniture, my pastel shepherdess statues, any available wall.

My parents' dining room in Huntington, WV. June 1999. Haloed by lung-filled balloons taped to the back of his chair, Joshua lifts a forkful of the dark chocolate cake I baked for his siblings-only pre-birthday celebration. Hershey's Special Dark Miniatures cover the cake, with Pillsbury chocolate frosting oozing between them. Joshua gets emotional about those Miniatures, quoting their wrappers in an almost tear-choked voice: "*Special* dark. Mildly *sweet*!" He equally loves Tootsie Rolls, which contain all the chocolate flavor of a pencil eraser, but I'd never mention the contradiction. Loose Tootsie Minis and Hershey's Miniatures line the bottom of the bright bags on the table, ready to ease the small let-down that hits when present opening is over.

Jennifer, Rebecca, and Joshua's bedroom. Summer 1997. Joshua lies in his unmade bottom bunk, toes anchored in the bed slats above him, playing an electronic game he found in a box of cereal. It's a baseball game, a three-inch-wide plastic diamond with flea-sized dots that dash around the bases. Between at-bats, the game beeps out a tune. Joshua's mouth is open: he's given the tune lyrics. *Her daughters love baseball, baseball is their love.* He loves me, I think, hearing him sing to himself as I snap the picture. He loves this home full of girls.

My parents' living room. Fall 2002. Joshua kneels in front of our family's empty oak film cabinet, a DVD in each hand, DVDs and VHS tapes in piles around him on the carpet. Two VHS tapes top the piles: *Roman Holiday*, a big winner at the 1954 Oscars, and *White Christmas*, a Bing Crosby gem. My family owns all those movies because they're enjoyable and they're clean. They were produced under the strict Hollywood Hays Code of the mid-1930s to late 1960s. Or, if they came before or after that code, they'd meet its standards for sex and language. In his hands Joshua holds *Dinosaur*, a Disney CGI flick released in 2000, and *Andre*, a 1994 movie with a little girl on the cover standing next to a floral-raincoat-wearing seal. Joshua's mouth is open in a snarl: "These are the only two movies we have that are *up to date*!" He wants us all to feel the irony. *Andre* and *Dinosaur* are NOT up to date. And *Andre* and *Dinosaur* are crap.

My parents' bathroom. April 2004. Joshua smiles into the toothpaste-specked mirror, one bare foot in the air, one bare foot on the bathroom floor. Rebecca stands beside him with a curling iron, styling his shoulder-length hair. I'm out of frame, back in his bedroom, trying to find the sharpest pants and polo in his closet. I can hear Joshua's linoleum-slapping dancing, Rebecca's singing. *That's what the Smoo is going to do. Impress the ladies at the dance!*

My parents' bedroom. August 2006. Joshua crouches on the floor by our parents' bed, holding up a palm-sized, googly-eyed donut puppet. Joshua has decided he wants to be an art film director, so he has dug out PaPa's ancient video camera, the one that captured Rebecca breathing in a blanket on the day of her birth and five-year-old me trembling with my red backpack in the doorway of my new school. He's propped the camera on a file cabinet, filming for a YouTube channel called Smoovies. All YouTube viewers can see: my parents' green blackout curtains, a lamp with a crooked shade, and Duncan the Donut, his circular body stretched open like a mouth. Duncan is lip synching "Please Please Please" by the Shout Out Louds. But the photo reveals Joshua on the floor, biting his cheeks to keep from laughing. Even his knees look happy. He's found his plan for his life.

Returning Cats

HUNTINGTON, WV

At my fundamentalist school's spring concert, my mostly white elementary choir performed Harry S. Miller's 1893 minstrel song "The Cat Came Back," a version with standardized grammar and diction to sidestep the written-in racism. Our choir sang Old Mr. Johnson's unkillable cat slow, straight, serious, as befitted our uniforms. Navy from the waist down, pressed white from the waist up, the girls with red ribbons pinned under our chins.

On the drive home from the concert, and for years afterward, my dad sang the song fast, a goofy approximation that ignored most of the lyrics. *The cat came back, the very next day. The cat came back because he couldn't stay away.*

I thought my dad must have particularly enjoyed that performance, more than the hymn arrangements we'd warbled during the rest of the evening, but a few months after the concert, he told me a story. When I was a toddling baby, my parents and I needed to live rent-free while our house was built. My dad's college bedroom in his parents' house was redecorated pink but still empty, so we crammed in, down the hall from the blue room where twenty-three-year-old Mark slept and did his homework for his associate degree in information technology at Marshall.

I knew that bedroom well: my grandmother kept it intact for Mark's weekend visits, and I'd sneaked in and stroked the fishing poles in the closet, the hunting rifles under the bed, the tube socks in the dresser. But I'd never imagined that room as setting for a story like this. Studying at the desk with its tempting notebooks and red pencils, Mark found my crying awful, all of us irritating. He belted "The Cat Came Back" through that room's closed door.

I learned a few years later that Mark was a returned cat himself. Before he studied computers at Marshall, before he got his IT job by another West Virginia river, he'd majored in agriculture at West Virginia University, across the state in Morgantown. Mark had dropped out of "dirt farmer school," as he called it, after his roommate pilfered his acne medication and a professor required him to castrate a bull. Later still, I learned how typical Mark's story was for Appalachia, how so many of us are torn between a desire to leave home and a magnetic love for our own broken patches of asphalt, for our own rocks, creeks, and hills. Even later, I found my choir's performance of that song, with children unconsciously performing brushed-up racism, to be a disturbingly on-point metaphor for some of my worst Appalachian experiences. Deadly inherited beliefs about people, medicine, faith, and science, dressed up with ribbons, tucked between hymns.

But when my dad told me that day about Mark's singing, I felt hurt that my uncle, who I knew loved me, had found me anything but adorable. I feared he didn't appreciate my baby brother. And afterwards, when my dad sang that song, I never heard it the same way. His voice was sarcastic, not funny, and the cat wasn't a survivor, he was a failure. My dad's voice carried the tension between siblings, the annoyance of children. The shame of moving back to your parents' house because you're not sure where else to go.

BLACKSBURG, VA

When I was eighteen, I decided to go to Virginia Tech for engineering, planning to pay my out-of-state tuition with my family-car-wreck money, scholarships, and loans. I'm still not certain why I did this. Perhaps because the only other person in my high school calculus class was applying to that program, and I was smarter than him. Perhaps because engineers make money. Perhaps because leaving my family felt more justified if I pursued a field of study Marshall didn't offer. Perhaps because I admired Cyrus Harding, a bossy engineer with every possible skill in *The Mysterious Island*, an 1875 novel by Jules Verne. I confused my admiration for Verne's creation of Harding with a wish to *be* Harding. I thought I wanted to build a city from a crashed hot air balloon, a beached whale, and a dried kernel of corn.

To prepare for my move, my mom and I bought everything new: desk, down comforter, eyebrow tweezers. We left my bedroom intact, even though reusing my old things could have saved us much-needed money, and my three siblings were still wedged together in a bedroom across the hall. Months before my move, and fifteen years after Mark moved out of his parents' house for good, MaMa had sold his bedroom furniture to create a sitting room where no one sat. When she told Mark, she reported, "He got real quiet on the phone." My mom and I were determined to avoid such trauma, even if it meant keeping a cradle of Cabbage Patch Dolls at the end of an empty twin bed forever. "You're *staying* in Blacksburg," my mom said, "but this is your home."

My brother and sisters didn't resent me for that empty room: they were, it seems, too young, too unused to privacy, too worried about our splitting-up sibling group to make demands. They all wanted to come along on my moving trip, to spend three more days together and see my new life, but my purchased hoard took up too much of the minivan. We had room for only one tagalong sibling, and I requested ten-year-old Joshua because he was cute.

I still stand by that choice, even though he danced and whined while my parents and I unloaded the van, and he acted indignant when my dad asked him to sit down on the hard dorm floor and keep him company while he put my furniture together. Joshua marveled at "Dietrick," the ordinary cafeteria, lending me a contrast to the terror I felt about my new life. And I was still sufficiently obsessed with my little brother to be entranced by his complaints. A fan of *The Monkees*, the 1960s TV series, Joshua repurposed "Last Train to Clarksville," the Monkees' Vietnam protest song, to express his boredom. *I'll take the last train to Virginia, and I'll meet you at the college, and I don't even know if I'll go home.*

During that move-in weekend, I threw away the humorous survey for incoming engineering majors, afraid my *no* answers would reveal me as a poseur to my new professors and classmates, my parents, myself. *Have you taken apart every appliance in your parents' house, just to see how they worked? Have you mixed chemicals at home, and was the fire department involved?* I rolled out my new rug, installed *Mathematica* on my new computer, filled my Napster queue with Christian pop songs that would educate my atheist roommate about Jesus. When my parents drove off, I took it bravely, though I'm thankful my mom waited years to tell me Joshua sobbed like a toddler on the ride back to Huntington.

But thrown-out surveys and concealed sobs can only go so far. Three weeks later, after no time at all really, I moved back. Still, my brain insists those weeks are important. Except for the week I planned my brother's funeral, I remember those days in better detail than any other time in my life. Nearly twenty years later and far from an engineer, I find myself plotting my Virginia Tech experience along Freytag's Pyramid, trying to shrink those weeks into a container I can understand.

Exposition: I get up daily for eight a.m. classes. I impress my chemistry professor. I sweat in my unairconditioned dorm. I eat hamburgers on the lawn at a welcome picnic. I hug the Hokey Bird, Virginia Tech's maroon-and-orange mascot. I resolve to succeed in a male-dominated profession. I subscribe to the *Believer's Voice of Victory*, a magazine produced by Kenneth Copeland, jet-collecting televangelist. I ride the city bus to Kroger and buy grapes.

Rising action: No one notices I don't drink because engineering students have no time to party. I make friends easily for the first time. Fresh from a high school where my classmate was expelled for writing the word "orgasm," where students were shamed for saying "gosh" or "golly," euphemistically taking the name of God in vain, I wish it were cooler in my dorm so I could close my window, shutting out the curses of the frisbee flingers on the quad. I struggle to calculate the changing pressure of a rising hot air balloon, the volume of water in a filling pool. I recite 1 inch = 2.54 centimeters in my sleep. My atheist roommate guffaws when she catches me watching Kenneth Copeland sermons on my computer. I go alone to a football game and get happily soaked, watching Michael Vick play in the rain.

Climax: My atheist roommate and I are in open war, her blasting rap, me blasting Christian pop, through our identical computer speakers. I reach for a grape and find them mold-fuzzed and shrunken. I call my family and talk to each of them, whimpering for an hour into the phone. I calculate how much money I'm spending and remember my ACT score earned me free Marshall tuition. In a brand-new sermon, Kenneth Copeland relates a divine prophecy for someone who has gone away to school and should have stayed home. I feel startled, grateful, and shamed. I spend a day with an intense, shaggy-haired, scarf-wearing young man who tells me he's been expelled and banned from campus, unreasonably, for stalking women. He leans over me in a tiny room as I play Chopin on a beat-up piano, tells me I have too much personality to be an engineer. When I see that young man again, two-stepping alone down a campus sidewalk, I hide behind an oak, but I believe he's right.

Resolution: I consider switching to pre-med because surgeons make even more money, think longingly about studying English. I remember Kenneth Copeland's prophecy. I realize that with the cost of one year of out-of-state tuition and fees, I could buy a little blue car. I walk to the bursar, the registrar, fill out the required paperwork for dropouts. I remember my *Believer's Voice of Victory* subscription, and I smugly imagine my atheist roommate at our mailbox, pulling out a new issue every month. I fail a math test on purpose, so I'll be too embarrassed to stay.

Dénouement: I call and ask my parents to come and get me. My dad leaves work early, tugs both bench seats out of the minivan, and drives two hundred miles. We push my rolling desk together under streetlights on the campus sidewalk, moving so fast our feet leave the ground. My dad drives through the night, stopping only for gas station coffee, crunchy with grounds from a leaky filter. Whenever he nearly falls asleep, he takes a crunch. At dawn the minivan rolls up my family's driveway. My mom hears the tires on gravel, runs outside in her nightgown, weeps and presses me to her chest. I go inside to sleep in my bed, next to my doll cradle, everything in place like I'd never left.

I still stand by my decision to leave Virginia Tech, even though I returned to the deep sheltering that allowed me to blissfully spend the day with an expelled stalker. Even though I returned to a homelife so immersive I didn't go on a real date until I was twenty-five. Even though I spent a significant percentage of the next few years sobbing on the living room floor in fights with my mother.

I avoided unpayable debt and bought a car I drove well into my thirties. I got to know my siblings as they grew up. I spent the months after my return teaching Joshua three-digit multiplication, and I got to see him every day during four of his twelve remaining years.

But there's one detail from those three weeks in Virginia I can't fit into my plot arc, likely because it disturbs the neat Prodigal Son ending that has allowed me to make narrative peace with that part of my life. The day before my dad drove me home, my friends bought and signed a Good Luck card. *Get out there and LIVE*, one of them wrote above her name. I thanked and hugged them, then I spent the last evening hiding in my dorm room, afraid they'd learn the truth. I wasn't getting out there, I wasn't all-caps living. I was slinking back home with ragged fur.

LEXINGTON, KY

Right before I left home for the second time, my family adopted two gooey-eyed kittens, one black, one white, balding from starvation and stress. We were dog people then, but we pitied them. My parents found Éowyn and Bo while driving into mountain neighborhoods, searching, as they had since Joshua's birth, for an affordable four- or five-bedroom house that felt as homey as the one they'd built when I was a baby. They were still searching for a house that would hold all six of us, though I was determined I was finally moving away.

In my four years at Marshall, I'd changed my major eight times, finally landing on history. I'd grown from a teenager who tried to use homework assignments to convert her professors to an adult who listened and thought. I'd ended my subscription to *Believer's Voice of Victory* after Kenneth Copeland wrote an article that cast Christopher Columbus—a man I now knew was responsible for indigenous slavery and genocide—as a prophecy-heeding follower of God.

I decided to earn an MA in Victorian history because it felt like the natural next step after my undergraduate studies. Because the University of Kentucky awarded me a prestigious fellowship, twice the money TAs received with no responsibilities. Because I was even closer to my siblings than I'd been at eighteen, and Lexington was only 120 miles from home.

I took Éowyn with me, but I felt guilty. The kittens thundered together around my parents' house, and they napped together with their black and white bodies tucked into a circle, a near-perfect yin and yang. My siblings and I chuckled at our sleeping cats' resemblance to the culturally appropriated symbol we saw everywhere on graffiti, bumper stickers, T-shirts, and tattoos. My mom had recently trashed her beloved *Mutts* collection after noticing that non-Christian black-

and-white circle inked among the cartoon dogs and cats. Formed of kitten bodies on my mom's corduroy piano bench cushion, the symbol seemed to mean cats existed on a different spiritual plane than humans, and these cats should never be apart.

Still, I took Éowyn, this kitten who woke me in the night by jumping on my chest and tearing my hair. I wasn't brave enough for a stranger roommate, remembering Mark's dorm thief and my Virginia Tech roommate stresses, and I couldn't handle opening my apartment door onto dark silence after a day at school.

On this move, my parents drove a minivan load of books and clothing, and all three of my siblings had a seat in my Beetle. My parents left quickly, but my siblings stayed for days, all of us munching frozen pizzas and sleeping together on a mattress I built from blankets, sweatshirts, and towels. One of my too-expensive apartment's boasted "luxury" features was a garbage disposal, and Joshua touched me with his fear that I might grind up a finger by mistake. Then I drove them all back to Huntington, back to their three-person bedroom, and I was alone with a kitten in my apartment.

I lasted four months in Lexington, but that whole year is a dreamlike blur, surely because I didn't sleep. I remember Foucault's panopticon, speeches in the Victorian House of Commons, drives to my parents' house midweek. The smell of manure from grazing racehorses, tiny soot-prints on white carpet from my cold "luxury" fireplace. Nights writing history papers and mornings writing fiction. Jealousy of my kitten, who knew nothing of Victorian politics. Furtive applications to creative writing programs. My four new pieces of furniture, crammed into my parents' storage building with rusty bicycles. Reunited kittens, cuddling and murdering blue-tailed skinks. "You couldn't take it, could ya" and a knowing look from the car mechanic's wife. Stress-induced depression, crying for weeks in my childhood bedroom, next to my doll cradle, under the gaze of a ceramic shepherdess who smiled down from a shelf. An MFA program acceptance letter my dad found in the mailbox while I was out. I asked him to tear it open and read it over the phone.

MORGANTOWN, WV

West Virginia University was eighty miles further from my parents' house than the University of Kentucky, but it felt closer. I felt soothed by the steepness of the sidewalks and streets, the brown river that traced the length of the city. My parents, my siblings, my ancient childhood beagle, and I were all cradled by the borders of West Virginia.

But this time I had no cat. Weeks before I loaded my parents' minivan, Éowyn chirruped her usual goodbye as she slipped through my parents' sliding glass door, then she left for good. Bo meowed into every corner of the house, then curled on the piano bench. The dark half of the circle, forlorn and alone. I considered taking Bo so we could grieve together, but my parents would have missed him. Kassie was Jennifer's darling—out of the question. I brought my little brother instead.

I had to attend two weeks of teaching workshops, and Joshua had three weeks left in his public high school's summer vacation. I found Joshua on his bunk in pajamas at two p.m., playing a handheld video game. "You can play games on my computer all day, and we'll hang out and finish unpacking my apartment at night," I told him.

"Sure, Sarbef!" he said. He put on some real pants, wadded shirts into a backpack. Then he tucked his tennis shoes under his bum on my front passenger seat and slept all the way to Morgantown.

Looking back, I'm surprised I chose to spend two weeks at the mercy of my teenage brother's anger issues, which were worsening every day. I left him alone for seven hours a day with a computer I couldn't afford to replace, in a new-construction apartment where I'd be liable for anything he damaged.

I'm surprised I didn't decide against bringing him because of his wandering streak. I risked losing him into that unfamiliar mountain college town, land of sun-bleached Natty cans, maple-lined river trails, rotting fifth-story porches, blocks of candy-colored Victorian homes, and slippery morning puddles of vomit.

If I worried at all, I can't remember it. I can only assume I was more afraid of being alone, two hundred miles from home.

During those two weeks Joshua didn't get angry, or at least not frighteningly so. If he explored, he was back by the time I opened the door. He was nearly as good company as I'd hoped, giggling with me when the guy upstairs got diarrhea, a rhythm of moan and flush. And he brought me to grateful tears when he surprised me with homemade brownies, an eight-inch-pan mix baked in a cookie sheet to a centimeter-thick crunch.

Joshua was otherwise profoundly useless. He watched cartoons on my computer when I needed it to write my syllabus. He napped on the loveseat while I unloaded boxes from my Beetle. My cathode ray tube TV teetered on a folding tray table beside my desk, and I slogged through my required evening work to the sounds of whatever awful program he'd found. Every night, I reassured my mother over the phone that I had, in fact, supplied her little boy with breakfast and lunch and sat with him while he ate his dinner. I wished I'd rented a larger apartment so I could have some space for myself.

Halfway through Joshua's visit, an email appeared one morning on the grad student listserv. Titled "Brewhaha," it was cowritten by two new male students I hadn't spoken to, but I'd noticed one for his curls and eyes-squeezed-shut smile, and both seemed friendly and kind. The email read, "We're bored as all hell. Let's all meet at the brew pub tonight at seven o'clock." I read that message over and over.

Bored as all hell. Was everyone else bored? I didn't have time.

Brew pub. A fundamentalist kid's nightmare. I'd made it through four years of college and four months of history grad school without a single drink, without setting foot in a bar. At twenty-four, I carried a driver's license with UNDER 21 blazed across the top because I'd renewed it two days before my twenty-first birthday, and I hadn't cared enough to go back and fix the mistake. Also, I doubted I could take my brother to that pub. I didn't want to leave him, I didn't want to lie to him, and I didn't dare risk telling him I wanted to go. I figured Joshua would support me entering a pub, even purchasing the first alcoholic drink of my life, but I feared what he'd tell my mother in a fit of anger or sadness when he got back home.

All meet. Was I missing my only opportunity to make friends?

Bored as all hell. For a half moment I wished for a different family, a different life, so I could join them in their pleasant profanity.

❦

One Saturday evening a couple days after I got that email, I heard a knock on my door. I opened it to find my upstairs neighbor, the guy with the hilarious diarrhea.

“You just moved here too, right?” he asked. I walked outside and stood barefoot on the hot gravel parking lot, closed the door behind me on Joshua, stretched out on the loveseat for a nap.

“Yes, I moved here from Huntington,” I said, smiling. The guy looked a little older than me, thick blond ponytail, the kind of plumpness under his T-shirt and running shorts that comes from Hot Pockets and cheap beer. He told me he'd just started medical school, and I found myself attracted.

After we chatted a few minutes, he said, “Hey, you wouldn't want to go out for a drink somewhere, would you?”

I blushed. Alcohol again. I said, “My teenage brother's here, and I don't go to bars.” But I meant, *Why don't we go to a restaurant that's kid- and Christian-girl-friendly and take my little brother?* That's not the nuance he heard.

His face darkened and closed, and he responded, “Hey, it wasn't a creepy-upstairs-guy date. I just wanted to get out of my apartment.” Before I could say anything else, he'd thumped back up the stairs, and when I went back inside, I heard him switch on his TV.

An hour later I woke Joshua to eat chili, a heavy, underseasoned concoction I'd made with half my usual ingredients. While he was eating, crouched on my thin Walmart rug because I didn't own a table, I told him I'd talked to diarrhea guy and it had gone badly. I asked if he thought I should take the guy some chili, to show I was up for being friends. “Or is the chili too bad?” I said.

“Well, it *is* bad, Sarbef,” Joshua said, thoughtfully chewing, “and he'll think you like him.” He stood up, cocked his cargo shorts to one side, and held out his half-eaten bowl. In a cartoonish, high-pitched girl voice, he said, “Hi, do you want some chili?”

“You're right, Smoo,” I said. My body turned hot. I joined my brother on the rug with a bowl.

While Joshua's advice probably came from shyness—he was as shy as I was—I think he was right. I asked his opinion because he had flashes of wisdom. I'd never been kissed, never been on a date, and that guy could have read the chili as a sexual advance. Because my brother was there, and I wasn't lonely, I had the sense to give up on men and friends for the evening and spend a safe, quiet night at home.

After I drove Joshua back to Huntington, I drove back to my new apartment, which suddenly felt enormous. With my brother gone, I finished my work easily, and I often found myself crying. For a while, it truly seemed as if every other new grad student had shown up to the brew pub that night and found their grad school soulmates, leaving me to fend for myself. I wished I could maneuver a buggy around a Walmart Supercenter with my family's fifty-item grocery list, or pick up my brother from high school, or wait in line for my parents' one toilet. In other words, I was bored as all hell.

I listened to the guy moving around upstairs, a guy who never asked me to go anywhere or do anything with him again, mentally replaying our conversation and reciting that Brewhaha email. If I'd had the courage to move across the state without bringing my home stresses and limits with me, I might not have been sitting on my loveseat alone.

Days after I drove Joshua back to Huntington, I got another group email, this time for a backyard party at the house of someone I didn't know. Thankful it wasn't an invitation to a bar, and thankful to see other people, I went.

At the party I found a thirty-two-year-old, redhaired, German-accented history grad student slouched in a lawn chair, legs stretched out in front of him, casually drinking a beer. He had mismatched, protruding ears that looked different from every angle, mesmerizing in their ugliness. He called to me across the yard—something like *hey, girl, come here*—and pointed to an empty chair. I sat down and chatted for an hour, then I spent those next few lonely months talking to him every night online. He'd read a Brontë book once, he'd studied nineteenth-century European politics, and he loved his mother, so I thought he understood me. With apologies to all kind men with this name, I'll call him Max.

I told Max everything: my family, my Christian high school, my disappeared cat, my newfound love of teaching writing, my lingering stress about leaving my program in Kentucky. Max talked about sex in a frank way I found disgusting and exciting, and he used my oversharing to target my insecurities. He told me if I'd had it in me to leave home and stay gone, I would have finished my history program. He assured me any grad student who didn't go to bars and drink would spend every moment alone.

But he told me stories, and I lived for those stories, never bothering to sort lies from truth. The bakeries his family owned in Germany; the year he wrote history articles in a monastery in the Alps; his near-Olympic career as a ski jumper, cut short by an accident on a too-warm winter day. His stories about his mother bound him to my heart. Max said he wouldn't exclusively date anyone while studying in the United States because his mother had chronic kidney disease, she'd raised him by herself, and she'd asked him not to. Such family loyalty, I thought. Such self-deprivation! American girls annoyed her, and she worried he'd marry one of them and stay.

During those three a.m. conversations, during my groggy days of teaching freshman composition, during my drives between Huntington and Morgantown, during my sleepless weekend nights in my Huntington bedroom I kept intact out of habit, out of security, out of selfishness, out of love for my family, and for no good reason at all, I thought about Max. I thought wistfully that he might have been the kind of boy I would have made mistakes with as a teenager, if I'd had the opportunity to make them. In short, because of my complete lack of relevant life experience, my years of reading the Bible and helping my brother with his math homework instead of talking to men, I approached this situation with the mindset of a curious fourteen-year-old child. Max took notice. When I admitted I was a twenty-four-year-old who'd never been kissed, he invited me to his apartment.

I hesitated. It was three a.m. and thunderstorm dark. I'd never done anything in my life I couldn't narrate to my parents. But it was time to change that, I decided. And deep down, I hoped to win over Max's American-girl-hating mother, marry Max in a German castle, have odd-eared babies in the United States or Germany, I didn't care which. I got in my car.

Rain-blind and unfamiliar with the mountain roads, I missed a No Left Turn road sign and barely avoided a collision with a speeding vehicle. I pulled into a ditch, shaking. If I'd died or, worse, ended up in a hospital, my parents might have figured out what I was up to and thought, I felt, deservedly less of me. Years before, I'd internalized *How You Can Avoid Tragedy and Live a Better Life*, a Christian self-help book with a wrecked car on the cover. I feared—and I knew my mom believed firmly—that life's problems, especially car wrecks, resulted from sin.

Still, I pressed on. I parked where Max had instructed, beside a storage shed at the bottom of a hill behind his apartment. My first sign should have been that he didn't come out to meet me. The rain had slowed enough that I could see him chuckling at his window as I slipped, repeatedly, getting muddier and muddier. My second sign should have been that he didn't care when I told him I'd almost been killed on the drive. "It's a No Left Turn," he said firmly, and that was that. My third sign: he acted angry when I teased him about the can of herring on top of his television. My fourth: his response when I discovered his poodle-print shower curtain. "You like dogs?" I asked, hoping. He shut me down quick. "Some girl put that up. She wanted to take a shower."

We snuggled on the couch, a movie playing under the canned fish. Instead of watching the film, Max watched me. He pushed my head toward the screen when I tried to look away from a battlefield amputation, snorting, "You're twenty-four." He commented gleefully when I kept my eyes on a sex scene. He told me to finish his Bud Light, and when I shuddered at the taste, he mocked me, then produced a fruity bottle from his refrigerator. I chugged it down. Finally, Max kissed me, and I wanted to kiss more, but he told me he never just kissed girls. If I wanted to make out, I'd have to have sex with him. Due to the drink I'd chugged, my fear of those dark, rainy roads, my wish to defy that book with the car wreck on the cover, and the curiosity Max had awakened in my body with that kiss, I spent what remained of that night in his smelly-sheeted bed. I told him I didn't want to have sex, and we didn't. Nevertheless, I find myself still too humiliated, more than a decade later, to describe what happened that night in his apartment.

I drove back to my apartment at dawn, and I spent the next day considering dropping out of my MFA program, wondering if Mark had been right about Morgantown, wondering if Max was right about me. Wondering if this was who I was: a person who gave up and went home.

But I didn't drop out. As soon as I quit spending all my energy on chats with Max, I realized my fellow bar-mingling grad students also went out to lunch, ate pizza at home while watching *Sponge Bob*, hiked in the Monongahela National Forest, and I was welcome to join them. I found Gideon, who gave me my *real* first kiss and loved me for five years. I learned that nearly everyone feels sad and lonely after a move to a new city. I learned that while refusing to enter bars can be socially limiting, no one cared if I didn't want to drink beer.

❦

Right after my run-in with Max, my parents gave up on house hunting and decided to add two bedrooms onto their house, finally a room for each child. "I don't need a bedroom," I told my parents, insistent. I thought about Mark's room, how he "got real quiet on the phone."

Mark had two years left to live, and I had no idea yet he was an alcoholic. But I knew, because he'd told me, that Mark had never bought the house he'd saved up to buy, that the only furnishings in his apartment were a bed, dresser, recliner, and stand for his TV. I feared if I kept my room, I might keep returning, bound forever to that house like my parents seemed to be. Or I'd move my four pieces of furniture from one crappy apartment to another, never building a real homeplace for myself.

Fears aside, I'd realized that to survive without my family, I had to move my full self elsewhere, body, brain, and spirit. I had to think outside of the car-wreck-cover books on my mother's bookshelves. I couldn't use visiting siblings as an opportunity to re-create my Huntington life, keeping myself insulated and lonely. I wanted my parents to view my single, adult self the way my dad's mother saw him when he got married, when she threw out his stuff and filled his bedroom with pink ruffles: a person who might need a place to sleep, but who wouldn't be returning. My siblings were so used to giving me my rights as firstborn, they might never openly sing "The Cat Came Back" when I encroached on their lives and space, but if I'd moved back yet again, I would have surely deserved it. It was beyond time for me to view trips to Huntington as visits to my beloved family, not opportunities to spend time at my true home.

So Jennifer kept the three-sibling room, and my parents built a big new bedroom for Rebecca. I moved my twin bed in with Rebecca; she planned to move out soon herself, and she enjoyed occasional room-sharing. I stashed the doll cradle in a closet and let my sixteen-year-old brother move his stuff into my room. Joshua covered the walls with comic book posters, piled stuffed animals on my dresser, shoved his bed against the interior wall instead of the window that looked out on the dogwood tree, and drowned out my fruity-body-spray, dusty-book, old-hamster-cage smell with a fog of unwashed socks. Within a week I could imagine that room had been Joshua's all along.

My mom taped my lost-dog whining over the homemade soundtrack she'd made of *Jesus of Nazareth*, a Franco Zeffirelli–directed miniseries from the 1970s that my siblings and I watched twice a year when we were growing up. When I was a baby, years before our family owned a VCR, my mom set up a cassette recorder next to the black-and-white set, switching out tapes when the machine clicked to a stop. She wanted to wash dishes and fold cloth diapers to Jesus's voice and the film's symphonic music, triumphant with an undercurrent of heartbreak. Then one day, perhaps halfway through scrubbing a baked-on dish, she heard my voice. She stopped the playing tape and pressed Record.

In the Bible, Jesus tells the Prodigal Son story to Pharisees, those stuffy religious know-it-alls, after they try to shame Him for eating with Israel's lowest lowlifes: drunkards, tax collectors, and harlots.

In *Jesus of Nazareth*, Jesus plunks himself down at a table with the lowlifes, and He parables directly to them. Before Jesus speaks, a half-drunk man lifts a goblet: "I drink to you in the name of all here." The line is funny because those sinners are nobodies, and the man doesn't see it, but then again, Jesus doesn't seem to see it either. Women with lipstick and earrings titter appreciatively in the background as Jesus begins speaking, a smile in his British accent: "I'd like to tell you a story."

When my family watched Jesus on screen, my mom liked to tell this story. Franco Zeffirelli was raised in a devout Roman Catholic home, but he left God. At forty-six he was in a horrible car wreck. As Zeffirelli bled in his car, he told God, if you let me live, I'll make films for your glory. He lived and directed *Jesus of Nazareth*.

The tittering stops when Jesus begins his parable. In the background, wind whistles past the tent where they're eating, flapping the door open and closed. On the cassette tape, the wind must have sounded like people listening. Watching the film, I can see the dinner guests' eyes widening, their jaws tightening. They're wondering if they have it in them to go home.

In *Jesus of Nazareth*, Jesus tells the parable of the Prodigal Son, but no actor plays the Prodigal. This leaves the audience casting around for a resemblance: the half-drunk man who gives the toast, harlots with earrings and exposed curls, bare-chested fishermen, Franco Zeffirelli, ourselves.

My dad and I found Scruffy repeatedly, but I have no memory of this. I'm sure my mom poured Scruffy an enormous bowl of Dog Chow, and I hope my parents let him eat it in the kitchen. But I only remember the searching. That loop around Twin Valley. My mom's calls to the pound. The burn in my throat when I screamed my dog's name, wondering if I'd see him again.

PART 3
RIOTOUS LIVING

The happy part of the Prodigal's journey lasts one-third of a biblical sentence. In that far country, he "wasted his substance with riotous living."

One Bible Storybook panel after the Prodigal takes his bag of money, he hunches in worn-out clothes outside a clay-brick building, a party visible through the windows. Inside, men drink ink-purple wine and laugh with a woman with exposed brown hair, a woman who, despite her modest pink dress, is surely meant to be a harlot. The caption reads, "All his money was gone."

The Bible Storybook leaves out a major part of the story, and Jesus does too. That moment when the Prodigal dismounts from a camel or disembarks from a ship, buys his first wine that wasn't grown and fermented on his father's land, strides around that far country with heavy pockets, grinning at women, exploring the new setting of his life. The parable omits the real enjoyment the riotous Prodigal must have felt in flashes at least–the enjoyment that made his elder brother so jealous.

Here are some old and enduring OED definitions of *riotous*, in use both during the years the KJV was translated and the years of my brother's life:

- Of life, conduct, etc.: extravagant, unrestrained, esp. marked by excessive revelry; wanton, dissolute.
- Of or relating to rioting or disturbance of the peace; taking part in or inciting riot; turbulent.
- Noisy, tumultuous; unrestrained.
- Of plant growth, branches, etc.: overgrowing, luxuriant; exuberant.

Surely because of the Bible Storybook and all my fundamentalism-infused years, combined with my current beliefs about social justice, I have a hard time picturing the Prodigal Son enjoying his excessive revelry. I don't want to picture an exuberant man enjoying a woman like a slice of cake, wetting his whistle with ink-purple wine.

Instead I picture my sad uncle Mark, drinking alone in his apartment until it killed him. I picture twenty-year-old Joshua, turbulently miserable, recalculating how long it would take him to buy a professional camera now that he'd spent a full year of call center salary on comic books and pot. I remember Mark, drunk on the phone in his final year, accusing my dad of mistreating him in childhood. I remember Joshua kicking holes in the door of a closet where I'm trying to hide.

I tend to ignore that happy, plant-focused definition and focus on *riotous*'s other meanings, the ones that sound to me, with my personal traumas, like violent episodes and addiction. I focus on the sad, judgmental versions: unrestrained noise that leads to death.

When I visited Haworth for the first time at twenty-eight, it was two years and five months before I lost Joshua and ten months after I sat with Mark in a Pennsylvania hospital during his final week alive. I'd flown to England to put my shoes on the floorboards that once held the writers of my favorite books, to see those tiny books they wrote together, to walk the moors in weather cold and damp enough to trigger tuberculosis. But I found myself focused on Branwell, not the sisters. In the Brontë Parsonage Museum, I lingered in front of the actual black horsehair sofa where Emily coughed up blood, the white baby bonnet Charlotte stitched before she died from morning sickness, one body buried inside another. But I found myself moved to the point of shudders by a mere replica of an artifact of Branwell's death at thirty-one, after he destroyed his body with alcohol and laudanum: Patrick Brontë's red-curtained bed.

In Branwell's last year, his father slept next to him, trying to keep his son from drinking, hanging or shooting himself, or burning the house with a forgotten candle. Branwell slept all day and moaned at night. Since my brother's early teens, I'd witnessed his daily escapes to his bunk, heard his suicide threats, heard him stalking around the house when he failed to sleep. In Mark's last week, I'd taken his keys from his sweatpants and driven from the hospital to his apartment, a place where the air hung heavy with moldering blood and vomit, and Jim Beam empties clustered around a recliner. The sisters' deaths moved me like the tragic ending to a fairytale. Branwell's was a death I could feel.

Hungry in Haworth, I wandered down the hill from the parsonage to the Black Bull. With my brain filled with Brontë biographies, I'd thought darkly of that pub as a place Branwell weakened his liver and heart. The pub's website spun the situation in a more cheerful, tourist-friendly light, claiming to be "Branwell's favorite." At the Black Bull, I pictured him in a corner, laughing with friends. As I sat there, an ocean from my family, nervous to be in a bar, chewing a hamburger alone, I found myself jealous of his ghost.

Before I left, a bartender noticed me for the young, female, American Brontë-tourist I was and offered to take me upstairs to see a scuffed mahogany-stained hardwood chair: Branwell's favorite place to sit. There was a rope tied arm to arm to remind enthusiasts not to sit down and smash the chair. I needed that reminder. And I needed this reminder that Branwell–like my brother, like my uncle, like the riotous Prodigal himself–wasn't always sad. Branwell laughed at the Black Bull. The Prodigal jangled his fresh bag of money. Mark fished at dawn with his brothers. During Joshua's most tumultuous, peace-disturbing years, he smoked pot in barns with friends, grilled hot dogs at the lake with his sisters.

I can't help focusing on the turbulent, unrestrained misery of these men. But I'm wronging them all if I forget their luxuriant, exuberant joy.

Moonstruck

In the King James Version of chapter 9 of the Gospel of Luke, a man brings his son to Jesus. Describing his son's misery, the man says, "A spirit taketh him, and he suddenly crieth out; and it teareth him so that he foameth again, and bruising him hardly departeth from him."

Matthew 17 describes the same father, the same boy—the same recurrent, terrifying illness—but in this chapter the father doesn't mention demons. In the KJV, the father in Matthew 17 tells Jesus his son is "lunatick."

Lunatick: a translation of the ancient Greek *selēniazomai*. The most direct modern equivalent is *moonstruck*.

After I moved to Morgantown, I visited my family first every weekend, then every two weekends, then once a month, unconsciously synching my drives to the phases of the moon.

In Morgantown, I worried about my brother, about my whole family, and I got lonely enough to hang out with Max, but I also reveled in the escape. I looked around at my full-size bed, my loveseat, my cheap brown rug, and marveled at the silence of my apartment.

From the safety of that silence, I chatted with my brother online about comic books, gummy worms, movies, and girls and pretended he was always okay.

In *Jesus of Nazareth*, a distraught father with a short gray beard herds his son to a stone porch, where people crowd around Jesus.

A boyish adult, the son has dark curls that seem too clean for his situation, but he looks possessed. He mumbles and slams himself against pillars and steps. His eyes blaze and dart at random. Chunky saliva covers the bottom half of his face. He tugs down a lit oil lamp that hangs from the porch ceiling and hurls it at the floor, barely missing his own feet.

Watching that scene as a child and teen, when my brother was unborn or still a boy who wrote songs about rockets and whined for video games, I felt moved, but revolted by the spit.

Watching it now, I notice that the possessed boy's too-clean hair curls just like Joshua's. I remember my brother slamming those curls against the hallway wall during the final five years of his life.

Lunatick is the linguistic offspring of the late Latin *lūnāticus*, derived from the Latin *lūna*, moon. During the late sixteenth-century decades when the KJV's translators were at work—when *lunatic*'s spelling, no matter how it varied, always included a *k*—the *OED* says the word meant "affected with the kind of insanity that was supposed to have recurring periods dependent on the changes of the moon."

I never saw a connection between my brother's illness and the size of the moon in the sky, though he certainly caused more trouble at night.

From 1554, in a translation of John Lydgate's *Fall of Princes*: "He was . . . euery moneth once Lunaticke."

When Joshua emerged from his room on my weekend visits home, sometimes it was daylight. Sometimes he joined my family at dinner, ate a bite of green beans. Sometimes he wanted me to drive him to a movie theater, and I obliged when I could, laughing at his legitimately good jokes, gritting my teeth through his too-loud music.

But too often he got up after nightfall. I shuddered at the click, pop, and slide of his always-stuck door opening, the puff of stale sock air that followed him as he walked. I gauged his mood by the speed and tone of his footsteps on our parents' laminate flooring.

From 1600, in a translation of Tomaso Garzoni's *Hospitall of Incurable Fooles*: "If the moone be euill placed, either it maketh men extatical, lunatick, or subiect to the kings euill."

Rereading the Bible now, I'm not surprised I see my brother's mental illness in Franco Zeffirelli's portrayal of an exorcism. Demon-torment throughout the Bible resembles mental or neurological illness. In First Samuel, in the Old Testament, an "evil spirit" often "troubles" King Saul, rendering him sad and restless. In the Bible Storybook's version, Saul slumps on his throne, resting his yellow-crowned head on his hand. When the spirit comes, Saul's servants call David—boy shepherd turned giant-slayer—who plays the harp until Saul is calm and well again.

Beginning the year Joshua walked to Tyler's, Joshua became stressed by the boredom and claustrophobia inherent in car rides, and he slumped, frowned, and cursed in his seat belt like a spirit-troubled king whenever my family went anywhere. If we let him play his CDs on full volume, drowning out conversations, passing cars, honking horns, he relaxed like Saul with the harp.

Medieval Roman Catholics noticed the resemblance between biblical demon possession and disability and illness they couldn't understand. St. Francis of Assisi, the famous garden statue who cradles baby birds and strokes the heads of fawns, was known in his own day for his exorcisms. In the thirteenth-century biography *The Life of St. Francis of Assisi*, St. Bonaventure's chronicles of the saint's exorcisms include this line: "One of the Brethren was afflicted with such an horrible disease as that it was asserted of many to be rather a tormenting from demons than a natural sickness."

But the Bible writers' choice of *selēniazomai* and the KJV translators' *lunatick* reveal an alternative historical explanation for unexplainable illness, a belief held by people who lived alongside—and surely overlapped with—believers in demon possession. When a person seemed to lose control of the brain or body, and when the illness came and went, some ancient and medieval Christians must have blamed the moon.

Sometimes at night my brother was hungry, up to microwave a hot dog. Sometimes he opened the door of the newly built bedroom where Rebecca and I lay in our twin beds, and he said, "Hey, Sarbef, Rebecca, want to watch a movie?" On those nights his footsteps were high-pitched and light.

But other times, we heard the deeper-toned sound of his footsteps, then a curse, and often a smash. If a lit oil lamp had dangled from our ceiling, my brother would have hurled it at the floor.

❦

In 1870 a group of British scholars began retranslating the Bible, seeking to correct the errors of the KJV. For one of these corrections, they replaced Matthew 17's "he is lunatick, and sore vexed" with "he is epileptic, and suffereth grievously."

Lunatic had dropped the k by 1870, and it meant simply "insane," not an illness that struck and receded with the phases of the moon. The translators reasoned that *epileptic* was now the clearest equivalent of *selēniazomai*, best fitting the intermittent nature of the illness, plus the collection of the boy's other symptoms—foaming, convulsing, falling into water and fire, gnashing teeth—described by Gospel writers Matthew, Mark, and Luke.

Current scholarly translations (e.g., the New Revised Standard Version, the American Standard), the versions preferred now for their accuracy and comprehensible language, have preserved this change. Turn to Matthew 17:15 and you'll find a man who tells Jesus his son has epilepsy.

❦

Everyone in the house heard my raging brother, and everyone groaned and got up. Joshua speechified about film and our family's failings. He took a menacing step toward a person, or a brass lamp, and two of us tackled him to the floor.

Then we all sat on him, a person on each leg, two people on his back, pressing his cheek into the rug, holding down his arms with our bare feet. All of us avoiding his eyes, which were not Joshua's eyes.

❦

When I compare my brother to the boy in the Bible and film, I realize that my brother's behavior was nothing like epilepsy. That epilepsy is fundamentally nothing like my brother's emotional disturbances, except that St. Bonaventure surely would have called either condition "such an horrible disease as that it was asserted of many to be rather a tormenting from demons than a natural sickness."

Also, both disabilities are intermittent—perfect for ancient-world and medieval moon explanations—and the intermittence makes both disabilities often invisible, giving the person with the condition the option of when—or whether—to talk about it in public. At least partly because Joshua's episodes struck most frequently at night, he seems to have passed for what his peers and teachers viewed as "normal" in high school. He directed plays and starred in them. He ignored his homework, but his teachers loved him for his jokes. He joined a group of awkward kids in grumpy T-shirts and ate cold Little Caesar's Hot-N-Readys in a park.

But I'm hesitant to say the boy in *Jesus of Nazareth* has epilepsy, any more than he shares my brother's undiagnosed condition. The scene is hardly a scientific portrayal of a specific ailment.

The father in the film doesn't say his line from Matthew 17:15, and so he doesn't diagnose his son with either epilepsy or madness. Instead he follows nearly word for word what the father says in Mark 9 of any current scholarly translation. Casting frantic looks at his son, the father pleads, "Rabbi, the demon has always tried to throw him into fire and into water to destroy him. If you can do anything, have mercy."

The boy's father in *Jesus of Nazareth* looks exhausted, like he's put every ounce of himself into keeping his boy alive, and his boy is all he's got left. I remember my mother sobbing in her nightgown, tangled hair in her face, a few hours into sitting on my brother on the floor.

I wonder if the curly-haired boy's parents ever tried sitting on their son. But in Luke, the father wails to Jesus, "Master, I beseech thee, look upon my son: for he is mine only child." I wonder if the sitting method is only practical in families like ours, with extra bodies to hold down hands and feet.

A wide variety of Bible commenters—including those who want to defend the existence of demons and those who aim to break the (still enduring) association between demon possession and epilepsy—like to point out that only the non-divine father, likely a man with a layman's ancient-world medical knowledge, describes the boy's condition as epilepsy or madness.

No matter the translation, and no matter if you read the story in Matthew, Mark, or Luke, Jesus diagnoses demon possession and tells the demon to leave.

❦

Film-Jesus watches for a few moments as the boy slams and writhes. Then He says, "Satan!" He fixes His ice-blue eyes on the boy and raises His hand. The boy writhes harder. "Leave him!" I remember watching Jesus's face and hearing that line as a child, feeling smug about of the power of my God.

Watching the film now, I ignore Jesus and focus on the boy. After Jesus kicks out the boy's demons, he lies still on the stone floor, apparently unconscious. According to the KJV Gospel of Mark, "He was as one dead; insomuch that many said, He is dead." In the film, the father stands frozen, afraid he's lost his son for good.

Holding Joshua's body to the floor, looking at his anger-wild eyes, I sometimes wondered if the brother I loved would come back.

❦

By 1611 the term *epilepsy* was new but available to the KJV translators, and the condition, also known as "falling sickness," was (largely) understood to be medical in nature rather than an affliction by demons.

The *OED* cites *epilepsy*'s first recorded appearance as 1578, as an ailment that could be alleviated by herbs. Rembert Dodoens, in Henry Lyte's translation *Niewe Herball*, says, "The same . . . is good for the Epilepsie, or falling sicknesse." Twenty-five years later, Shakespeare used the word in *Othello*: "My Lord is falne into an Epilepsy, This is his second fit."

The KJV translators' choice of *lunatick* feels particularly deliberate. Like Franco Zeffirelli, they could have used the word *epilepsy* and didn't. They saw the word *selēniazomai* and the list of symptoms, and they still decided to blame the moon.

When the sun began to rise, my family felt Joshua's muscles relax. His neck fell limp against the rug. We let him up, and he sobbed his apologies, looking at our faces with soft, clear eyes. "I didn't want to hurt you, Mama. I didn't want to hurt you, Sarbef." I know, I know, we all told him.

In *Jesus of Nazareth*, the son opens his eyes after a few moments and focuses them on his father's face. He says, "Father." The onlookers maintain their safe distance. The father weeps and hugs his son against his chest.

I understand why nearly 150 years of translators have translated *selēniazomai* as *epileptic* or *epilepsy*, but against reason I prefer the KJV *lunatick*. While I would never let anyone apply that word to my brother, he certainly fit under its umbrella of intermittent mental illness.

Lunatick allows me to imagine my brother into the possessed boy's story. A story, like the parable of the Prodigal Son, where a miserable young man has a happy ending.

Lunatick allows me to think of my brother's anger as an unstoppable force. Moon-driven. Beyond mental illness. If I use the word *lunatick*, there's nothing to forgive. Joshua couldn't help smashing his parents' house. He couldn't help harming me and my family.

And *lunatick* allows me respite from finding ways to blame myself.

From 1564, in John Strype's *Ecclesiastical Memorials*: "All this trouble . . . was when you were lunatike and not your owne man."

We thanked God silently as we got up from the floor and returned to our beds, but we didn't throw our arms toward the heavens. I'm sure my mom hugged Joshua, but no one sobbed with joy and relief.

We hoped Joshua would sleep. We hoped he'd get up and be the funny kid in high school. And we knew he'd get angry again.

Lost Photographs

My parents' hallway. March 2006. Dressed in plaid pajama pants and a T-shirt, Joshua stands in front of my mother's craft closet, one fist raised, the other in contact with the door. *Bang, bang.* This photo seems to come with sound. He's already checked the closet for his laptop, dumping baskets of tape and scissors, clearing shelves of construction paper, and now he's sending a signal to our mother. She hid his laptop for a threatened week on Friday afternoon, after she snooped in his bookbag and found Fs on a report card. She told him she'd bought him that computer for school, but that's obviously *not* how *he's* using it, and she wishes she'd never bought it at all. Now it's Saturday, and what, truly, is Joshua supposed to do if he can't watch his pirated films? Joshua's set jaw is flecked with unshaven stubble. The top of his nose wrinkles under his glasses. *Bang, bang.* Within minutes, my mother will appear with the laptop. He'll grab it from her hands without a word.

Spring Valley High School Auditorium in Huntington, WV. May 2008. Joshua runs up the aisle between the rows of audience seats in a T-shirt and jeans, moving from the back door to the stage. The houselights are on, so he's visible along with the audience, including Jennifer, Rebecca, and me. Joshua's brandishing a wooden baseball bat, eyes ablaze. Nearly everyone in the audience is laughing: everyone but me and my sisters. I just look stressed in the photo, but I'm cycling through emotions. Terrified of Joshua, then furious at those teachers, teens, and parents for laughing at my brother. Then thankful and relieved. No one else sees what my sisters and I see. It's hilarious to see friendly Josh pretending to be crazy.

McDonald's parking lot in Huntington, WV. Thanksgiving 2009. Joshua sits in my Beetle's front passenger seat, head in his hands, glasses on the car floor, shoulders shaking with sobs. I'm in the driver's seat, holding two melting chocolate milkshakes. Joshua's been sobbing for fifteen minutes. He began in a theater across town, at the ending of Spike Jonze's *Where the Wild Things Are*. Little boy Max floated toward home on a boat, away from a howling, heartbroken Wild Thing, and Joshua went to pieces. His reaction startled me. He chose the film for the director; we didn't read that book as children. And Joshua simply does not cry during films. Soon he'll sit up, accept a milkshake, refresh himself with a slurp. He'll say, "I don't know what the fuck happened in there, Sarbef."

Spring Valley High School Auditorium. May 2009. Joshua crouches in the shadows in a giant cotton trash bag, dressed in a cheap bunny suit. Maybe he looks like an eighteen-year-old in a goofy costume, or a tossed-away toy, but the audience knows better. Joshua's the play's director, and its surprise star. For the first few performances, Joshua managed from backstage, dealing with missed cues and prop mishaps, but then the girl playing the bunny was injured in an unrelated accident, and Joshua put on velveteen. Joshua is committed to the performance: he emotes the velveteen rabbit's sorrow and fear as he spends the night in that bag, waiting to be burned with scarlet fever bedsheets. But underneath the rabbit's sorrow, there's pride in Joshua's eyes. Pride that transforms rabbit ears and a cotton-ball tail into the clothes of a king.

My parents' street. July 2009. Joshua strides home at sunset on the still-hot asphalt, coughing just a little, smoking a grape-flavored cigarette. He's been sad this summer, waiting for college, tortured by endless dull errands. The financial aid office. The mall for dorm sheets he wouldn't use for months. But today, a miracle. A useful college errand! Our mother drove him to the Department of Motor Vehicles for a non-driver's ID. Back home, he ran into his bedroom, pocketed the cash he'd earned mowing, consulted a YouTube video titled "How to Smoke a Cigar." Then he slipped out the window and walked to Clay's. The grape cigarette in the photo will be illegal in two months, a federal effort to curb tobacco use among teens. A decade later, I feel that irony, but I can't say I'm angry. While I'm aware of smoking's risks—PaPa's congestive heart failure, my great-aunt's lung cancer, the tripled risk of suicide attempts for people with mood disorders—I'm not sure I could have snatched away that cigarette. From the set of my brother's shoulders, I can tell he feels like director David Lynch in his promotional photos. Like Woody Allen in *Manhattan*, when he puffs away, claiming he "looks so incredibly handsome with a cigarette." Joshua smokes his way home in the warm evening air. It's one of the best moments of his life.

The Man Who Lived among the Tombs

After a few months of sitting on Joshua during my weekend visits, I demanded over the phone that my mom take Joshua to a doctor. I threatened to never come home again, to spend Christmas with my boyfriend Gideon's family or alone in my apartment. Joshua got stronger every time we sat on him, and sometimes he got in a punch or a hair pull before we tackled him to the floor.

I told my mom I was afraid, and I *was* afraid. Still, I was bluffing. When my brother was at his worst, I loved more than feared him, and I knew I'd always go home.

In the 2014 *Early Science in Medicine* article "Demonic Possessions and Mental Illness: Discussion of Selected Cases in Late Medieval Hagiographical Literature," art historian Carlos Espí Forcén and psychiatrist Fernando Espí Forcén examine one of Jesus's exorcisms along with exorcisms from hagiographical literature and art. They grant the demoniacs speculative diagnoses that include schizophrenia, mood disorders, epilepsy, and Tourette syndrome. I find this proceeding highly interesting, though I don't mind believing Jesus cast out actual demons, and the scholars admit their diagnoses are "slippery" and "anachronistic."

The Espí Forcéns leave grumpy King Saul undiagnosed, but they bring him up to illustrate the difference between Old and New Testament demon torment. Old Testament demons tormented from outside the body, and they responded to treatments like David's harp. New Testament demons entered the body—one demon inside the boy with seizures, perhaps thousands inside the man in their chosen biblical case—and getting rid of them required an exorcism.

My mother and I both loved Joshua and wanted him well. The New Testament–Old Testament issue is where we differed. My mother believed literal dark spirits plagued Joshua from without, like the spirits David drove away with his harp.

I must note that, now, my mom supports her anxious daughters taking their medications, approaching pharmacy counters herself so we won't run out of pills. She's still no fan of doctors, but such feelings are no match for her love for her children. If Joshua were alive, and medication made a real impact on his shifting moods, I'm sure she'd do just about anything to keep him on it. But at that time, no one in our known family had taken medication for mental illness, and she hadn't seen such tangible proof. So—due (from my perspective) to my mom's traumatic past with her mother, and to psychiatrist-hating preachers who blame the devil and weak faith for mental illness, and to her interlinked distrust of modern medicine and intensely sincere faith—my mom called Joshua's illness a "spiritual problem." Joshua's dark spirits would depart if my family prayed and waited, if he showed a real interest in God.

I believed then, and I believe now, that Joshua's demons were integral to his brain, and he needed to manage them with a modern-medicine exorcism.

For their biblical example, the Espí Forcéns analyze the Gerasene demoniac, a man whose demons introduce themselves to Jesus as "Legion." The story is included in the Gospels of Matthew, Mark, and Luke and left out of the Bible Storybook and *Jesus of Nazareth*.

While crossing the Sea of Galilee with his disciples, Jesus falls asleep in the bottom of the boat. A ship-smashing storm blows in, so the disciples wake Jesus. He calms the wind and sea with His voice, and the boat glides to the Gerasene shore. From the Gospel of Mark: "And when He was come out of the ship, immediately there met Him out of the tombs a man with an unclean spirit, who had his dwelling among the tombs."

A few days before my threats, I'd crept into Joshua's room when he lay in his bunk after a night on the floor. Crouched on the end of his bed, I'd told him I'd read about bipolar disorder, and thought he might have that or something like it. I'd told him mental illness can sometimes cause people to punch their sisters. I'd told him his violent episodes weren't his fault. I'd told him he needed to go the doctor, and I'd promised to get our mother to take him.

Please understand: Bipolar disorder does not equal violence. I have no wish to contribute to the stigma of mental illness, or to the irrational fear and discomfort so many otherwise kind people feel toward the mentally ill. That fear and stigma—and my family's fear of that fear and stigma—is part of the web of genetic, physical, and emotional circumstances that cost my brother his life. But I believe it's an injustice to my brother if I blame only him, and not his illness, for the nights my family spent on the floor.

The Espí Forcéns diagnose the tomb-dwelling Gerasene with a mood disorder—a category that includes bipolar disorder and major depression—citing a list of symptoms that might match my brother's, if my brother's episodes were exaggerated in a nightmare. They note the Gerasene demoniac's "decreased need for sleep," his "self-mutilation," his "increase of energy with psychomotor agitation," and his decision to "live isolated from society" in a graveyard.

I have no idea what I read online twelve years ago that made me suspect my brother had bipolar disorder, and more specifically bipolar I. But after reading the chapter "Bipolar and Related Disorders" in the current *Diagnostic and Statistical Manual of Mental Disorders*, the DSM-5, I still hold this belief.

I know this diagnosis is particularly "slippery," since I have no medical training, and "anachronistic" because my brother is dead. I'd be thrilled if Jesus reanimated my brother's ashes, allowing a professional to prove me wrong.

I felt bold enough to ask my mom to take Joshua to the doctor because I'd seen a crack in her defenses. The night before I talked to Joshua, my mother had sat next to me on his anger-stiff body, her bum holding down the crook of his knees. She'd sobbed and said, "I thought I'd gotten away from all this when I didn't have to live with Mother."

In the late 1960s, after her divorce from PaPa, Granny quit her nursing career to sleep, worry, and chain-smoke on her black vinyl couch. In her late teens, my mom began supporting herself, her mother, and her younger brother with shifts in the blouse department of a downtown store.

The night my mother sobbed on my brother's back, she was fifty, with the body of a woman who'd carried four babies to term, wearing a middle-aged woman's cotton nightgown. But the tone of her voice, those sobs, allowed me to see her at twenty, younger and slimmer than I was, shuddering in front of that black vinyl couch as Granny accused her of anything, everything. Granny wasn't violent, but her words were a violence. Granny got off that couch to tug my mother's belongings toward the door, threatening to put them into the street, or to unplug the phone when my mother expected a call.

According to the DSM-5, people diagnosed with bipolar must meet the criteria for a manic episode at least one time in their lives. Depressive episodes and hypomanic episodes are common among people with bipolar I, but they're not necessary for the diagnosis.

Criterion A for a manic episode: *A distinct period of abnormally and persistently elevated, expansive, or irritable mood and abnormally and persistently increased activity or energy, lasting at least 1 week and present most of the day, nearly every day (or any duration if hospitalization is necessary).*

Criterion A: In the last five years of his life, sometimes Joshua barely slept for weeks. He went to school or work by day. He wrote, drew, or stared at his computer screen in the evenings. At night he stalked up and down the hallways, looking for someone who would talk to him or watch a movie, or looking for a fight.

The Gerasene demoniac cried "night and day . . . cutting himself with stones."

❦

Exhausted by my threats, and perhaps broken down by that particularly terrible night, my mother took my brother to a self-proclaimed "natural doctor," a man with an MD and a soft voice who asked patients to call him his first name. I'll call him Paul. He dealt in chakras, chelation therapy, and other treatments that had not been FDA approved.

My mom normally wouldn't have put up with chakras, or anything that smacked of a far country, but she didn't trust the medical system, and Paul didn't either.

Paul wasn't the kind of doctor I'd meant, but I thought he might be a start.

❦

Criterion B: *During the period of mood disturbance and increased energy or activity, three (or more) of the following symptoms (four if the mood is only irritable) are present to a significant degree and represent a noticeable change from usual behavior: 1. Inflated self-esteem or grandiosity. 2. Decreased need for sleep (e.g., feels rested after only 3 hours of sleep). 3. More talkative than usual or pressure to keep talking. 4. Flight of ideas or subjective experience that thoughts are racing. 5. Distractibility (i.e., attention too easily drawn to unimportant or irrelevant external stimuli), as reported or observed. 6. Increase in goal-directed activity (either socially, at work or school, or sexually) or psychomotor agitation (i.e., purposeless non-goal-directed activity). 7. Excessive involvement in activities that have a high potential for painful consequences (e.g. engaging in unrestrained buying sprees, sexual indiscretions, or foolish business investments).*

Criterion B: 1. Joshua believed the screenplay he was writing would change film (though it feels like a betrayal of my brother to say it couldn't). 2. See criterion A. 3. When euthymic (between episodes),

Joshua was either silent or a decent conversationalist, talking for short periods, then pausing to at least pretend to listen to a response. When manic, he could hold forth all night. 4. "Sarbef, my thoughts are racing. I can't keep my thoughts still in my head." 5. I'm not sure about this one. 6. Joshua stomped up and down the halls, and into the hills, unable to calm his body or brain. 7. The year before he died, he went on pot-purchasing runs with awful friends into parts of downtown Huntington where people frequently get shot. He texted Rebecca from the worst block in town: "I'm in the trunk."

The Gerasene demoniac runs through the graveyard and up and down the mountains, shredding his ankles and stone-bruising his hardened feet.

When my mother was in her early twenties, several family members and a man she was dating convinced her briefly to have Granny committed to the State Hospital. I'm guessing someone saw a crack in my mom's defenses. Nearly everyone who loved my mother said institutionalization was for her and her mother's own safety. And if my mom didn't have her mother committed, my mom would never get married, never have children. She'd ride the city bus home to that smoky house every evening, wondering if her mother had managed to carry her clothes, books, and radio to the street.

My mom signed the commitment papers, but she couldn't go through with it. Police and state hospital staff came for my grandmother when she was home alone. My mom was at work, folding blouses. She got a call on the department phone: "Miss, we'll need your permission to break down your door."

On the phone with the police, my mom pictured her mother trembling in a back room with matted hair and a nylon nightgown, trying and failing to light a cigarette. She pictured her mother with a beehive and a turquoise dress, driving my mom and her brothers to church. My mom screamed *No!* into the phone.

I was in Huntington when Joshua went to the doctor, reading or writing in the bedroom I shared with Rebecca on visits home, and my mom told me about the appointment from the hall. She began, "I took him to a doctor, Sarah Beth, God as my witness!" and I knew everything was over.

When I joined my mom in the hall, Joshua stood beside her, saying nothing, his face flickering between expressionless and proud to have so much attention on his brain. "Well, 'Paul'"—my mom used air quotes for emphasis— "wouldn't let me go in there with Joshua, but Joshua told me all about it on the way home. That man played psychologist, tried to blame everything on Joshua's parents. He asked Joshua if we were 'infantilizing' him. As if I don't want more than anything for him to grow up and do something with his life!"

Paul had asked to talk to Joshua alone at the appointment, which made my mother instantly suspicious. I'm sure she'd been hoping to explain the situation, to emphasize Joshua's tiredness, downplay his anger. She'd probably hoped to come home with vitamin supplements that would make everything okay.

Criterion C: *The mood disturbance is sufficiently severe to cause marked impairment in social or occupational functioning or to necessitate hospitalization to prevent harm to self or others, or there are psychotic features.*

Criterion C: One night when I was in Huntington, less than a year before Joshua died, he came to Rebecca's and my room and said his brain kept telling him to kill himself. I should have driven my brother to the hospital. But I was the Prodigal's older brother, too steady and respectful to cause my mother a serious trauma, and Rebecca was the same. "You're sleeping in here, Smoo," Rebecca told him, and I got up and gave him my bed.

The Gerasenes have tried to keep the demoniac in chains—an ancient-world version of institutionalization—but "the chains had been plucked asunder by him, and the fetters broken in pieces." Under the demons' influence, the man chooses to live alone among the tombs.

My mom's boyfriend and family members were wrong. My mom married my dad, who understood she needed to take care of her mother.

They rented an apartment a few blocks from Granny, and Granny did so well alone they built a house across town, the one where I grew up, stopped by every few days to check on Granny's stores of cigarettes, coffee, 7UP, Crisco, Ritz crackers, teabags, sugar, chicken, canned fruit cocktail, chocolate drops, milk, and romance novels.

My siblings and I grew up with a grandmother who sometimes screamed at us, who told wild stories about the neighbors, who sometimes threw us out of her house. But mostly she sewed us clothing, cooked us hot-plate fried chicken, played Yahtzee, told better jokes than our parents. It seems like Granny needed a safer, happier version of what the Gerasene demoniac sought in the graveyard: her own space and time alone.

When Joshua's mental illness began in childhood, my family felt like we'd been through this before. We weren't frightened by his rage. We hoped Joshua's new bedroom would give him the space and privacy he needed. We didn't expect him to turn his closet into a tomb.

Criterion D: *The episode is not attributable to the physiological effects of a substance (e.g., a drug of abuse, a medication, other treatment) or another medical condition.*

Criterion D: Once, in college, my brother suffered from paranoia and hallucinations after smoking synthetic marijuana. Joshua's friend found him in his dorm room and called an ambulance. Joshua texted Rebecca: "I'm in the hospital." Paranoia and hallucinations were not among my brother's usual symptoms.

No translation of any of the Gospels mentions the Gerasene demoniac eating or drinking anything.

I knew what my mother meant by "played psychologist." She meant the field of mental health was a pseudoscience, practiced by villains, and here was this natural doctor hack, pretending to practice a pretend field. She'd told my siblings and me about the psychologists whose classes she'd taken at Marshall, who'd taught that intelligent people couldn't believe in God.

For my mother, *psychologist* also meant any mental health professional with the power to diagnose, and therefore entrap. The word included the State Hospital doctors, nurses, therapists, and staff, as well as the (apparently kind) man who diagnosed Granny with paranoid schizophrenia. With that diagnosis, my mom and her brother had Granny declared incompetent, so they could sign Granny up for disability without Granny's signature and (later) sign Granny up for her hated dead ex-husband's (PaPa's) pension, so they could buy Granny's coffee and cigarettes and pay her utility bills. For Granny, diagnosis-incompetence had been one concept, a horrible necessity infinitely preferable to institutionalization. Not long after Granny talked to the doctor, she couldn't legally vote or drive, and it meant next to nothing when she signed her name.

Psychologist also meant the threat that had hung over our heads whenever Granny went to the doctor or the hospital. "Your mother needs to see a psychiatrist," nurses, social workers, and opticians told my mom after one conversation with Granny, their tones ranging from worried to threatening. We knew from experience that Granny wouldn't reliably take any kind of medication. She once poured a bottle of cholesterol-lowering pills down her toilet, claiming the treatment "ate off her heel." And we knew she'd die, quickly and terrified, if we allowed a social worker to place her in any kind of home.

Since hypomania isn't necessary for diagnosis, and its criteria overlap with mania, I'm leaving it out, but I know my brother had depressive episodes, experiencing at least the required five of the list of symptoms. 1. *Depressed mood most of the day, nearly every day.* (Check.) 2. *Markedly diminished interest or pleasure in all, or almost all, activities most of the day, nearly every day.* (At his worst, he couldn't even enjoy films.) 4. *Insomnia or hypersomnia nearly every day.* (When he was sad, my brother slept every available moment or not at all.) 6. *Fatigue or loss of energy nearly every day.* (If I took him to the mall, he'd find a bench or patch of carpet and nap.) 7. *Feelings of worthlessness.* ("Sarbef, I don't feel like my life is worth anything.") 9. *Recurrent thoughts of death (not just fear of dying), recurrent suicidal ideation without a specific plan, or a suicide attempt or a specific plan for committing suicide.* (A year before Joshua died, my mother found him crying in the closet, a belt around his neck. She dragged him out and didn't sleep for a month, watching him every moment he was home.)

My brother appears to have experienced the added bipolar I specification of "rapid cycling," since he experienced far more than the required four manic and/or depressive episodes in a year. It wasn't unusual for him to experience four episodes in a month, with mania often sliding into depression (a common experience, the DSM-5 states, for people diagnosed with bipolar I). However, it also wasn't unusual for him to experience whole months of euthymia, experiencing no episodes at all, allowing me to have an occasional happy visit, and allowing my mother to hope he'd turned a corner and everything now would be okay.

The Gospel of Luke reports that "oftentimes" Legion had "caught" the Gerasene demoniac, which caused the Gerasenes to attempt to chain him. I wish the Bible gave a glimpse of a moment between those oftentimes, when the man ate figs, drank from a well, washed blood and grave dust from his face.

I wasn't surprised Joshua had told our mother everything about the doctor visit. Out of loyalty, surely, but likely also aiming to wound. *Infantilizing* was a barb. I felt it myself as a pseudo-parent, his eight-and-a-half-years-older sister.

Yes, Joshua was the last child, the baby brother. Yes, my mother, my sisters, and I helped him with his homework, made his bed, microwaved the hot dogs he ate for lunch.

Once, a year after Joshua walked to Tyler's, I called him to the kitchen before the hot dog sat hot and plump in a bun, next to a glass of grape juice. He scoffed, "I don't want to watch you make it!" and stormed back to his video game or nap.

Still, I'm not certain of what Paul was driving at when he asked Joshua if his parents were "infantilizing" him. Maybe we were. But it seems to me now that it's somewhat beside the point. On a webpage titled "Why does someone develop bipolar disorder?" the National Institute of Mental Health admits, "Doctors do not know," but provides some reigning theories. Genetics, since multiple cases of bipolar disorder often appear over several generations of families—often in families with cases of schizophrenia. Also, the structure of a person's brain.

❦

Jesus talks to the demons, who puppeteer the man, using his voice box to call themselves Legion. The demons know their time is up, so they start begging. They point out a herd of swine, wallowing by the nearby mountains, and they ask permission to move into those pigs.

Jesus tells Legion it's fine (to keep the demons out of people? because pigs aren't kosher?), and the swine are immediately restless, with a need to self-harm, or at least harm those demons. They charge "violently down a steep place into the sea."

❦

Standing in the hallway, my mother continued: "He gave Joshua a prescription, a real weak antidepressant's what he said it was"—she patted her purse—"but, as my daddy always said, 'I'm putting it in file thirteen.'"

I never saw Joshua's prescription. I felt bereft about this wasted opportunity to try medication, but Joshua was a minor. My mother's child, not mine. And the prescription might have done more harm than good. Like my mother, I'd heard the 1990s reports and rumors of Prozac-linked suicides. And I know now that SSRIs can bring on potentially deadly manic episodes in people with bipolar disorder, so at-risk patients must be under knowledgeable care if they take them. Care from someone more qualified than Paul.

❦

The people who feed the pigs see it all, and they round up the Gerasenes, who decide to check things out. The people find the mass pig suicide frightening, and surely some of them find it financially ruinous, but they're even more upset when they see the local crazy man "sitting, and clothed, and in his right mind," using his own voice box to talk to Jesus.

Instead of thrashing about naked in the graveyard, the Gerasene demoniac passes alarmingly for sane. The townspeople might run into this man when they worship or sell their pork. They ask Jesus to "depart out of their coasts."

"Institutionalize your mother," many people told my mom, though Granny could live alone and well in her own home.

Just before the conversation ended in the hallway, Joshua told me he'd asked Paul if he thought Joshua had bipolar disorder. My mom spoke Paul's response in unison with Joshua: "That diagnosis wouldn't be appropriate at this time."

Of course a diagnosis wouldn't have been appropriate. Paul was a "natural doctor," not a psychiatrist or licensed counselor. I'm sure he didn't want to be sued. But he could have referred Joshua to another doctor, one who could have figured out the truth. If Paul made a referral, neither my mother nor Joshua mentioned it. As far as I know, Joshua never talked to a doctor about his mental illness again.

Please understand: I don't blame my mother, and the last thing I want is for anyone else to blame her, or for my mother to blame herself. My mother acted on the basis of love, her own traumas, and sincere, unshakable faith. That faith gave her the strength to care for her mother as a teenager. It gave her the strength to live on after she found her little boy dead in a closet.

I know my mother believes, even now, she saved Joshua from medicine that might have harmed him, from a diagnosis that might have made him seem to the world, or to feel, like her legally incompetent mother, or like a man who runs naked in a graveyard, tearing his skin with stones.

I also know a diagnosis and treatment might not have stopped him from eventually killing himself. Reading medical manuals, journals, and websites, I keep coming across the same information. People with bipolar disorder are at least fifteen times more likely to kill themselves than the general worldwide population. As many as 30 percent of people with bipolar disorder attempt suicide; males are statistically more likely to succeed. Lithium is the only medication proven in long-term studies to bring down the death rate—a far cry from a "real weak antidepressant"—and I'm not confident my brother would have been better than Granny at taking pills. Bipolar disorder is so deadly the National Institute of Mental Health includes a message at the bottom of every page about the illness, providing a phone number for readers considering suicide.

And I know I'm infantilizing my brother if I credit or blame my mother for the fact that he lived, undiagnosed and unmedicated, to twenty-two years old. A strong-willed legal adult, Joshua was capable in his final four years of purchasing and peddling pot, capable of getting hooked on cigarettes and coffee (both anathema to our mother), and, for a time, capable of convincing our mother to drive him fifty miles on winding mountain roads so he could have sex with his girlfriend. I told Joshua when he was seventeen, and again and again in the five years that followed, that I thought he had bipolar disorder, that he could likely manage it with treatment. I think it's unfair to Joshua to underestimate the power of his own choice.

And if I take a step back, look at my brother not as my brother but as a mentally ill young man in West Virginia, whose ancestors have lived in Appalachia for two hundred years, I find it difficult to blame him, myself, my mother, or even the horrible preachers we all watched on TV. According to the Walsh Center for Rural Health Analysis's 2020 report, *Appalachian Diseases of Despair*, suicide rates have long been higher for people ages 18–65 in Appalachia than that same group in the rest of the United States. In 2011, there were 18.9 completed suicides in every 100,000 people in that group, versus 15.4 in the rest of the country. By 2018, suicide had risen overall, but more steeply in Appalachia: now 22.7 per 100,000 in that same group as compared to the rest of the country's 17.5. The report blames widespread poverty, some of the lowest education rates in the country, high rates of uninsured people, and lack of health care in rural areas, all of which breeds untreated mental illness and despair.

Those factors didn't directly affect my brother—college student, son of college-educated parents, kid on his parents' health insurance until twenty-six (if he'd reached it). But the American Psychiatric Association's 2018 report *Mental Health Disparities: Appalachian People* also considers the culture behind the statistics—17 percent higher suicide rate than the rest of the country—and they list some factors that surely did.

An "acceptance that life is difficult" (why even try to fix it?). Why should my mother try to reduce her blood pressure, when she's only had a mild stroke? Why not sit through the night on your brother and son, hoping it's the last time?

A historical reliance on "herbal remedies" and "folk medicine" due to generations of isolation without access to traditional treatments. Growing up, my siblings and I drank so much home-brewed colloidal silver, poured so much of that potion into our infected ears, I'm surprised we didn't all turn gray.

The same report lists the region's positive "protective factors," though I'm tempted to lump them with the negatives because I know well they can harm as well as protect. Here's a "protective factor": strong "spiritual beliefs," tied to a "culture of honor," based on a desire to feel "worthy" of "one's community, family, nation, or God."

I thought Joshua looked disappointed as he slunk back to his bedroom. He had five years left in his life.

Dream Cities

In the windswept, tuberculosis-ravaged West Yorkshire town of Haworth, Branwell Brontë dreamed of London. In a rural neighborhood outside Huntington, West Virginia, Joshua dreamed of New York.

Branwell fell in love with London as a little boy, reading his pastor father's political and literary magazines. Joshua fell in love as a teen, watching films.

In London, Branwell planned to astonish the painting professors at the Royal Academy of Arts, penning world-shaking poetry in his spare time. In New York, Joshua planned to direct and produce an art film based on the screenplay he worked on whenever he felt like writing: a high school drama teacher has sex with a male student, then kills himself in the shower with a razor blade. Joshua would hold his film premiere in a basement theater, with a tiny audience who noticed every angle, word, and shaft of light.

To prepare, Branwell studied maps, poetry, bloody mystery stories, political oratory, and drawings. Joshua watched Woody Allen's *Manhattan*, *The Muppets Take Manhattan*, and a documentary about a New York tour guide.

I'm guessing Joshua was the New York expert of my family's corner of Wayne County, West Virginia, but no one was interested. Twenty-first-century travel is too easy, information too available online.

In Haworth, outside of his home circle, Branwell's knowledge made him a delight. In *The Life of Charlotte Brontë*, Elizabeth Gaskell describes Haworth innkeepers' "unfortunate habit" of sending a note to Branwell, asking him to leave his father's parsonage and walk down to their pubs whenever they had customers from out of town. The innkeepers hoped those customers would match Branwell pint after pint, "beguiled" by his "flashes of wit." Once, Branwell beguiled a customer from London. Gaskell says Branwell chatted about the city's "habits and ways of life," its "places of amusement." He whipped out a pen, mapped time-saving shortcuts. Before he ambled home, Branwell astonished the traveler, revealing he'd never been to London in his life.

❦

In the summer of 1835, eighteen years old, Branwell wished to move to London. Whether he was ever there, even for an hour, has been a matter of historical debate. What's sure: Branwell drafted a letter to the Royal Academy asking for information about how to apply. "Where am I to present my drawing?" he asked. "At what time—? And especialy Can I do it in August or September . . ."

What's also sure: that same summer, Charlotte wrote to a friend describing the teaching job she'd just taken away from home. Charlotte hated teaching, so she explained. Her father was about to incur heavy expenses, paying London prices for her brother's paintbrushes and gin.

One year after Branwell wrote that letter to the Royal Academy, he penned a short story called "The Adventures of Charles Wentworth." His story's small-town protagonist traveled to Verdopolis, a "mighty city of Africa" Branwell and Charlotte had invented together as children. When Wentworth first arrived in Verdopolis, he strode "through his room in a pleasant sort of excitement," but within minutes the excitement "ebbed off." In the morning, he woke with the "delightful" realization that he didn't have a single "relation in the city." Then he left his hotel and walked around Verdopolis with a "wildish dejected look," feeling "the want, that restless uneasy feeling with which rest is torment." Returning to the hotel, he "stretched himself on a sopha, and listlessly dreamed away his time until dark."

"Branwell undoubtedly went to London," gothic novelist Daphne du Maurier wrote in her 1960 biography, *The Infernal World of Branwell Brontë*. In lieu of evidence, which she admits is nonexistent, she speculates that "The Adventures of Charles Wentworth" is based on Branwell's trip. Biographer Winifred Gérin takes that short story even further in her 1961 book, *Branwell Brontë: A Biography*, breaking down Wentworth's journey into a blow-by-blow account of Branwell's London experiences.

Wentworth visited "St. Michaels Cathedral" (Gérin reads this as St. Paul's), but he almost decided against going in, fearing disappointment. Wentworth visited museums, felt "cast down and melancholy" before works of art (Branwell perceived his own hopeless lack of talent, failed to take himself and his artwork to the Royal Academy). Wentworth fortified his sad self with "little squibs of rum" (Branwell headed to a pub, drank away his father's money). Finally, Wentworth made his way home, nearly as penniless as the pig-feeding Prodigal.

In fairness to Du Maurier and Gérin, Wentworth's visit to London sounds like everything Branwell ever attempted in his life. Branwell's short biography on the Brontë Parsonage Museum's website reads as a litany of failures.

In 1838, twenty-one-year-old Branwell set up a portrait studio in Bradford. The bio: "He made many friends among the artistic community of the Bradford pubs, but failed to make a living." Then he began to get sacked. "Sacked within a year" from a tutoring position in Broughton-in-Furness. "Sacked" from a position as a railway clerk, after he "missed a discrepancy in the accounts." "Sacked" from a tutoring position at Thorp Green over an affair with his student's mother. After he "found himself back home in disgrace after a fourth failed career," he descended into laudanum, hard drinking, "self-pity," and nightmares.

That bio skips over the London plan, but it's easy to imagine it in: Branwell traveled to London to apply to the Royal Academy of Arts, but he got drunk and went home.

Biographer Juliet Barker doesn't care for imagining in details. As far as reliable evidence shows, Branwell never went to London in his thirty-one years, and he certainly didn't go in 1835. Barker laments previous biographers' tendency to fill in factual holes by "trawling through the Brontës' fiction," calling that practice a "subjective and almost invariably pointless exercise."

Barker says Branwell's letter to the Royal Academy is no proof of his journey. Branwell tore it up and wrote poetry on the scraps. And that fall, after the supposed trip, Branwell's father wrote to Branwell's tutor in a nearby Yorkshire town, expressing pleasure that his son hadn't headed to London before he was ready. Du Maurier and Gérin had imagined Branwell drinking in London pubs, dashing around shortcuts, just as Branwell had imagined himself.

I agree with Barker about the dangers of looking for autobiography in an imaginative writer's fiction. I knew about Joshua's screenplay when he was living, and I didn't take it as evidence that he'd suffered statutory rape by a teacher, or even that he was he attracted to men (though, on this second point, I wondered). But I feared then—and I know for sure now—about the screenplay's roots in Joshua's own thoughts of suicide. So while I wouldn't look to "The Adventures of Charles Wentworth" for a record of Branwell's journey, I can't help trawling through that story for insight into the writer's state of mind.

"On a sudden, the tears came" as Charles Wentworth stood on a sun-drenched dock in Verdopolis. "A feeling like a wind seemed to pass across his spirits because he now felt that not even the flashes of glory which those streets and buildings had struck from his soul . . . could preserve his thoughts from aimless depression."

Perhaps Branwell recorded his fears about visiting London: even in Verdopolis, Wentworth couldn't be happy. Or perhaps Branwell wrote that story to console himself, imagining the worst after he didn't get to go.

At nineteen, Joshua wanted to move to New York City. He wanted to wake up every morning alone, stacked in a building that smelled of strangers. He wanted to spend his days chain-smoking and walking around.

Like Branwell's father, my parents knew their teenage son wasn't ready for his dream city. He had no idea how to find a job, how to sign a lease, how to buy his own ticket from American Airlines, Amtrak, or Greyhound. They offered Joshua the dorms at Marshall: affordable and close enough that they could reach him at once if—or, as it turned out, when—his semester was a Branwell Brontë–level failure. In August 2009 he moved his clothes and stuffed manatee into Twin Towers, a fifteen-story dormitory that eerily echoed New York.

Downtown Huntington is a concrete haven amid Appalachia's slurry-orange creeks and hill-climbing cows. It boasts streets and sidewalks poured Manhattan flat because they lie in close parallel to the Ohio River. Before his move, Joshua had viewed downtown Huntington as a destination for forced minivan trips to church, the doctor, or dentist. After his move, Joshua realized a few dozen blocks of half-empty, crumbling buildings was still a city. His sister Rebecca, several cousins, and former students from his high school lived in the blocks around him, but there were thousands of people he didn't know.

Downtown Huntington gave Joshua an easy supply of pot; the Thirsty Whale, a bar that served him Long Island iced teas without even a fake ID; a whole campus of benches and sidewalks where he could smoke cigarettes without hiding from his parents; and Bailey, a moody photographer who was—it seems—thrilled to have sex with him. It gave him a life eleven miles from the home where he felt comfortable enough for his rages to turn violent. Eleven miles from his parents and the KJV Bible etched with his name.

Downtown Huntington also gave him New York. A month into the semester, Bailey spotted a flyer on campus for a weekend bus trip. The bus would travel north all night on Friday, south all night Saturday, giving its riders one glorious day. My parents gave Joshua spending money and asked him to take his cell phone.

Usually Joshua struggled with travel: the cramped limbs, the same voices for hours, the recirculated air. For that trip, Joshua listened to music on an iPod, opened his window to the cold night, stretched out in his own seat, traded comic books with Bailey across the aisle.

When the bus emerged at dawn from the Holland Tunnel, Joshua called my parents. "Mama," he gasped, looking around at yellow cabs and skyscrapers, at the precise patch of sky that might be visible in his someday films. "It's so great. It's just so great. I can't believe it."

Joshua rode a ferry to Ellis Island. He smoked a cigarette on the banks of the Hudson River, and he smoked another in Central Park. He walked all over Manhattan, surely stepping on a square of sidewalk that had held Woody Allen or Jim Jarmusch. If Joshua had had a week in New York, I suspect he would have had time to become exhausted and worried, even manic or depressed. He might have skulked around Manhattan with Wentworth's "wildish dejected look," feeling "that want, that restless uneasy feeling with which rest is torment." Instead, he was—it seems—happy all day before he got back on that bus, flunked all his classes, and lived his last three years in our parents' home.

After Joshua's funeral, Rebecca found the disposable cameras he'd filled on that trip, long forgotten under his bed. Ocean waves, ferry railings, clouds between skyscrapers, subway seats, street signs. A photo a minute until he ran out of film.

Since I lost my brother, I've often feared his short adult life was like Branwell's, all frustrated hope and wasted talent. Misery without the addiction. I can't shake the resemblance: the screenplays left unfinished, the classes he failed, the comic books he planned to write and didn't. A beloved city he touched only in dreams.

Then I remember those photos, my historical evidence. Joshua made it to New York.

Beaver Pond

"I love winter for the textures," my dad said. I followed his eyes to neon patches of moss, plush clumps of dead grass, a leaf shining under a puddle. We were walking the trail to the Beaver Pond in Lavalette, West Virginia, one year before we lost Joshua for good, and two years after Mark died.

An early daffodil stopped us in our tracks, domestic yellow between wild green lichens. Until the 1970s, when the state claimed the land for a park, this trail had been somebody's farm. "Look," my dad said, stooping toward the petals, "some old lady's flowers are still alive."

My dad and I walked the Beaver Pond trail with Uncle Mark the summer I was five years old. I know, more than remember, what we looked like. My pastel blouse, Mark's jogging shorts and T-shirt, my dad's worn-out work clothes: scuffed black dress shoes, threadbare oxford shirt, khakis worn at the cuffs. The three of us jumped stone to stone across the stream, turned our shoes sideways when the path plunged downhill, dodged caterpillars that dropped from June leaves.

A copperhead lay coiled on the path, and my dad moved it with his walking stick, his tan arms wielding that carved pine with the power of Moses's staff. I complained I was hot, so Mark knotted the corners of his white cotton handkerchief and dropped it on my head. "That'll keep the sun off you." I felt better immediately, tamping down the dirt in my explorer's hat.

Finally we reached the Beaver Pond, a thirty-by-fifty-foot watering hole a farmer had created by building a dam across the stream. The pond lived up to its name. Beavers slapped the water with their wide, flat tails. Beavers whittled tree branches with their teeth. Beavers lounged in a swimming hole they'd built with their own wall of sticks and mud.

When we reached the pond, I sat down on a rock to watch the beavers while my dad slid a chunk of nightcrawler onto my fishing hook. Dragonflies—red, violet, bottle green, zebra striped—dive-bombed gnats, their lacy wings humming inches from my skin.

Mark carried his tackle to the far side of the pond, probably taking a breather from five-year-old me. I asked my dad if I could fish beside my uncle, and he told me I could if I was quiet. "Mark doesn't like anybody to scare off his fish."

Pole in hand, I crept along the bank until I stood beside Mark. He kept his eyes on his red and white bobber. "Hi there, Sarah Beth," he said softly, and I beamed. He didn't cast my line for me like my daddy would have, but he didn't tell me to go away. I sat in Mark's shadow and tried to keep still. Maybe I wiggled. A startled beaver scurried up the hill behind the pond, less than fifty feet away from our fishing spot. I was spellbound for those seconds by the beaver's full round body, hidden until now in the murky water. All four paws hurrying, its tennis-racket tail bouncing between the trees.

I held my breath as my dad and I neared the end of the trail, waiting for the pond to burst into view as we rounded a bend and emerged from the tree canopy. But when we rounded that bend, the pond was missing. The farmer's dirt wall and the beaver dam had washed downstream, leaving the rocks where little girls used to sit and puddles barely large enough for frog spawn. We searched for beaver relics and found a few dried-out sticks, gnawed to sharp white points.

My dad and I stared across the invisible pond, and I knew we both saw Mark on the opposite bank, whistling softly and casting. Maybe we hadn't buried him in a cemetery twelve miles away. Maybe he hadn't missed the last two family Christmases, too sick and sad to leave Pennsylvania. Maybe my uncle had been at this lake all along, needing to fish by himself. My dad and I walked toward Mark, straight across the pond bottom, avoiding the puddles, stepping between clumps of weeds that looked like sheaves of wheat.

The bank was empty when we got there, so my dad looked ahead to the hill, the one the beaver had scrambled up twenty years before.

"Sarah Beth, do you remember that No Trapping sign?" I wasn't sure, but said yes. "Look at that speck of orange behind that tree. It's gotta be the sign. Let's climb up and read it." So we climbed, using saplings as handholds, tugging ourselves up the hill.

We wanted to see if the sign still said the same thing now that all the beavers were gone.

In the Bible, famines are at least as common as shipwrecks. The Prodigal should have seen this coming. "And when he had spent all, there arose a mighty famine in that land; and he began to be in want."

When I'm craving a glimpse of the Prodigal at the height of his riotous living, the Bible Storybook irritates me with that single, prudish, post-joy panel when "All his money was gone." But when I get to the part of the story when the Prodigal runs out of money, I'm thankful for that image of transition, when he finds himself shut out of life's party, and he's not yet ruined, just sad.

My family owned our Bible Storybook because my mom had heard about it from Jimmy Swaggart, a famous–then infamous–evangelist with the fervor of an Old Testament prophet. In the 1970s, my mom listened to Swaggart's radio program, one of her spiritual life rafts while she cared for her mother in her late teens and early twenties. In the 1980s, I watched Swaggart with my mom on TV. I found his broad pink face offensively ugly, but when his Louisiana accent gave the word *Jesus* four enunciated syllables, I felt like he was grasping an electrical wire that ran from his body up to heaven.

Every broadcast, Jimmy Swaggart sat down at his grand piano and seemed to make all the keys sing at once. "Bar-style," some critics accused him, though Swaggart railed against rock-and-roll so powerfully he convinced Walmart in 1986 to remove *Rolling Stone* and rock albums from their shelves. Reading the Bible Storybook with my mom and sisters at night, I felt, indistinctly, the evangelist hovering above us at his shiny black piano, cheering on our study of the scriptures.

Along with rock and roll, Jimmy Swaggart preached against adultery, publicly denouncing pastors for cheating on their wives. Then in 1988, at the height of my Bible Storybook enjoyment, he got found out. Some men–connected to one of those humiliated pastors–captured photographic evidence of Swaggart meeting a sex worker at Tony's Motel in Metairie, Louisiana. According to Art Harris's *Washington Post* article "Jimmy Swaggart and the Snare of Sin," Tony's was a place with flashing "neon lights," boasting "adult movies, water beds and rooms by the hour." Swaggart had been meeting women there for "two or three years," driving a Lincoln Town Car that matched his wife's, combing his thick blond hair over his face as a disguise. My mother, not one to whitewash, told six-year-old me our family's favorite TV preacher had been "caught with a prostitute in a motel."

The Assemblies of God demanded Swaggart stop preaching for a year, seek counseling for his marriage, for sex addiction. But Swaggart wasn't having it. He'd preached against Christian counseling–atheistic psychology infiltrating the church–and he didn't need a break. He put on a dark blue suit and stood behind his pulpit, his church pews full. A TV camera zoomed in on his broad pink face, which he pointed toward heaven. Tears dripped from his chin. "I have sinned against you, O Lord," he said.

Swaggart's church and TV audience must have sensed the Father grabbing their beloved, pink-faced prodigal, cradling him in His arms. The Assemblies of God defrocked Swaggart; he set up an independent ministry and got more TV-watching, money-mailing followers than ever. Even my mother forgave him that time.

The Bible Storybook's Prodigal has all his clothing and props from the previous panel, minus the bulging leather bag. When he slouches outside the window, his yellow hat and red cloak, so crisp in his wealth, look dumpy and loose. His once-trim beard has grown scraggly. His white undergarment has torn at his neck.

The Bible Storybook Prodigal's eyes, so sad under that sad yellow hat, and his chin lowered over that torn undergarment, remind me of my brother when I peered into his bedroom, where he lay in bed in the middle of the day, his bug-bit hands tucked partway under his face, half-open eyes staring at the blue carpet.

In 1991, just months into my family's new Bible Storybook, Jimmy Swaggart got caught on a Friday morning in Southern California, driving a Jaguar this time. A police officer pulled into a lane behind the Jaguar, and Swaggart swerved into the opposite lane, trying to stash his dirty magazines. When the officer pulled Swaggart over for his terrible driving, the officer spoke to a woman riding with him. Later that day she told KNBC-TV in Los Angeles why she was in the car. "For sex, I mean that's why he stopped me," she said. "That's what I do, I'm a prostitute. He asked for sex. He was shaking."

In 1991, Swaggart didn't mention the sex worker to his congregation, but he told them he'd been depressed. He said that before the police picked him up, he got out of the Jaguar and sat under a palm tree, leaving the woman in the car. He felt an "oppressive spirit, like hands that gripped" him. I wonder if he imagined himself as spirit-tormented King Saul in the Bible Storybook, slumped in his chair under a palm.

Next, it seems, Swaggart got back in the car with the woman and considered killing himself. He said, "If I hadn't known I would go to hell"—for suicide? for dying unshriven? for murdering the woman in his car?—"I would have pulled that Jaguar in front of an eighteen-wheeler." He thanked the officer for pulling him over, saving his life.

Swaggart's son released a statement that said his father was stepping down from ministry for a time, but Swaggart appeared behind his Louisiana pulpit the next evening, told a story. A *Los Angeles Times* reporter heard it all. The previous night, Swaggart said, he'd tried and failed to read his Bible for hours, and at four a.m. he'd "whimpered like a hurt little dog." He'd said, "God, if you're there, if you're really there, tell me what to do," and he'd slept for two hours. At six a.m. he'd woken up, and "the Holy Spirit was rolling all over" him. He had his answer: return to the pulpit, face his congregation. My mother still quotes what Swaggart told his congregation that day: "The Lord told me it's flat none of your business." She quit listening to his sermons. His ministry limped forward, never the same.

Jimmy Swaggart: *The psychological way and the way of the Cross are diametrically opposed to each other. . . . As for preachers who claim that the two can be melded, it shows either a terrible ignorance of the Cross of Christ, or else, gross unbelief.*

Two days after Swaggart returned to the pulpit, the *Los Angeles Times* interviewed three psychotherapists about the minister for the article "Swaggart Seen Unlikely to Seek Treatment." Two were ordained ministers themselves, and one identified as a "Christian therapist." They said Swaggart's sneakiness and denial were symptoms of sex addiction, but they didn't expect him to be treated. When it came to mental health treatment, Swaggart was no hypocrite. He viewed his sex addiction as demon-torment and sin.

One of the psychotherapist/ministers also used demons to describe Swaggart's situation, paraphrasing one of Jesus's parables. In the book of Matthew, Jesus says an "unclean spirit," once cast out of a man, "walketh through dry places, seeking rest." The fate that scared Legion so badly they asked Jesus to let them possess the pigs. Overcome with weariness, the spirit returns to his old home and finds it "empty, swept, and garnished." Ecstatic, the spirit rounds up seven roommates "more wicked than himself, and the last state of that man is worse than the first." The psychotherapist said, "He left the house unsettled because he did not seek treatment, and seven demons entered therein. In that sense, he's even worse than he was in 1988."

The Prodigal could have got up from that window, become a hand on a ship, seen the world, drowned quickly and cleanly in a shipwreck. He could have sailed or walked somewhere with corn and rain, somewhere no one knew him as a beloved upper-class son or a broke, partying money-waster, and sought a kosher way to make money. He could have trudged home before he looked like he'd emerged from a tomb.

The Prodigal didn't possess the strength, knowledge, and foresight he would have needed to make a change before disaster. Why? Bible readers can't know for sure. Jesus didn't talk about the Prodigal's Granny with unmedicated schizophrenia, his long-held habits of laziness, piano-playing televangelists who preached the evils of psychology, his fiercely loving and protective parents and sisters, or the generations of righteous self-reliance in the region where he lived. All I know: the Prodigal moped outside the window until everything rotted away.

PART 4
STARVING WITH SWINE

After the Prodigal runs out of money, that one-time heir takes a job feeding swine. We're not told what benefits come with the job, but they must not include food. Near starvation, the Prodigal asks the pig owner to let him share the "husks that the swine did eat," and the owner says no.

My brother lived primarily on candy bars, licorice, cigarettes, and marijuana from the age of nineteen to twenty-two. When he was home, our parents bought apples, Angus beef hot dogs, and orange juice, begged him to eat, but his cheeks look sunken and his eyes languid in a photo of his last Christmas morning alive.

There are no photographs of Branwell Brontë, but on my first visit to Haworth, I saw "A Parody," a sketched self-portrait from Branwell's last year. That sketch was an eerily fitting piece of the museum's current special exhibit, "The Infernal World of Branwell Brontë," its title taken from Daphne du Maurier's biography. Du Maurier explains that the Brontë children used the phrase "infernal world" to describe their fictional kingdoms, fearing and reveling in the potential wickedness of their imaginations. I experienced that same feeling when writing my spookier Sunshine Books as a child. But throughout the biography, and in the museum exhibit, Branwell's "infernal world" meant his wild creativity, his inability to face reality, and the restless despair that plagued his mind.

In "A Parody," Branwell lies in Patrick's curtained bed in a room without walls. The church's tower and graveyard hover in the background. Branwell himself is shirtless, a bedsheet covering him from the waist down. When I sat with Mark, his arms and chest were shrunken above a monstrously swollen belly, his beard as ratty as the one worn by the Bible Storybook's pig-feeding Prodigal. Dying alcoholic Branwell looks far healthier than my underfed twenty-one-year-old brother, healthier than my brother on the best day of his life. Lush muscles, an abundance of hair. Still, Branwell's face reveals his life-threatening misery. A skeleton stands at the foot of the bed, extending one bony arm over Branwell's body.

In the last year of his life, Joshua created a self-portrait through a secret YouTube channel, one where the viewer must click through a graphic content warning. Rebecca found the channel by chance, after watching Joshua's film reviews on his usual channel, Smoovies. When Rebecca mentioned the new channel to Joshua, he asked her to "please oh please" never watch it. She respected his wishes, and I did too, for years after he died. Some content is amusingly perverse: a zoomed-in image of my brother's bare feet as he sits on the toilet and audibly urinates. Or odd and sad: a ventriloquist dummy, his lips closed tight around an unlit cigarette, narrating humanity's fall from grace in the Garden of Eden. "My mom says God created people because He wanted a family," Joshua laments, slumped against the wall in his bedroom. He sounds angry to be alive. But some content is genuinely disturbing. Lying in his bed, Joshua wraps rubber bands around his neck, plastic wrap around his face. Joshua invented a word to name that channel, one I won't give because the channel still exists. The name of that channel is infernal.

At twenty-eight years old, I loved "A Parody" because my brother sketched too. Cartoons that featured a version of himself with startled eyes, a round nose, and thin wisps of hair. Cartoon-Joshua complained about girls, commented on global politics, dreamed on a hilltop with a goat. *A cartoon*, I thought. *Smoo would love this.* But I looked again at the headstones and skeleton, decided against showing the sketch to my brother.

In the Bible Storybook, the pig-slopping Prodigal's tunic is missing its sleeves. His cheeks are hollow, shaded gray. He clutches a wooden bucket in the back left corner of the pen, his body dwarfed by six fat pigs.

Branwell and Joshua traveled to a far country and starved without leaving their parents' houses. There's more than one way to disappear.

Somewhere on Earth

On Friday, March 12, 2010, nineteen-year-old Joshua stepped out of my mom's green minivan on the Marshall campus and vanished. I'm sure he knew it was Jennifer's birthday. My mom had hyped the ice cream cake for weeks, telling even me—I lived six hundred miles away that year, in upstate New York—that she'd ordered Jennifer's favorite, layers of chocolate, vanilla, and fudgy crunch.

Still, I don't think Joshua ruined her day on purpose. He just needed to run away.

I first learned of Joshua's disappearance in a brief phone call from my mother. "He's gone. Please pray." I knew *he* meant Joshua. The tone of her voice—and my sinking stomach—felt so familiar I assumed he'd walked off again into the hills. I assumed he'd filled his pockets at Clay's and kept on going, puffing a Marlboro as he strode.

My mom told me during that call that Joshua was missing with no cell phone. She didn't think he had the change to use one of the university's few remaining pay phones, the cash to buy a sandwich. Then I got the story in bursts from my parents on Google's Gchat, creating a record I've read many times.

Those Gchat transcripts give me a strange, hopeless joy. The same feeling I experienced as a child in the years before we adopted our first family beagle, listening to that tape of myself whining to look for Scruffy. I could relate to my cassette-tape self: she had no dog. And I liked hearing myself believe Scruffy could come home.

When I read those Gchats, current me knows the end of this story: *this* time, Joshua will be okay. And while past me is frightened enough to sit on Gchat into the wee hours of the night, she believes Joshua is alive. Past me doesn't offer to drive or fly home. In fact, she still plans to board her flight to London on March 13—her first trip to England!—and she has the wherewithal to worry over her unpacked suitcase, electrical adaptors, and currency exchange. Past me promises her mother, "I'll pray for Smoo," and I can tell she means she'll pray for her live brother, somewhere in Huntington, or at least somewhere on earth.

In mid-January, two months before he disappeared, Joshua returned to classes at Marshall. New semester, fresh start.

During Joshua's previous semester, he'd reveled in the freedom of the dorms, but he hadn't gone to class, and he'd drank so little water he'd contracted a near-deadly kidney infection. My mom had used the infection to appeal for a full, last-minute medical withdrawal, keeping his GPA unmarred. For this second attempt, he lived with my parents. My mom taped his schedule to the refrigerator, tugged him from his bed, and drove him to the listed buildings at the listed times. She sat next to him at the kitchen table, nagging him about homework, making sure he ate mashed potatoes and finished glasses of juice.

Rebecca, a Marshall senior, kept her own copy of Joshua's schedule in her downtown apartment. She took freshman-level Music Appreciation with him on Monday nights, sitting in a cramped classroom from sixty-thirty to nine p.m. as a bushy-bearded professor played recordings of African drums.

On the first night of that class, Joshua sat with Rebecca, doodled a bearded drummer in his notebook. Then he noticed a classmate, Michael, an unhealthy-looking kid who wore basketball shorts in the January cold. During Joshua's dorm semester, he and Michael had gotten high and bought snacks at Speedway, the gas station where undergrads bought cases of Natty Light, elderly Black women from the adjacent section 8 housing bought lotto tickets, and police monitored both populations. Joshua and Michael smoked cigarettes outside the classroom building after class, reminiscing about their near-miss run-ins with the cops. After that conversation, Joshua's Music Appreciation grade was doomed.

Every Monday, Joshua and Michael hid somewhere and smoked pot during the class's fifteen-minute break. Rarely, they came back for the second act, relaxed and giggling, filling the classroom with the skunk stench on their clothes. Joshua didn't bother to turn in work, even when Rebecca typed up a version of the homework that looked nothing like hers and printed it out with his name at the top. Joshua also didn't sign the professor's attendance record, passing it on to the next student even though attendance was part of the grade. Every week, two-thirds of the class signed their names at the beginning of class then left at the break, causing the professor to sigh disgusted sighs only full-class attendees could hear. But Joshua, something of a man of honor, never signed the sheet. To him, passing a class wasn't important enough for casual lying, and he refused to restrict his ability to leave.

Along with Joshua's schedule, my mom kept a copy of Marshall's academic calendar. She'd circled Friday, March 12: the last day to drop a course without a kidney infection. Driving Joshua to school on Jennifer's birthday morning, my mom turned down his CD, reminded him of the drop date, and asked how he was doing in his classes.

Joshua said, "I'm doing good, Mama," and turned the volume back up. She didn't believe it. Rebecca had told her he was failing Music Appreciation, and my mom had suspicions of her own. After my mom dropped him off, she parked her car on a metered street and walked onto the campus.

On Gchat my mom wrote, "He told me he was going to class. I noticed he didn't go in the Rec building. I followed him and watched him light up a cigarette."

It's important to note my mother was shocked. Joshua had smoked heavily for nine months, mostly while living with our parents, but he'd smoked on walks around Twin Valley or risked fires in the woods behind the backyard. My mom had washed his nicotine-infused button-downs, but her sense of smell was poor. So when Joshua lit that cigarette, my mother witnessed her baby boy joining her addicted-till-death mother, joining her father who only quit after he'd smoked away his heart. In her love for Joshua, my mother must have forgotten (or forgotten to worry) that his descents into depression or fury were triggerable. She must have forgotten cigarettes can take fifty years to kill a person, but it only takes moments to die.

I imagine my brother on a university park bench on a cool spring day, one leg crossed over the other, left arm folded against his chest. I like to think he was happy for a moment before my mom stood by the bench in her mom jeans glory, before she tore the cigarette from his hand and stomped it under her so-comfortable-looking walking shoe. Before she asked him if he was failing everything again.

❦

After my mom confronted Joshua, she said, "He took off." At noon she drove to their usual meeting place, and he slouched into the minivan with his bag.

He said, "You're right, Mama." He'd smoked through the semester. He'd only gone to Music Appreciation to see Michael and Rebecca. He needed to drop all his classes, or he'd earn a transcript of Fs.

But Joshua hadn't dropped anything yet. He needed to collect a handwritten signature from each professor (genuine or forged) and turn in the signatures to the registrar before the office closed at five. My mom demanded Joshua get back out of the minivan.

She told me, "He got an evil glimmer in his eye and got out. Haven't heard from him since. I wish I had drove him home." When my brother got that evil glimmer, he was already far away.

❦

Later that night I got on Gchat to wish Jennifer a happy birthday, and I asked her if Joshua "just didn't come home" or if he was "having a problem," meaning—though I didn't have this language—a mood episode. Jennifer lived with my parents that semester, and I figured my mom had told her the story in full. My dad saw my unanswered message on a shared family computer, and he replied: "Problems."

My dad later clarified, combining my mom's account to him of Joshua's words when he exited the car with a description of Joshua's mental state: "Very mad sad if you want me to get out I'll get out." I knew "mad sad" well. I suspect now, based on the DSM-5, that "mad sad" was a "mixed episode." A state combining depression and mania, when I wasn't sure if my brother would bash his head against a wall, try to write an entire screenplay, disappear into the shower for hours, threaten to break every person and object in the house, walk across West Virginia, or collapse in his bed.

"She greatly regrets how she handled it," my dad said. Without discussion, my family all knew what we feared: Joshua was hungry and cold as a lost, scraggly dog, or he'd landed, perhaps deservedly, in a Huntington jail.

If I could have believed Joshua was just taking a day for himself, an independent adult, perhaps I wouldn't have worried. If I could have believed Joshua had realized he was mad sad and set off on foot to any of the nearby clinics, hospitals, or counseling centers, away from my family and our futile, insistent help, that might have given me reason for genuine hope. But I knew Joshua didn't have it in him. Like my parents and sisters, I feared he'd taken his journey into a far country without a pouch of money, skipping the riotous living, jumping directly from departure to despair.

My dad added, "School is suddenly not very important."

The day Joshua disappeared, my mother wrote him an email, hoping he'd somehow find himself at a computer. Her plea for a prodigal's return makes me cry.

> *Joshua, My Beloved Son,*
>
> *Please come home. We have steak, ice cream cake, Cheetos, strawberry crush pop, everything for a nice birthday party. We miss you. I'll help you find a good job that you like and gives you some pride. Then when you are more ready, you can go back to school sometime. You know that we will help you all we can.*
>
> *We love you so much,*
> *Mama*

My mom's email offered Jennifer's party as a returning prodigal's feast, but still, my mom cared about his older siblings. She repeatedly reminded me, mid-Joshua conversation, "Sarah Beth, you better go pack."

And she told me Rebecca was "saving the day" by "staying real upbeat" for Jennifer's birthday. Rebecca took Jennifer to a movie. They sat by the exit with their phone ringers on in case the family called.

Some days can't be saved. Early on March 13, I drove fifty miles in rural New York darkness to learn my flight had been cancelled and rescheduled for two days later, due to storms and high winds far away. I feared my flight would be cancelled again, that I'd never see the Atlantic Ocean through an airplane window, that I'd never walk on the West Yorkshire moors. I cried on the drive back from the airport. After I unpacked my computer, I found a Gchat message from my mother: "Jennifer's birthday was ruined. We were too upset to eat the cake."

❦

That same morning, my mom told me she and my dad were going to "'hang out' all day" in the student center, a place Joshua would surely turn up if he returned to, or had stayed on, the Marshall campus. The quotation marks around "hang out" underscore her irritation. Joshua had already put her through a full day of misery, and surely he'd cemented that semester's transcript of Fs. Now my parents had to wait for Joshua to possibly show up in the student center, like two prodigal's fathers staring at the road.

My parents "hung out" for hours in a giant room with a central fireplace, lounge chairs, and couches, updated versions of the furniture where they'd chatted together thirty years ago, as dating students. Now they were middle-aged parents surrounded by kids who napped with their heads on their backpacks, who jumped and squealed when their friends walked in, who bobbed to music in their headphones while munching stale Pizza Hut breadsticks. One of my parents watched the street entrance and one watched the back, a Snickers and a bottle of orange juice next to them on a chair.

My parents left the student center for dinner. They came back to find Joshua standing by the fireplace, wearing a bedraggled version of the outfit he'd worn when he got out of the minivan. He didn't look angry, just tired and sad. Next to him stood Bailey, his onetime travel companion to New York. He hadn't mentioned Bailey in months, and he'd mentioned her with such boredom-laced bitterness, no one had thought of her at all.

When Joshua saw our parents, he cowered and shook. Perhaps he feared they'd shame him in front of the breadstick eaters, or perhaps he feared something worse, something I can't imagine or understand. My dad walked up to him, holding out the candy bar and juice. He put his hand on Joshua's shoulder, said, "Come on, let's go home." Joshua accepted the offering and walked with our parents, head drooped, my dad's hand still resting on his shoulder.

❦

On one of my recent visits to Huntington, my mom told me finding Joshua in the student center is one of her favorite moments with my dad. "David was just like the Prodigal Son's father. He'd already forgiven Joshua and just wanted him home."

I cling to that moment too, along with my Gchats, along with my Scruffy whining. They all remind me of past me, that self who could take a break from lost brother worry to wish her sister a happy birthday and mope about a weather-delayed trip. That self who believed it didn't matter if bad things happened to her family—car wrecks, disappearances, suicide attempts—because her family would continue on, alive. Joshua's reappearance in the student center reinforced my conviction I was right.

I like to conjure up an image of that day in the student center, built from my parents' stories. I try to remember myself remembering, to filter the image through the self who disappeared on the day of Joshua's suicide. My brother takes the candy bar, lets my dad grip his shoulder, shuffles to the minivan with sad eyes. My live brother is on his way back to my parents' house, and I feel relieved, but not surprised.

Oh, good. He's back, past me thinks, adding books to her London-bound suitcase. Our prodigal has returned on earth.

Lost Photographs

Walker's Branch Road in Huntington, WV. April 2012. Twenty-one years old, Joshua walks to Clay's in the dark while I sit in his desk chair, combing JSTOR for evidence for his political science paper. After half an hour I hear a rap at the window, push aside the blue curtains, open the pane. Before he climbs inside, he hands me a condensation-damp plastic shopping bag: two malt liquor tallboys, two giant bars of Hershey's Special Dark chocolate. Sipping our drinks, taking bites of our chocolate, we coauthor a passing paper before dawn.

My parents' dining room. July 2012. Joshua stands in the dining room, ten feet from away where I stand in the kitchen, browning ground beef. He's wrinkling a computer printout, complaining about his community college schedule I put together. "History!" he says. "You know I hate history. It makes me so miserable, Sarbef." In the sad tone in Joshua's voice, I can hear toddler-scuffed tennis shoes, tiny grass-stained pants, but I barely look up from the frying pan. I tell him he needs that class to graduate, though I know something else could be substituted. I tell him I picked the classes based on the time slots, to minimize our mother's two-hour roundtrip drives into Ohio, which is the truth. "Why don't you just *work*?" I ask Joshua, words I'll remember forever. He laughs, drops the schedule on the floor, and walks to his room.

Marquee Cinema in Huntington, WV. Mid-August 2012. Joshua accompanies me, Jennifer, and Rebecca to a showing of Jay Roach's 2012 comedy film *The Campaign*. Two weeks later I won't remember a single scene. My brain will replay only the minutes after, when we left him behind at the library. But years later I'll remember his warm, breathing mass of skin, bones, muscle, organs, and blood slouched beside me. The burst of air when he genuinely laughs. The buzz of his whispered criticisms.

On Joshua's Last Christmas . . .

he got up for breakfast. He'd spent his recent free hours in hibernation, emerging from his bed to smoke, to absorb enough water from coffee to keep alive. But that morning he sat with my family at the breakfast table, ate a cinnamon roll, several bites of chopped up fruit, and then he stayed up all day.

he had gifts for everyone. Turquoise hairpins for me, red mittens for Rebecca, a toboggan with lion ears for Jennifer. As we tore off the paper, he watched us and grinned, neglecting his own gift pile on the floor.

he didn't get angry, and our parents didn't have their usual holiday fight.

he sat in four-sibling symmetry with his sisters around a board game. Inspired by the American version of *The Office*, the game was miserably complex except for one clear task: players were instructed to shout, "That's what she said," à la Michael Scott, after any accidental innuendo. We resisted at first—the sexism, the heresy of sex jokes in our mother's house—then we committed, eating sliced summer sausage as we played.

he posed for a photo, sitting on the futon, wearing the new slippers his sisters had gifted him for midwinter smoking, fanning shrink-wrapped Jim Jarmusch–directed films. I could see bruise-like bags under his glasses, and his cheeks looked sunken, but there was real happiness in that head tilt, in that open-mouthed smile. There was Christmas tree light on his face.

I felt alarmingly happy. I feared my family was living the joy that comes one Bible Storybook panel before sorrow, and soon we'd have to pay.

Rhododendrons

Afternoon sunlight. Cooper's Rock State Forest in northern West Virginia. Summer 2012, sometime after my May breakup from Gideon, my boyfriend of five years, and before Joshua's August suicide. I stand on a ninety-degree, twenty-five-foot cliff overlooking the Cheat River. Broken branches and maple leaves ride the current. I'm thirty years old, hanging out with a group of undergraduate students, taking a heartbreak-dazed respite from my life.

The way out to this cliff is four-wheel-drive vehicle only, up and down gravel, between tangled walls of shiny-leaved rhododendrons. I recognize their blooms from my fourth-grade West Virginia Notebook. My mother bought a pink polyester clump at a craft store, and I rubber-cemented it onto cardstock, penned "*Rhododendron maximum*, the West Virginia state flower." These blooms are both brighter and paler than my example, cream mixed with magenta. Unmistakably alive.

A male student jumps first. He's jumped here before, he can swear it's safe. The rest of them flash into the water. Perhaps these students haven't heard the stories about fall deaths from these West Virginia rocks, drownings in these West Virginia rivers. They likely didn't watch the crappy Christian movie about the girl who breaks her back on a cliff just like this one, with their own backs pressed to cold metal folding chairs in a Pentecostal Sunday school class.

After a few minutes the students reappear in their soaked jean shorts and bikinis, crawling on all fours up a trail. I skitter to the edge, embarrassed by my dry shorts and shirt. "Just jump out," the guy who's been here before tells me. "Jump as far out as you can, so you clear the cliff."

"Right," I say, and I jump right away. Straight down because I'm terrified. Because in that moment, I don't care enough to try. My body arcs toward the wall, cotton grazing moss-greened limestone. I plunge feet first into the water, inches from a boulder on the riverbank. I scramble onto that boulder, shake both legs, both arms, run a finger down my spine. I crawl up the trail, tremble on the cliff until it's time to get into a student's SUV, head back down the gravel road, past the rhododendron blooms that will fall off and float down the river.

After Joshua dies, I'll think back to this jump. How close I came to killing myself. I'll wonder: when Joshua stepped into his closet, prepared his leather belt, did his thoughts resemble mine when I stepped off the cliff? I thought, *Maybe I'll die, but it won't matter.* This moment isn't my life, just a pink polyester version of my life. Tomorrow I'll close the notebook and walk away.

While my parents were adding Rebecca's bedroom to their house, Bo, the remaining black half of the sibling-cat circle, got fed up with the builders' racket and left. He was gone so long we gave up on looking. A search for his sister, my family decided.

A year later, my dad drove home to fetch something while my mom was in the hospital, and he spotted Bo, nearly as starved as the day we found him as a kitten, eating from a neighbor's outdoor trashcan. Bo had been to the far country. He'd long run out of money. He'd tired of begging for food with the swine. My dad rejoiced, gave Bo meat from the refrigerator, cheered my sick mom with online miracles of lost cats that went home.

Bo fattened back up, this time without muscle. He wore his journey in a baggy flap of stomach. But he stayed for years, until the months before Joshua died, so long we thought Bo had forgotten his journey. Then Bo ran away again, this time for good.

I'd like to imagine Bo stayed away because he found his sister, that their well-fed, elderly bodies are curled together.

But I know too much about leaving and returning siblings. I'm sure one of them is dead.

PART 5
RETURN

"And he arose." The Prodigal stands up and walks out of that pigpen. He's not going to sit there and shrink until pigs eat what's left of his body.

My brother got out of his bed and buckled a belt around the bar in his closet.

Branwell Brontë—according to Elizabeth Gaskell, who cited "one who attended Branwell in his last illness"—felt his death coming and staggered to his feet, keeping a promise he'd made to himself when he realized he was going to die. I imagine him upright in a beige muslin gown by his father's red-curtained bed, staring through the stone and plaster walls of the parsonage, locking eyes with the beckoning skeleton in the churchyard.

And he arose. The Prodigal casts off the remaining threads of his coat like a risen corpse tossing away a shroud.

Joshua squatted until he passed out, cast off his sad brain with his month-worn boxer shorts and his mosquito-scarred calves.

Juliet Barker dismisses Gaskell's account of Branwell's death, with his planned exit, as "second-hand" info, "embroidered" by "village gossip." But in Barker's version, Branwell still arose from his bed. She says he "started convulsively, almost to his feet, and fell back dead into his father's arms."

My mother held Joshua, but his body wasn't warm like Branwell's. His spirit was miles down the road.

How to Plan a Funeral for Your Twenty-Two-Year-Old Brother

STEP 1: ADMIT YOU HAVE A BODY.

On Thursday, August 30, 2012, after four hours of sleep, you wake up feeling like the world has shifted. Like the sun might have come up on the wrong side of the nearly windowless apartment you share with Rebecca in Morgantown.

Last night, Rebecca talked to Joshua from midnight to one a.m., Joshua in his musty bed two hundred miles away in Huntington, in the house where you learned to read. Then at three in the morning, when you realized Rebecca was also awake, you climbed under her queen-size duvet and the two of you talked about your brother, only calling him Smoo. You were both worried about him, but Labor Day weekend was two days away. You'd see Smoo on Friday and hug him. Sometime before dawn you stumbled back into your room, and you and Rebecca fell asleep. But now it's nine a.m. and you both know something has shifted in the universe.

Since it's a Thursday, you don't have to put on khaki pants and enthusiastically harangue a classroom of hungover WVU freshmen. You get up and steep a strong cup of black tea, determined to conquer that world-upside-down feeling with a terrific writing day. Rebecca throws on a T-shirt and jeans and calls your mother as she sets off for the university alone.

When Rebecca tells you the story later that night, you'll imagine them both: your mother pacing the kitchen on her beige cordless phone, glancing every minute at the pendulum clock on the wall; Rebecca walking through downtown Morgantown, cell phone to her ear, passing twenty bars, five churches, at least ten homeless men sweating in their winter coats. Your mother and sister talk about how close Joshua is to finishing his associate degree, how thankful your mother is that she'll see her girls tomorrow night.

When Rebecca reaches her graduate student office, they both hang up, and Rebecca starts typing a paper for a course she'll drop that afternoon. At precisely noon, Rebecca's phone rings.

"Rebecca?" your mom says, her voice quiet. She speaks in the dead dog, dead grandparent tone, with an edge of something new and worse.

"What?" Rebecca screams, knotting her long brown hair in her hands. "Tell me! What! Is it Smoo?"

Always a roundabout speaker, your mother continues, "Rebecca, I've been watching the clock. Since Joshua didn't have school today, I thought I'd leave him alone till noon, but I just checked, and he's not in his room." Empty bed, empty chair at Joshua's desk.

Rebecca asks if he could possibly be out buying cigarettes, and your mom says no, she's been up since six, and Joshua hasn't left his room. Then your mom says, "Rebecca, stay on the phone. I know he's not in the closet, but I'm just going to make sure."

By "in the closet," your mom doesn't mean *hiding during a panic attack*, like your anxious poet friend, or *seeking a space to pray*, like your mom when you were little. She doesn't mean *sorting through his shoe collection*. A few months earlier, your mom heard a whimper in the middle of the night. She went into Joshua's bedroom and found him in the closet, a belt looped around the clothing rod and his neck. He raised his head and sobbed, "I don't want to die," and she dragged him out of the closet and held him.

That night, many mothers would have called the police and put their sons in the hospital. But since your mom feared the potential life-destroying consequences of policemen, hospitals, and mental illness diagnoses, her response was a suicide watch of her own. For months after Joshua's attempt, your mom lay awake at night, bursting into his room nearly every hour. Often she found him watching an art film in a cannabis cloud, or enjoying porn, bedsheet over his erection—he knew his mother might appear at any moment. Joshua fumed, but he rarely locked his door against her, perhaps thankful for this lack of privacy, for the possibility that if he despaired again, someone might catch him in time. Lately, though, Joshua has been rather happy, almost hopeful. Last night, your mother let herself sleep.

Rebecca knows what your mother means by "in the closet." She grabs her hair at the crown and turns white as she waits, knocking her knees against her desk, rapping her shoes on university linoleum. She already knows he is in there.

❧

Your mom calls your dad, and Rebecca calls you. Your mom says to your dad in his pharmaceutical plant office, "You need to sit down and close the door." He finds his keys, mutters something to his boss, speeds home with the radio off.

When Rebecca calls, you're sitting on the living room floor in your pajamas, printed-out essays in rows on the rug, ready to brag about a writing breakthrough. Maybe if you can talk first, whatever she has to say will disappear.

But before you can speak, Rebecca says, "He did it. He killed himself."

You run outside, leaving a wrinkled track through your essays, desperate to get into the sunlight. "What?" you say, breathing heavily. You dig your bare toes into the dirt patch behind your apartment that an old man mows with gasoline. "Who?" You know who, and you knew what "he did it" meant before she clarified. When your parents or siblings say a single word, you hear paragraphs in the tones of their voices, and you've wondered all morning if the world felt upside down because your Smoo no longer lived there. But still, your brain needs the name with the action.

"Joshua killed himself," she mumbles, but you understand.

"No, no way." Despite years of fear, you're completely unprepared, like your leg has been suddenly lopped above the knee. You know that bloody stump is going to hurt, but you're too surprised to feel anything yet.

"Joshua killed himself," Rebecca says again. Later you'll replay this moment and think about how she used the name "Joshua," as if it weren't your Smoo who had hurt you this way.

"He hung himself in his closet. Call Mommy," she says, and hangs up.

"It's okay. I'm okay. We're okay," your mother says when you call, willing you to be as calm as she is. As calm as she needs to stay so she, and perhaps her whole family, can survive.

"Mommy," you say. "Are you *sure* he's dead?" On sappy teen TV, when young men hang themselves, it takes them forever to die. There's plenty of time for their mothers to find them, for repentant bullies to bring carnations to the hospital psych ward. You feel a Smoo-shaped hole deep in yourself, but still, maybe shit TV hasn't lied.

"Stay on the phone," your mother says. "I'm going to check." The line goes silent, and you picture her standing beside a pile of Joshua's handmade puppets, hand in the closet, fingers pleading for a pulse.

"Sarah Beth, his face looks real distorted. I think . . ."

"Can't you call the paramedics? Can't you do CPR?"

But you don't mean CPR. You mean tell Lazarus to crawl out of his tomb, tell Jairus his dead daughter is only sleeping. Find an Old Testament prophet with dead-raising power in his dried-up bones and chuck Joshua's body into his grave. Three years later, your mother will get angry at herself. Why didn't she stand there and scream, "In the name of Jesus, Joshua, come back to me"?

But in that moment, your mother knows it's not a day for a miracle, or at least a miracle that's more spectacular than her continued ability to stand.

She says, "Sarah Beth, he's cold."

STEP 2: LET THE BODY GO.

Still in your pajamas, still barefoot, still on the phone, you run around the corner to your friend Ann's house. Her turquoise two-story is where you do your laundry, where you watch Ann's children perform raccoon plays, where you chat about books over wine and Ann's brownies. Today you need a place to lie on the floor, and laundry and raccoons mean safety. Ann is home, thank God. Her husband hides the children from your grief, and you lie down on the hard blue carpet on her glassed-in front porch. Ten years older than you, Ann seems to know you need a mother, a mother who isn't standing with her son in a closet. Ann covers you with a red fleece jacket and sits down beside you on the floor.

But don't forget: you're still on the phone. And you've remembered things get dicey when people keep unreported bodies in their houses. Face against carpet, you say, "Mommy, you have to call the police." Your mother hesitates. You understand. She's in this in-between place, the place after she had a breathing son, but before uniformed men barge in and jot on a pad, "Cause of death: asphyxiation by hanging." In this in-between place, it seems like time might move backwards. Like it could turn into yesterday, and she could pry Joshua out of bed and drive him an hour to school, his music so loud the hatchback would start trembling.

Besides, it's *her* body. All 110 pounds of it. Pointy pigeon chest. Shoulders that hunch forward. His receding hairline. Teeth that would have been braces-straight if he'd been the sort of person to wear retainers. Legs scarred from that summer he went to camp, and he picked his bug bites till he nearly hit bone.

"Mommy, you really have to. We'll get in trouble."

Your mother sighs. "Okay."

In the background, you hear your father stagger in. Your mother tells you she loves you and hangs up the phone.

STEP 3: CALL YOUR EX-BOYFRIEND.

In May, you and Gideon broke up. You wanted children. He was afraid to get married. He saved like a miser for land of his own where he could shoot squirrels and deer. Two hours ago, the breakup seemed necessary. Now, three months apart have washed away and you only remember five years together.

You gasp into the phone, "Joshua's dead," and he acts the way only your life partner could: this is his problem too. He drops his dissertation about eighteenth-century French diaries and says, "I'll be right there." Rebecca's with you now. A professor drove her to Ann's house and offered to drive all the way to Huntington. But that four-hour drive is Gideon's job. Aside from you and your sister, Gideon is the only person in Morgantown who has eaten chicken at your parents' kitchen table. And he cared about your brother. They agreed Werner Herzog is a filmmaking genius and Quentin Tarantino is a derivative hack. You and Rebecca plod the four hundred feet to your apartment—her in her rumpled T-shirt and jeans, you in the red jacket—and find Gideon standing in the parking lot.

Gideon waits on your couch, running shoes in your wrinkled essays, while you and Rebecca pack. Whenever you go home, you tick through your categories: work, hygiene, clothes, pets, teabags (your mother doesn't keep caffeine in the house). But this time all you can remember you need is a dress and shoes to wear to the funeral. Who needs clean panties or a toothbrush when you're standing at the end of the world? Rebecca also barely packs. Later she'll tell you she firmly believed the family would kill themselves together when you all got home.

As you stand in front of your bedroom closet, deciding which dress would forever be *the dress you wore to your brother's funeral*, you have a horrible thought. Your Smoo, his face "real distorted," in an open casket in Reger Funeral Home. You call out for Gideon to find your phone, like you did when he loved you, and he brings it within seconds. You touch your cheek to his thrift-store plaid shirt and squeeze his hand *thanks*—those beloved calluses from two decades of chin-ups. When he's back on the couch, you phone your mom again.

"Don't get him embalmed!" you say when she answers, unable to waste time on "Hello" or to say your brother's name or nickname and "embalmed" in the same sentence. "We need to get him cremated." Your parents' finances are tight already, and you know the cost difference between cremation and a fancy casket. Plus, Joshua's body in his prom suit, in a dark box forever next to your cancer-eaten great-grandmother and your dad's liquor-dead brother? The idea is more than you can bear.

"You think so?" your mother replies, her voice unnaturally steady.

"Yes, I really do."

Aside from oldest child bossiness, you aren't sure why you have a right to demand this, and you aren't sure your mother will say yes. When PaPa was dying—you were eight but you remember—he asked his children to have his body cremated. Your mother refused, insisting, "Daddy, funerals are for the living."

You know funerals are for the living, and that's why you want your brother cremated. You need his body to be gone, like he jumped on a bus and disappeared.

"I really think so, Mommy. Cremation's so much cheaper, and we don't want an open casket funeral."

You hear your mother shudder, then sigh, a strangely hopeful sigh. "I'm so glad you called now. That man from Reger showed up here with the policemen, and he keeps sticking a paper at me and saying, 'Ma'am, you have to sign this so we can embalm.'" Her voice goes nasal when she imitates him. "Sarah Beth, it's making me sick."

You know that man from previous family funerals. Fat, mustached, serious. He looks like he was born in a suit. You try and fail to imagine him in your house, his black tasseled loafers on your brother's blue carpet.

"Well, you know what, Sarah Beth? I'm going to go back in there, and I'm going to tell that man *no*." Your mother's voice sounds triumphant. Here is something your family can control.

STEP 4: GET THE FAMILY TOGETHER.

Two cats in carriers, dress in a tote bag, shoes on your sidewalk-dirty feet, you climb into Rebecca's red Subaru Forester she bought herself. If Rebecca's in a car, she drives. The day after she got her driver's license at eighteen, she drove you, her six-years-older sister, to Cincinnati. But now Rebecca's slumped in the back like a sleepy child, and Gideon—a *man*, her *sister's ex-boyfriend*—sits behind the wheel.

First stop, Fairmont, West Virginia, to pick up Jennifer. She recently began a veterinary technology program in Fairmont, so she has an apartment twenty miles closer to home. All you've told Jennifer is "Something bad happened" and "We're coming over right now." She doesn't have anyone yet in Fairmont—no friends with glassed-in porches, no professors with offers to drive to Huntington—so if anyone were to tell her about Joshua before you got there, she'd be utterly alone. You stay on the phone with her all the way to Fairmont and refuse to answer any questions. She doesn't ask the big one—*Is Joshua dead?*—even though she knew the minute you called. She knows it's easier for everyone if she pretends Joshua's chain-smoking in Huntington while you grind your teeth through afternoon traffic.

When you get to Fairmont, Jennifer's waiting in the parking lot in the scrubs she wears to her veterinary technology program. She handles the onset of shock as well as anyone could—no tears, an intense *oh-no!*—then you run up the filthy carpeted steps to her apartment, even though speed is useless. If you take those steps four at a time, your baby brother will still be dead. Her cat carrier on her lap, funeral dress in her backpack, Jennifer scoots into the backseat next to Rebecca.

The Subaru is small enough for a general conversation, but the front and back exist in separate universes. From your front-seat perch, you imagine that backseat in the family minivan, fifteen years ago, on a trip home from the Columbus Zoo. You sat alone in the middle seat, studying the cracked library binding of a Brontë novel, wishing you wouldn't get carsick if you read it. In the back, Jennifer drank can after can of root beer and pretended it made her drunk. Her voice loud and wobbly, she held up a can and declared, "It's root beer with the root crossed off." Rebecca munched cookies and crackers and admired her new elephant bracelet from the gift shop. Joshua wrote songs about his new rubber giraffe and his new plush gorilla with a tag that claimed he loved jazz, and the toys danced along on his sisters' laps. *Big Papa . . . loves Teddy*

Grahams. Joshua's voice was deep and slow, the way he thought a gorilla might sing. *Big Papa . . . plays in a jazz band.*

There's no middle seat in the Subaru. You're next to Gideon, knees up and pointed toward his jeans, the way you sat in his unairconditioned pickup last summer in Tennessee. You rode to Gideon's family's farm, where you gave the cows sweet feed and shoveled manure into buckets for the garden. You went to the pawnshop and dug through DVDs. On the way out of the shop, Gideon paused to peer at the tarnished silver chains and the ten-karat relics of failed marriages. Then he squeezed your shoulder and grinned. He used the nickname he gave you because you lagged when the two of you got ready to go anywhere. "Someday, Pokey, I'll get you a ring."

But it's August 30, 2012, and those days in the truck and the minivan are gone. In the back of the Subaru, Rebecca sits dull and silent, while Jennifer chatters, no one will remember about what. In the front, you stare at Gideon's profile and his curly ponytail, secretly seething at him for driving the speed limit. If he went slower, you'd have more time to prepare for a house that rings with the silence of no brother. If he sped up, maybe you could get to Huntington so quickly you could catch Joshua alive.

Gideon takes his eyes off the highway every three seconds to catch your eye, smile, and squeeze your knee. "You all right there, Pokey?" he asks once a minute, as if it's the only sentence in his head. It's your job to reassure this man you love, so you shape your lips into a smile.

As you roll closer to home, you pass the mall where Joshua bought his CDs, the church where he escaped from the nursery. The white wooden roller coaster at century-old Camden Park where Joshua operated the rides in summer and fall. The polluted creek where he fished for bluegill. The lone maple in a cow pasture Joshua declared "the most beautiful tree in the world."

You reach the house where Joshua killed himself, and you stumble out of the car. Your parents are waiting in the driveway, but they're people you haven't met: this old-looking couple with no son. Your mom grabs you, then Jennifer, and Rebecca and your dad crowd in. Gideon hesitates, and then he adds his arms and body to this urgent hug, this phalanx against the coming grief-storm. Your mom stretches her arms wider so she can squeeze Gideon's shoulder. He belongs here.

If you could stay forever in this tangle of sad bodies, you wouldn't have to scrape up the energy to walk up the steep driveway, to climb the back steps and open the door. You wouldn't have to free the cats from their carriers. You wouldn't have to pee and wash your hands. You wouldn't have to help your parents find something for dinner, and you wouldn't have to try to eat. You wouldn't have to remember there are times on the clock when humans should be in bed, and times when humans should be up and moving. But the sun's going down, faster now that the summer's ending, and you've got a funeral to plan. Arms fall limp, bodies stiffen, and you take a dazed step back. Your parents and sisters grab the cat carriers and your skimpy travel bags and trudge into the house.

You're left alone in the driveway with Gideon. During a quick planning session for how you'll all get back to Morgantown—he'll take the Subaru, you and your sisters will borrow a car from your parents—you find yourself wanting to kiss him, but some faint distance holds you back. When you both fall silent, he takes your hand and strokes your fingers, and you reach up and peck him on the jaw. Then you drop your chin and smile up with your eyes, a look that says, *It's your turn now*. If he kisses you back, if he really kisses you, he'll come in and spend the night on the futon. At dinner, you'll set the table with six plates, not five like someone is missing. When you get back to Morgantown, he'll take out his Crockpot and fix you beans, carrots, and potatoes without salt.

Gideon lets go of your hand. "No, Pokey." He kisses you on the forehead like a child.

You've forgotten the last three months, but Gideon remembers. He gets into the Subaru and drives away.

STEP 5: SPREAD THE NEWS

After a night of Nyquil sleep, you wake up and remind yourself your brother is dead. It's Friday, your first full day without Joshua. You haven't woken up from one of your old dead-brother nightmares, a realization that mixes horror and relief. In those nightmares, Joshua, in a manic rage, bludgeons your parents to death with an earth-colored jug lamp your mom threw out when you were ten. You aren't there, but you watch it all. Before the cops arrive, Joshua's rage melts away and he weeps over his parents' blank, bloody faces, and he quickly finds a way to kill himself.

You realize you feel safer without your brother in the house, then you feel guilty for your relief. You remember your four-year-old Smoo who bounced around the house in undershirts you embroidered with Snoopy and Woodstock, and you contemplate dosing yourself with more Nyquil. If you drank the remaining half bottle, perhaps you would sleep for several days, and three days from now you could surely handle everything. Finally your oldest-child duty rises to the surface, and you get up and find the remains of your family huddled on the family room futon.

No one else in your family drank Nyquil, so no one else slept, but your family has to leave the house anyway. You have to go to your dad's parents' house and tell them their grandson hanged himself in his closet. Yesterday evening, you and your mother and Rebecca made calls: your mom's two brothers, your dad's one living brother, aunts and cousins, your friends, Joshua's closest friends, and Bailey, even though she and Joshua broke up a year ago for good. But your grandparents are too old and too deaf to learn such news on the phone, and no one had the energy last night to drive the seventeen miles to their home across the river in Ohio. Your family decided to gift them an extra day in a world where their grandson is alive. But now the sparrows are singing, dragonflies are diving for gnats, and sunlight is streaming through the east windows. Your grandparents' bonus day is over.

"Come on, everybody," your mom says weakly—a faint imitation of her usual get-up-and-go call—and the rest of you drag yourselves into motion. Your parents could run this awful errand without you and your sisters, but there's only five of you left, and you're in this together. No one wants to be home alone.

In a drawer—you're avoiding closets right now—you find shorts and a tank top that, like all your clothes, belong to the former, live-brother era of your life. In this outfit you walked around New Orleans three days after your breakup, achieving a blistering sunburn and trying furiously to be happy. In this outfit you read on your parents' porch swing three weeks ago between Joshua's continual interruptions; he described how the nicotine strength varied cigarette by cigarette in his current pack of Marlboro Reds. You put on this costume of your former self and prepare to sit in your former self's place, in the middle seat of your parents' minivan.

But when you slide open the side door, the seat is missing. Your dad has removed it to haul an appliance, and so the van is down to five seats: two in the front, three in the far back, a spaced-out version of the coupes your parents drove when you were a child. You climb into the back, and your sisters slide silently in beside you, Rebecca clutching a palm-sized stuffed elephant. Your parents take their seats in the front, and for a minute you feel like you've traveled back in time: you're eight, Jennifer's five, Rebecca's two, and Joshua hasn't yet been born.

Then your dad drives out of Twin Valley, over the same asphalt an ambulance driver covered yesterday. Lights and siren off, your twenty-two-year-old brother in a body bag in the back.

❦

At your grandparents' house, Rebecca and Jennifer take a few steps up the front sidewalk, then collapse in the shade of your grandparents' groomed bushes. Your oldest-child duty gives you the courage to make it to the front porch, but no further. You sit down on the six-by-six carpeted concrete slab and wait for your parents to finish getting out of the car. MaMa and Grandpa have lived in this house for a decade, and you realize you've never really seen their porch before. The frayed carpet on the corners. The individual grains of soil around the potted pansies. The half-scrubbed flyspecks on a lone plastic chair.

When your parents reach the porch, they don't sit down beside you, but they don't go inside, either. "Those pansies need watering," your dad says.

"You're right," you say, then no one speaks for several minutes. Maybe you'll sit on the porch all day.

Finally MaMa opens the door and stares down at you, and up at your parents. She used to be a gorgeous five-foot-six blonde, three inches taller than your mother, but she's lost eight inches to osteoporosis.

"What's going on out here?" she demands. "I *thought* I heard a car."

MaMa knows something's up. Ever since you can remember, your family has barged right in if the door was unlocked, or rang the doorbell and knocked until someone unlocked it. Never in the thirty-year history of your life has your family waited silently on your grandparents' porch. But in terms of *what* exactly is up, MaMa is genuinely in the dark. She has no clue this sword of Damocles has been dangling over your family, no clue her grandson was mentally ill. To your grandmother, Joshua's the happy little boy who splashed the water out of her pool, who broke her ironing board surfing down the stairs. He's the quiet young man she paid to mow her yard until late July, when she found a cheaper mower at her church.

Still on the porch, your dad begins, "Mom," but his voice breaks.

"I'll tell them," you say, and you step into the air conditioning and wait for your parents to follow. Your sisters shake their heads *no* and stay in the bushes. Once your parents are inside, you close the door and direct your grandmother to her pink wingback chair, the place she sits on Christmas morning. Your grandfather is sitting on the couch already, one side of his face drooped with Bell's palsy. The palsy has developed in the past couple weeks, since your last visit, and even with your brother-suicide shock, it makes you feel sad to look at him. Speaking is difficult for Grandpa just now, so he begs for the news with his eyes.

"Well?" MaMa demands again, and you sit next to her thin, bent body in the chair.

Your mom settles in an easy chair, your father on the couch next to Grandpa, then you will yourself to speak. "Joshua killed himself. Joshua's dead. He hung himself in his closet." You speak so loudly your near-deaf grandparents can hear you, so loudly it feels like acceptance.

MaMa's reaction is immediate. A deep, single-note wail, over and over. She thrashes so hard you're afraid she'll topple into the floor. You wrap your arms around her arms and soft belly and squeeze her crooked spine against your chest. She stops wailing for a moment to cry, "I was at the hospital with Elwood all night. He was getting tests!" Then she cycles through several rounds of wails and "I was at the hospital all night" and "Not this today! Oh God, I can't take anymore!"

You look over at your grandfather. He's silent, but his eyebrow is raised and his mouth is open on the unparalyzed side of his face, and both of his blue eyes are wide. Your father's hand rests on his father's arm.

Finally MaMa calms enough to moan, "How on earth did this happen?"

You're about to say the words "bipolar disorder" when one of your parents interrupts you, you won't remember which, declaring, "Joshua was on drugs."

"Drugs!" MaMa screams sharply, into your ear, and the wails begin again. One of her hands breaks free and tangles in your hair. "I didn't know he was on drugs!"

He wasn't! you want to say, but you can't. You can't speak because it's true: your brother smoked pot, took unprescribed Adderall, experimented with God knows what. He left his pipe, carved into the shape of a panda, on his pillow when he died. Weeks later, his toxicology report will come back clean, no drugs in his system, but you believe now, and you'll believe after the report comes back, that Joshua numbed himself with cannabis before he stepped into his closet. Still, Joshua wasn't a junkie. To most people in the Huntington area, *on drugs* means heroin addicts, people who skulk around bus stops, who ignore their families and forget to eat or go to work, who shiver on benches by the Ohio River. Your brother lived in a disgusting bedroom, but he washed his hair and brushed his teeth, made calls for a telephone survey company, operated those Camden Park carnival rides. He was about to earn an associate degree, the same level of schooling your grandparents' darling Mark achieved, and Mark had a great job until a few months before he died.

And the real reason you can't speak: your parents need something to blame, and "drugs" is a safe place to put their hate. Safer for them, it seems, than bipolar disorder, which is slippery and genetic and somewhat treatable with possibly fat-making, stupor-inducing, suicide-triggering medications your brother never once tried. A disorder that could resurface in their grandchildren. A disorder that might make your grandparents call Joshua "nuts." A disorder your parents—after all the medical articles you've quoted to them, describing Joshua's exact symptoms—don't seem to believe he had. Years later, you'll read the National Institute on Drug Abuse's 2021 study of the correlation between marijuana use and increased suicide attempts in people between 18 and 35, especially those who had experienced major depressive episodes, and you'll wonder if both you and your parents were right. But right now, you know every member of your family is blaming themselves. If marijuana can take some of that heat, why not let it?

You curl yourself tighter around your grandmother, resigning yourself to your grandparents' belief that your Smoo is a dead addict, and then a minor miracle happens. MaMa stops wailing and sits up almost straight, revelation flashing in her eyes. "You know something?" she says in her rare storytelling tone. "What happened with Joshua, it's making me think about poor Mark." You know your grandmother would never connect poor Mark with drugs, despite the alcoholism, so drugs are apparently forgotten. You let go of her and slide down onto the immaculate carpet to listen. It's easier to breathe on the floor.

"I've never told anyone this before, not even Elwood," MaMa continues, looking intently at her husband. "One day, when we were in that house up on Thomas Avenue, I was sitting in the TV room with Mark." He lounged on the floor, and your grandmother sat on the couch behind him, massaging his neck, playing with his late 1970s floppy hair. Mark was twenty, nearly thirty years from drinking away his liver in a lonely apartment. As MaMa lifted a thick blond lock from her son's neck, she gasped. A horrible red stripe, like the burns her little boys got on their hands when they played on a rope swing.

"What's this?" MaMa demanded—not tactfully, you're certain—and he ran upstairs and slammed his bedroom door.

A couple days later, Mark drove across town to a Marshall class, and his mother took the opportunity to search his room. "And you know what I found?" she asks. "Buried under a bunch of junk in his closet? A hangman's noose!"

No one says anything. It's a moment of silent connection, brains and souls hugging like your family's bodies yesterday in the driveway, and any word might destroy the bond. You imagine Mark fashioning his noose, maybe finding the rope in his father's storage building, tying a knot he learned in those 1960s boys' guides that taught your dad and his brothers to train dogs, build rockets, breed aquarium fish. Then you imagine your own brother. You watch him remove two feet of clothes on hangers from his closet and tug the belt out of that day's jeans.

After a couple silent minutes, your grandmother stares down at you on the carpet, her face lit with a new inspiration. "You aren't still dating that boy, are you?"

"No," you say.

"Oh! Thank! God!" she yells, face and hands toward the living room ceiling. "When you brought that boy here to meet me last year, I kept thinking, she loves that boy, and he's scared to death of getting married."

"You were so right!" you say, remembering Gideon sitting stiffly on your grandparents' couch, and for a moment you feel a flash of triumph. You are *not* still dating that boy.

MaMa smiles, despite her dead grandson, despite her dead son, despite that crappy night she just spent at the hospital. She didn't notice her grandson's mental illness, but she was dead-on about your dead-end relationship. She looks so calm, you can leave.

You get up to walk out, and your parents stand to follow. But your Grandpa points at the seat next to him on the couch, asking you to sit beside him. You force yourself to look at his face, the sagging lips and eye socket Joshua saw a few days before he killed himself. The night after Joshua saw Grandpa, he told Rebecca over the phone that Grandpa was dying, and he couldn't take it. Rebecca told him Bell's palsy wasn't fatal, or likely even permanent, but now you wonder if Joshua believed her.

Joshua wasn't close to Grandpa, but Grandpa was a symbol of your and your siblings' childhood, of summer days in the aboveground pool Grandpa built out of vinyl and wood. Of the years before Joshua often became uncontrollably angry and horribly sad. Grandpa had already sold the house with the pool, and now he seemed to be disappearing too. You feel like you understand why Joshua couldn't handle Grandpa's drooping face, and you suddenly feel as angry at Bell's palsy as your parents feel at drugs.

But you know the real culprit. It's the fire in the brains of those young Childers men that compelled them to loop ropes and belts around their necks.

"Thank you," Grandpa says, his voice slow and strange. "Thank you for holding my wife."

You hug him and his drooping face, and you escape outside to join your sisters.

STEP 6: SURVIVE THE CONSULTATION AT THE FUNERAL HOME.

Next stop, Reger Funeral Home. The place your family held Mark's funeral three years ago, Granny's funeral five years ago, funerals for Grandpa's brother and several of MaMa's sisters. Now your Smoo is in there.

Rebecca and Jennifer won't go in, so they sit on the side steps, the noon sun baking the shining backs of their bowed heads, their tanned arms they've wrapped around their knees. There's an awning over the back door, but that's the hearse and ambulance entrance, the door that opened yesterday for your brother. You open the door behind your sisters for your parents to walk in, but your dad stops and hurries back to the car. He returns with Rebecca's elephant.

"You forgot him!" he says, stooping to hand her the toy.

"Thanks." She smiles slightly and hugs the elephant to her chest. Your dad seems to wish, like you, that you and your siblings were four live, happy children, playing with toy animals on the way back from the zoo.

Inside the building, you and your parents shuffle across the velvet carpet to the consultation office, where you sit down in too-plush chairs. The black-suited man who hovered in your brother's bedroom yesterday, brandishing embalming papers, is now in his element, at his oak desk with his laminated price sheet.

"First off," he says, his face and voice solemn, "I want you to have the opportunity to pay your respects. Would you like to have a moment with Joshua?"

"No," your mom says, a tremble in her voice, "I've seen him." Then, more loudly, "And Joshua's not in there, you know! He's in heaven. That body's just a shell. That's not him!" Your dad nods his agreement.

You give the man a look that telegraphs *wait a moment*, and he turns his attention to you. "Miss, would *you* like a moment with Joshua?"

"Maybe?" you say, and everyone sits in silence for a full minute. Your parents watch your face, horrified. Your mom found Joshua in the closet, your dad saw the body bag: you know they want you to say no. Still, you feel Joshua's body's presence. Your brother is somewhere in this building. You couldn't see his green eyes, but you'd see his brown eyelashes, those dark places at the outside corners of his eyelids. This is your last chance in your life to see Smoo's body before it's burned.

Ten years ago, when your beloved dwarf rabbit died in the night, your mother carried her to your bed in a towel, soft ears visible above the terrycloth. "You need to hold her," your mother said. She told you about studies she'd read about stillborn infants: mothers who held the tiny bodies recovered more quickly. Their brains and bodies understood their babies were dead, so they accepted the death and said goodbye. You held the bunny and recovered quickly, likely because it was a bunny, but still, you wonder if seeing Joshua might help. You want to hold your Smoo's hand, tanned from mowing and smoke breaks, to kiss his oxygen-starved forehead. But you're afraid of recording a memory of your brother's body. You'd remember his "real distorted" face for the rest of your life.

You think of the last time you saw Joshua, three weeks ago now, the final image that's currently replaying in your mind. It was your last day of your final summer visit to Huntington, and you and your sisters stayed as long as possible, four siblings in a row at a matinee. After the film, Joshua had an hour before his shift at the call center, and he wanted his sisters to walk with him downtown. "Hey, I've got an idea!" he said. You could get a coffee, visit a comic book store, listen to him talk while he smoked.

"I'm sorry," you told him. "We've got a four-hour drive, and it's going to get dark. We'll give you a ride to work."

One block from the call center, he got out of Rebecca's red SUV at the Cabell County Public Library, a four-story brown building where homeless people read magazines and parents like yours take their children to get books. You and your sisters told him you loved him, promised you'd come back on Labor Day weekend and eat hot dogs with him at the lake. He stood in front of the library and lit a cigarette, sad eyes following the car until it disappeared. Right now, that memory feels horrible: why didn't you all quit your jobs, drop out of school, and walk around Huntington for the rest of your lives?

But in that horrible memory, your last image of Joshua is handsome, upright, breathing. Nothing like a body after a hanging. And you figure those baby studies are right. If you saw and touched Joshua, your brain and body would accept that he's dead.

"No," you say, and the man smiles sympathetically behind his desk. Your mom squeezes your arm and whispers, "Thank you, God."

You make the rest of the decisions quickly, speaking for your parents. You know what they want. Yes, we want to use the Reger Chapel for the funeral service. Please have the service next Friday, we need time. No, we don't want a closed casket at the visitation. We don't want to buy a casket at all. Please cremate him, and don't tell us when you do it. Bury his ashes in the family plot at Spring Hill. No, we don't want a recommendation for a place to purchase a headstone. Joshua's not dead, he's gone: he left his family for heaven. Joshua boarded a chariot for Glory, or he jumped on a bus and disappeared.

STEP 7: FIND A VENUE FOR A GRADUATION PARTY.

On the drive home from Reger, your mom cranes her neck to stare at you and your sisters in the far backseat. "We need to feed people after the funeral," she declares. She wants to rent a big room, serve food, play upbeat Christian music and Joshua's most palatable favorite tunes, invite everyone who ever loved him.

"Yes, let's do it!" you say, but you feel hesitant. You know food after funerals is perfectly normal, but if you took your mom's plan and added an enormous chocolate cake with "Congratulations!" in a green sugary script, you'd have the graduation party your mom described to you two weeks ago. The party she wanted to throw next May when—as it seemed two weeks ago—Joshua was going to actually finish his associate degree.

But the closer you get to home, the more you like this idea. Who cares if you're throwing a graduation party without the graduate? You're still proud now that he's dead. And if you play the Shins, Andrew Bird, Men Without Hats, maybe, for half a second, you'll feel like Joshua just stepped outside for a smoke.

And the main reason you want to throw this party: you're desperate for something to do. Yesterday evening, before your Nyquil sleep, your ears were on hyper-alert. You listened for the *thunk* of Joshua opening his bedroom door, his footsteps on the laminate flooring, the flick of his lighter on the back porch, his voice: *Hey Sarbef, wanna watch a movie?* The funeral's in six days. If you have to sit in your parents' house for six days, listening to nothing, you're afraid your parents will have to bury you too.

When you get back to the house, you search for Huntington venues on your mom's computer, and alas, the only good list is for wedding receptions. Photos of beribboned white chairs on bright green lawns. Rooms of lace-draped, candlelit tables. You've seen this list before: you did some tentative research eight months ago, when you thought Gideon might buy that pawnshop ring. The morning's breakup triumph washes away, leaving you feeling spinsterly and nauseous. Still, you hit Print and sort through the options.

If you're *looking for something rustic*, there's the lodge at Camp Mad Anthony Wayne. You can two-step away the evening on a hardwood dance floor, then roast marshmallows around the campfire in your wedding gown.

If you're *looking for romance*, there's the hilltop room at the Rose Garden, where you can look down on the Gertrude Jekylls and Buff Beauties. You can stroll through fallen petals when you need a smoke.

You consider the "Historic Z. D. Ramsdell House," the Civil War–era, chandeliered home your mother rented for your grandparents' fiftieth wedding anniversary. There's a picture of your extended family from that day on your grandparents' living room wall: MaMa and

Grandpa looking fourteen years younger; you with curled bangs and braces; Mark, red-faced but alive. Joshua stands at the front in his Easter Sunday suit, knees apart and bent, arms raised and crossed, pretending he might karate chop the camera. But the Ramsdell House only holds fifty people, and why spoil a good family memory?

You decide on the Westmoreland Women's Club—seats eighty, no dance floor, no memories except that day twenty years ago when your family potlucked with people from church—but someone has it booked for the week.

So you call about the lodge at St. Cloud Commons, run by the Greater Huntington Park and Recreation District. Full kitchen, space for a hundred guests. You've never been in the lodge, but you've been to the adjoining park: the place where you attended your high school's soccer games, where your dad launched rockets with his brothers forty years ago. You hesitate for a moment, but you hated high school, and Mark already messed up your dad's rocket memories by drinking himself to death. A woman on the phone tells you to come into the office for paperwork, and all five of you get back into the minivan.

All five of you walk into the narrow park office, where a middle-aged, dyed-blonde woman stands behind a desk. She looks like she could chop a whole winter of wood, like she could hurl a heroin addict off a park bench. When your mom asks to rent the lodge, the woman responds, "What's this for? A wedding?" She eyes you and your sisters, maybe wondering which girl is going to wear white tulle and cause sticky champagne spills on her lodge floor.

"No," your mother answers, gripping your father's arm. "We want to have some food there after our son's funeral."

The woman mutters, "I'm sorry for your loss," and hurries the paperwork.

On the car ride home, you stare at the hills, stretch your legs in the empty middle space, and think about the Brontës. Now Joshua has died first, just like Branwell. After that, the Brontë sisters fell like dominoes. Emily at thirty, on the horsehair sofa. Anne at twenty-nine, in a hotel by the sea. Branwell died heartbroken, Anne and Emily died single. Except for Charlotte, who died at thirty-nine, shortly after she got married, their family had funerals instead of weddings.

Two weeks later, back in Morgantown, when you're feeling grief-stricken and dramatic, you'll go to Ann's house and talk Brontës over brownies. You'll say, "People in other families get married, and we die."

STEP 8: PUT SOMETHING IN A BOX.

When someone dies suddenly, there are so many phone calls. *Please cancel Joshua Childers's student loans. Please close Joshua Childers's bank account. Joshua won't be going to work at the call center tomorrow, or ever again.* After your mom phones the college where he nearly earned his degree, his advisor calls back and says they've got something for her. In May a professional photographer snapped Joshua holding a camera to his eye, a picture for the school brochures and website.

"We didn't end up using it," the man says—your mom remembers this well, Joshua was sick with disappointment—"but we've still got the picture! We had a nice big print made and everybody signed it. We wanted you to know how much Josh meant to us." You imagine your brother's photograph taped to a wall in a cinderblock hallway, professors and students with Sharpies in hand.

On Saturday morning your mother drives the twenty miles and picks up the picture, the final image she'll have of her son. The school is closed, but Joshua's advisor meets her there anyway. The signatures are, fortunately, not on the picture itself, but on a foot-wide strip of white at the bottom, like a 24-by-48-inch Polaroid.

"Isn't it gorgeous?" your mom says when she gets home. She cradles the picture against her stomach and looks down, blocking Joshua's face with her long curly hair. When she sets the picture down, you see your brother holding an enormous camera with steadiness and confidence, like a guy with a decent-paying job. You see that receding hairline that was driving him crazy, smiling lips and dull green eyes. Your mom blocks the signature strip with her arm and says, "Look, we're going to take it to Michael's and have them cut this part off. Think how gorgeous it's going to look in a frame!" It *is* a nice photograph, printed well, but since you never saw it when Joshua was alive, it feels like a portrait of him dead.

Your mom herds you and your dad and sisters into the car. Time for the daily funeral excursion! This time to Michael's to get that picture framed. Your mom's going to put it on a stand at the party. In lieu of the guest of honor, in lieu of a body.

On the way to Michael's, someone realizes it's noon—damned mealtimes, three times a day—so your dad stops the minivan at a pizza place. The pizza takes forever, leaving your family to talk funeral plans and shudder at the new asymmetry: three people named Childers on one side of the table, only two on the other.

When the pizza comes, it's impudently delicious, defying your appetite-free grieving, and the deliciousness makes everything worse. You know your brother's body is at Reger, but you feel like he's sleeved in cardboard, under the backseat of the minivan. You want to take that picture and start running. You could hide together on a mountaintop, or you could crouch in the mud by the Ohio River. Anything to keep that picture from getting framed. You put your head on the table and bawl aloud, long blond hair in your greasy plate.

"Sarah Beth," your mom says, half sympathetic, half pleading. She's afraid if she cries, she'll cry for years. Your dad weeps silently, set off when any of you cry. Rebecca takes your hair out of the pizza grease and squeezes your arm.

"Getting that picture framed," you gasp between sobs, "makes Joshua feel more dead." You don't care about those signatures, but cutting them off feels like a violence. And encasing that picture in glass and wood forever: something about it feels like a burial.

"Sarah Beth, I know," your mom says, though you're not sure she understands. "But it's such a wonderful picture. It'll be so nice for everyone to see it. Joshua looks so handsome. Just like David at that age." She grabs your dad's hand, and he cries harder. At Michael's, your mom takes the picture in alone, and the rest of you wait in the minivan.

After the funeral, the picture will hang on the wall in Joshua's room, in place of the live boy who watched movies there, in place of the body that once hung in the closet. For years, your mother will take you into Joshua's room and point to the picture. "Isn't he beautiful?" she'll say.

You'll feel like she's looking into his coffin.

STEP 9: SCREAM ABOUT THE CATERING.

Two days before the last time you saw Joshua, you walked with him and Rebecca in downtown Huntington. "You know what I like to do sometimes?" your brother said between Marlboro puffs. "I like to go to Jimmy John's and get me a Turkey Tom."

"Let's do it," you said, and the three of you ate sandwiches on outdoor metal tables in the heat.

You replay this memory on Sunday evening, when you're talking to your mom about catering for the party. First, you decide against hot dogs, Joshua's favorite food. Your mom says, "Sarah Beth, I know we're not the Rockefellers, but I'd like it to be a *little* classy," and you're afraid hot dogs would make you cry until you puked. Then you rule out those convenient platters of chicken from Chick-fil-A. It's the summer of 2012, Chick-fil-A's CEO has just spoken out against gay marriage, and everyone you know is boycotting the chicken chain or hitting the drive-thru for every meal. Your mom supports the Chick-fil-A mission, but she doesn't want guests to talk hate and chicken at her son's funeral. Finally, you ask your mom about Jimmy John's. She says, "Better than hot dogs," and everything seems to be settled.

Then your mom's two brothers knock on the door. They've brought a wife—your aunt Rachel—and a brand-new girlfriend. The girlfriend never met Joshua, but she seems frantic to help, to prove herself part of the family. She carries in a five-pound freezer-section lasagna and plops it on the table with a hard-frozen thud. "I knew you wouldn't feel like cooking, so I brought your dinner for tonight!"

"Thank you so much," your mom says, patting her back in a half hug.

Your uncles cry and hug you, tell you they'll miss your brother, and you know they mean it. Then everyone settles down on the family room futon and armchair and asks your mom for the finding Joshua dead story. You, your dad, and your sisters go hide in another room.

Half an hour later, you decide the story must be over, so you head back into the family room. Aunt Rachel has heard about the funeral after-party, and she's deeply interested in the catering. A retired schoolteacher, Aunt Rachel has voluminous gray hair and a velvet quilted coat her mother handmade thirty years ago, and she shares your mother's burning need to talk about Jesus. When your mom says, "Sarah Beth picked Jimmy John's," Aunt Rachel gets up from the futon.

"Sarah Beth!" she calls, then spots you in the doorway. She walks over and drapes her arm around your shoulders. "You can't have Jimmy John's. It *has* to be Chick-fil-A."

"What?" you say, jerking away. You aren't surprised: she annotates every issue of the Billy Graham Evangelistic Association magazine, *Decision: The Evangelical Voice for Today*. But actually you *are* surprised. Aunt Rachel knew your brother—not well, it's true, but it seems like anyone would know his funeral was hardly time for an argument about chicken.

"You have to order Chick-fil-A!" she repeats. "You have an opportunity here to take a stand for your faith."

You feel a scream welling up. You've always been scrupulously polite to this woman—she paid for your childhood piano lessons, she's offered you so much Campbell's soup—but right now you feel capable of saying anything. One option: *I hate you. Get out of my house.* Another: *My brother SUPPORTED gay marriage.* Or: *Fuck you.*

Your mother sees your scream coming. You see her fear on her face, so you manage a substitution. "You are NOT going to use my brother's funeral as a political statement!" You wave your hands as you yell, enjoying Aunt Rachel's widening eyes, and then, like a teenager, you run into your bedroom and slam the door.

Your outburst must end the visit. You hear car engines starting. You feel a satisfaction that turns to panic. You find yourself in the warm night air, stumbling barefoot down the front yard to where your uncle and Aunt Rachel parked on the street.

Aunt Rachel is climbing into the sedan, but when she sees you, she stops and stands on the pavement, car door open, eyebrows raised.

"I love you!" you call before you reach her. Then you give her a fierce hug. You're not a bit sorry, but you do love Aunt Rachel. It wasn't you that screamed, it was your grief.

"I know you do," she says, returning your hug. She gets into the car, and your uncle drives away.

When you go back into the house, you put the still-solid lasagna in the freezer. You feel your mother watching you—you know you've humiliated her—but instead of shaming you, she starts laughing. "If we wanted to eat at midnight," she says between gasps of laughter, "that lasagna would make a lovely meal."

STEP 10: FIND A WOMAN TO PREACH THE FUNERAL SERMON.

It has to be a woman. That much is certain, though your brother didn't care about feminism. Your mother can do what she wants at her son's funeral, and she wants to make those Huntington people squirm.

In the Bible-thumping churches in Huntington, West Virginia, only men can serve as lead pastor. In one evangelical church out of a hundred, a woman will preach the sermons, but she'll list her husband as lead pastor on the bulletin and sign, even if he only operates the video camera. Your mother took your family out of those misogynistic churches a decade ago and served as the family's pastor herself.

Last Sunday morning, your mother sat on the cat-shredded couch, commanding respect with her shoulders and eyes as she led the family

Bible study called Service. Despite her ill-fitting jeans and her misbuttoned blouse, she looked more like a queen than a pastor. You weren't there, but you're certain of what she looked like: King James Bible open on her lap, relevant passages marked with folded Kleenex. Your dad sat slumped on the couch beside your mom, and Joshua snored on the loveseat under the window. You and your sisters joined Service via speakerphone: you and Rebecca in Morgantown on your bed, Jennifer in Fairmont with her crochet needles in a ratty recliner. Your mom read a Bible chapter, prayed an interminable prayer, then she strode across the carpet to Joshua. She shouted into the phone and his ear, "You can wake up now! Service is over."

So your mom's your only pastor, and she can't preach her son's funeral. And she doesn't want one of those women with the video-camera husbands. She calls Bonnie, her childhood friend who lives in Maryland. Bonnie's not a pastor, but you've heard her pray with a pastor's cadence and authority over Kentucky Fried Chicken at the park.

Joshua barely knew Bonnie. You remember him speaking to her only once, at a church picnic when he was five. Joshua bounced past the picnic shelter, snatching a third Coke from the cooler on his way to the swing set, and Bonnie noticed he'd gotten tall. "If you keep growing that fast, we'll have to put a brick on your head!" she said. She shared a knowing chuckle with the other ladies. Joshua paused mid-bounce, just long enough to respond. "Well, I'll put tape on your glasses."

Your mom's friend doesn't remember that story, or apparently anything about your brother, but the situation can be easily remedied. Bonnie and her husband Roy drive the few hundred miles to your family's house two days before his funeral. They're due for a Huntington family visit anyway: it's no inconvenience at all! When they arrive, Bonnie and Roy stand on the family room rug and yarn about the stress of navigating Appalachia with a GPS. The talking dashboard in their car sent them down a backroad with five burned-down trailers and a place that sold beefalo burgers. Bonnie sinks into the futon, bracelet-covered wrists in the air, and says, "At least we made it here, praise the *Lord*!" She accepts a cup of herbal tea from your mother and takes out a pen and a leather notebook. Your dad and sisters wave and disappear, but your oldest-child duty holds you in the room. After your mother sits on the futon, you settle on the rug by her feet. Bonnie leans toward your mother and you and intones, pastor-like, "So, tell me about Joshua."

It's exactly the question you want Bonnie to ask, but you suddenly have nothing to say. As a child, your brother named a guinea pig Carl and a newborn bunny Joshua, after himself. His nose turned fuchsia when he went sledding. He liked to fart loudly in his bottom bunk and ask a sister to join him under the sheets. As an adult, during Camden Park's yearly Spooktacular, he wore a black hood, wielded a bladeless chainsaw, and frightened passengers on the park train. These aren't facts for rich blue cursive in a leather notebook. Your mom provides the basic details: twenty-two years old, most-of-the-way through an electronic media degree, born again as a child though he'd recently backslid. You fetch Joshua's high school trophies from the hall shelf—second place in the state in puppetry one year, first place the next—and Bonnie writes a single word, maybe *backslid*, maybe *puppets*.

"We're so glad *you're* preaching the sermon," your mother says. "Not somebody who wouldn't understand, and talk about"—she runs her hands nervously through her long brown curls—"his suicide." Some of the Bible thumpers in the audience will certainly believe Joshua's in hell, that people can't transport themselves to heaven through their closets.

"Of course. That stuff is no one's business." Bonnie grabs your mother's hand. "You just want to celebrate Joshua's life."

You can't take any more, so you go out onto the deck to sit on the swing. Roy had the same idea, so you listen to tales about his only child, a young man about Joshua's age who adores living in Japan. "Matt's making a TV show over there. Can you believe it?" Roy asks you. "He talks like he's going to stay there forever." Roy shakes his silver haircut and stares off toward your family's unmown lawn. If he could see past the woods behind the backyard, past the mountains, for seven thousand miles around the curvature of the earth, maybe he could see his son laughing without him.

A week ago, you would have felt sympathetic, but Japan's so much closer than heaven.

STEP 11: REMEMBER WHO THE FUNERAL IS FOR.

Your mom drove to Reger the night before the funeral to set everything up, so your family arrives the minute the visitation begins. The visitation is half an hour—the shortest timespan your mom deemed a legitimate length for a visitation—and your family wasn't about to add a moment with an early arrival.

When you step onto the visitation room's too-plush green carpet, you find at least thirty on-time mourners. You glance around for Gideon, though you know he's in Morgantown, and you squeeze your arms against your chest as you look at the place your dead family members have rested, though you know Joshua's not-yet-cremated body is hidden away in cold storage. Instead you see your brother's newly framed portrait, surrounded by flowers in boy-friendly colors and two floor lamps spaced coffin-width apart. An occasional relative respectfully approaches the photograph.

Your grandparents sit on the chairs that line the walls, MaMa sipping a Styrofoam cup of black coffee from the lounge. She's an expert at surviving funerals at Reger. In an alcove, a group of your adult cousins and Joshua's high school friends are watching the photo DVD Rebecca put together. You walk over to the TV, and Joshua's friends ignore you, but your cousins hug you, dropping tears into your hair. After you extricate yourself, you see minutes-old Joshua, round-headed and bald. One-year-old Joshua in the clothes dryer. Three-year-old Joshua and his sisters in MaMa's red wooden swing, dripping swimsuits sheathed in white terrycloth cover-ups.

The newer pictures include ill-taken shots of Joshua, arms slung around his high school friends, and those friends laugh appreciatively when they see themselves on the screen. During family shots, they look sulky and bored. You feel suddenly territorial over that hidden-away body, angry at these stupid kids who don't care that Joshua was your Smoo. You want to say, *Look! Joshua belongs to me and my sisters. Watch us pose in front of the lion enclosure. Watch us dance around the forsythia. Watch us open presents every Christmas of our lives.* Then you remember you suggested adding those friend photos to the slideshow, a courtesy to those friends. Right now, you're not sure why you cared.

One of your cousins, a dark-haired woman in her forties, is crying over every photo, re-watching when the slideshow begins again. She's transfixed by the giraffe- and *Toy Story*–obsessed little boy—her relative!—who is born, grows up, gets hollow eyed, then disappears. A black-suited Reger employee appears with a box of tissues, passing your tearless mother to hand the box to your cousin. She accepts a wad and sobs harder, and you want to scream. You, your sisters, and your parents have the rest of your lives to mourn Joshua, but this cousin, a woman who saw Joshua maybe ten times in his life, is sobbing violently because it's the only time she'll need to cry. She'll feel lousy tomorrow, but she'll be over it in a week, a month tops.

Afraid you'll have another Chick-fil-A-type outburst, you stalk off to find the coffee. The lounge is empty, so you pour yourself a cup and sit on a leather loveseat. After a few deep breaths and a nasty sip, you have a revelation: your cousin's tears are the whole point. You, your parents, your sisters, your grandparents are facilitators of other people's grieving. For most people in this room, something awful happened to someone they genuinely cared about a little bit, and they need this space and time to cry it out so they can move on. You dump five packets of powdered creamer into your coffee and join your sisters. The three of you stand so close your dresses touch, three quarters of the group that once crammed together onto a sled, took turns under the spigot in the bathtub, shared two seat belts in the back of your grandparents' car.

At the end of the visitation, Bailey arrives in a wrinkled black dress. She walks over to your parents, waving tentatively and sniffling. She looks legitimately sad. The ex-girlfriend in you yearns toward the ex-girlfriend in her, and you rush over to hug her. You introduce Bailey to your sobbing cousin as "Joshua's girlfriend," and Bailey beams through her tears, the grieving widow. You've given her the recognition she came for.

STEP 12: SURVIVE THE FUNERAL SERVICE.

The thirty-minute visitation ticks by at last, and the Reger men herd the mourners down a hall. The visitation room is windowless, but sunlight illuminates stained glass in the chapel, and you can hear your leather sandals slapping the brown linoleum. Your feet have been silent for the last half hour; you focus on the sound of your shoes.

Your shoes carry you to the front row, the pew of honor, the pew that in all past family funerals in Reger Chapel you've left to more important or more insistent guests. This time your little brother is dead, and everyone expects your shrunken family to sit in front where everyone can watch you. Part of the play you have to perform. In your role as grieving oldest sister, you're suddenly conscious of the dress you brought from Morgantown: a sleeveless denim shirtdress that hits above the knee, with side slits that nearly reach your panties. Jennifer's in a long floral dress with a sweater, Rebecca in a pressed white blouse and gray pencil skirt she'll toss in the kitchen trash can tomorrow, teaching clothes turned funeral artifact. You look like the sister who's headed to the beach, but you remember why you chose this dress: wearing it, you feel completely like yourself. The girl who drinks tea. The girl who hugs cats and bakes brownies. The girl who loves Gideon, though she ought to stop. The girl who will always love her Smoo.

Bonnie clicks up the steps to the heavy wooden pulpit in her high-heeled pumps, in tasteful polyester, with her classy French twist. She reads the obituary your mother wrote, sounding solemn and strong as any male Huntington preacher, and then she launches into her sermon. Within seconds, you find yourself squeezing both sisters' hands, then dropping their hands so you can grip the pew, holding yourself in your seat. You won't remember the exact words, but the sermon's gist is this: Joshua turned away from God, started smoking marijuana, and became so bound by the powers of darkness he took God's greatest gift, his life. Bonnie widens her eyes and raises a clenched fist when she gets to the suicide. Bonnie doesn't say it, you're 99 percent certain Bonnie doesn't mean it, but the sermon makes it sound like Joshua's in hell.

You realize your mother must have gotten chatty when you were out on the deck with Roy, talked about the drugs that stole her son, but you know this isn't your mother's fault. Your mother is holding your father's hand, breathing hard, eyes focused on the floor. This isn't the sermon she asked for. If she could have preached her own son's funeral, she would have described her daddy hugging his grandson at heaven's gates, the dead family beagles sniffing Joshua's knees. You feel a chill from the air conditioner, and you wonder if this is how Emily Brontë felt in the churchyard at her brother's funeral, her cape ruffled by the chill that led to her death.

At the closing, Bonnie asks everyone to bow their heads and listen hard for the voice of the Holy Spirit. If the mourners don't want to end up like Joshua, drugged out and dead, could they please raise their hands as a sign they're coming back to God? You refuse to bow your head, so you look up at Bonnie. You see her staring at the back row, at Joshua's friends in their pilled black dresses and faded black T-shirts, clutching flowers they bought at a grocery store. They're staring back at her, hands down.

Tomorrow Bonnie will tell your mother on the phone, "I preached that whole sermon for Joshua's unsaved friends, and I was devastated when none of them raised their hands." Today you place your hands on your stomach, willing yourself not to vomit. Like you, Bonnie seems to have realized this funeral is not for your family. For Bonnie, the funeral is for those kids who chuckled at the fuzzy photographs of themselves smiling with your brother, those potheads who are walking on a rotten covering, about to drop into the pit of hell. Years later, you'll manage to empathize—this ultra-devout, eloquent woman from a male-dominated church got a chance to preach, a chance to possibly help some absolutely non-Christian people—and you'll realize what an awful task it must have been to preach a sermon for a dead young man, her son's age, that she didn't know. But right now, you feel like this sermon is another part of your brother's tragedy.

During the altar call, you feel a squirming at the end of your family's pew. In the space next to Rebecca, a space your family left open without thinking, seeking a space for six, not five. Joshua's dead, but he isn't gone yet. Your brother stands up and walks outside, cigarette and lighter already in his hands.

After at least one full horrible minute, Bonnie ends the prayer, her disappointment palpable. She follows your mom's wishes exactly in one way, at least: she invites everyone to the lunch celebrating Joshua's life over at the St. Cloud Commons Lodge. But you know she's forgotten something important. The black-suited mortician notices too, and he scurries up to the front as the crowd begins to stretch and gather their purses, asking everyone to remain in their seats. Maybe that man felt the misery in the air from wherever he lurks during funerals, or maybe he took the missing element personally, as funerals must be conducted properly at Reger Funeral Home. He motions with both hands for everyone to sit, then says, "I would like to offer Joshua's friends and family the opportunity to speak."

You bolt up the steps to the wooden pulpit, passing Bonnie as she hurries down to her seat. You're holding a eulogy you worked on all week, during the time you spent in your bed between funeral errands. Still, you feel you have a choice to make. You could have a public meltdown, here in front of your aunt Rachel, your surviving uncles, your living grandparents, your best friend from college, your professor from undergrad, some ladies that still attend your former church. You could scream that your brother wasn't a drug addict, mental illness killed your brother, and if your brother's in hell, you want to join him. You wonder if anyone in the audience would cart you off to the hospital's psychiatric ward. You wonder if your mother would have a heart attack.

Instead you place the eulogy on the pulpit and read about what it means to be a Smoo. Who your brother was during the years, and then the days, when he was well. *It's a perfect day when a Smoo sits in the back of a canoe, fishing line in the water, reeling in catfish after catfish. A Smoo loves not only the taste, but the scent of hot dogs; he uses them as fresheners in his sock drawers.* You can feel your brother smoking outside the chapel; you wonder if he can hear you through the stained-glass windows. *A Smoo thinks it's important enough to head to the store at midnight, just to buy licorice. A Smoo dances alone in his bedroom with a puppet, then talks a sister into dancing with him.*

STEP 13: DANCE.

The funeral over, you ride in the backseat of the minivan to the St. Cloud Commons Lodge. When you get out of the van, you breathe in the field where Mark launched rockets with his brother, the bleachers where your Smoo languished during a soccer game, demanding hamburger-shaped gummies and Styrofoam cups of Coke. The dry pool where MaMa's sister swam, six decades before she died of lung cancer. In the pool's center, there's a fountain with a one-foot gap at the base; you imagine your future great-aunt's lithe teenage body plunging down and through that hole, young, happy, fearless, and alive. The park is crawling with dead siblings. It feels like a relief to walk inside the lodge, a place where—as far as you know—none of those dead siblings ever went.

You spent the morning at the lodge, stacking plates and forks, peeling open tissue boxes, lounging listlessly while friends unfolded tables. But when you walk in, you notice a change: Joshua's portrait set up by the giant stone fireplace, transported by Reger. You knew the picture would be there, but its presence still shakes you. You wonder if it rode to the lodge in a hearse. Suddenly weak, you walk over to the food table and grab a tiny catering version of a Turkey Tom. You hate turkey, but that sandwich feels like the only choice right now. You collapse into a metal folding chair at one of the tables, and a minute later you're joined by your dad's living brother and his wife.

No one knows what to say, so after you thank your aunt and uncle for coming and your uncle answers, "We're supposed to be here at a time like this," and there's nothing to say because he's right, you fill the silence by exclaiming, "Joshua's doing so well in school!"

After a pause, your uncle replies, "Uh, that's great," and he and his wife look at each other uncomfortably. When you began the sentence, part of your brain had forgotten Joshua's suicide for a blessed half-second, and the other part wanted to assure your physics teacher uncle—the designer and builder of the rockets your dad and his brothers launched—that your brother was smart even though he was dead. By the end of the sentence, you have fully remembered Joshua is lying somewhere at Reger, waiting for the next opening at the crematorium, but you don't correct yourself. You let your aunt and uncle glance at you sideways, taking focused sips from their plastic cups. Yesterday you found yourself talking to Rebecca about your brother in the future tense—*when Smoo learns to drive*—and for one second you wondered what car he would use. In those moments of denial, you feel whole and happy; you're not ready to let those moments go.

After a few minutes your grandparents arrive and sit down next to you without drinks or food, a silent request. "Hey, how about I get you some food? We've got some good sandwiches up there!" You force enthusiasm so your voice will be loud enough for them to hear.

"Okay, honey," MaMa says, squeezing her soft fingers into your forearm. You hurry away, but slow down when you get to the table. You open a fresh bottle of Coke, fill two plates with the most neatly wrapped sandwiches, the snappiest pickle spears, and the chip flavors your grandparents eat at home. Your dad notices you from across the room and hurries over to help you carry, both of you finding relief in small and necessary actions. When you sit back down, your grandmother unwraps her sandwich and lays it on her plate, folding the paper on the side like she might use it to wrap a Christmas gift. Your grandfather's face looks better already, which makes you feel relieved—you can look at his face without flinching, and fewer mourners will gossip about that sag-faced old man—but also so much worse. If only Joshua could have stuck around for another week. You ask your grandmother if she likes her sandwich, hoping to distract her from the funeral she just sat through, but she doesn't seem to hear your question. "Honey, where did your mother find *that woman* to do the funeral?"

Your aunt and uncle stop eating and listen, and you wonder if they're merely curious, if they were upset by the sermon, or if they minded having to sit while a woman read the Bible at the front of a room.

"That's my mother's old friend," you say, looking around at everyone at the table. Your aunt and uncle nod and go back to eating. Normally you'd feel resentful at your grandmother's tone on "that woman"—you know exactly how MaMa feels about women in authority—but you're too annoyed about the sermon to care.

"Well, I couldn't hear a word that woman said. She spoke so quick!" MaMa turns to your grandfather. "Could you hear anything that woman said, Elwood?"

"Nope, not a thing."

You smile for the first time in days, nearly laugh with relief. "Could you hear me when I read?"

"Better than that woman, honey, but not really. You send it to Elwood in his email and I'll have him read it to me later."

"I'll do that," you say, and you lean over and kiss her.

About forty-five minutes later, when the metal bowl of ice has melted and Joshua's friends are on their fourth Solo cups of Dr. Pepper, when second cousins have asked you to sort through the sandwiches because they'd like to take home BLTs, some new guests arrive. The Huntington family of kids you and your sisters babysat for years, now ages six through twelve. They burst in through the lodge's back door, all sun-bleached hair and tanned knees, so happy you wonder if they know they're at a funeral.

At this point in the afternoon, you and your sisters are hunched in folding chairs next to Reger's boom box, listening dully to the mix of your mother's contemporary Christian and your brother's indie rock, but when you hear the kids' squeals, you stand up. You take a step toward them, and they're on top of you, cycling through you and your sisters, hugging you so hard you crouch to keep from falling. The third-born, an eight-year-old boy, stops hugging first and hits the food table. He grabs one sandwich in each hand, holds them above his head, and yells, "This is the best party ever!" You laugh so hard you almost start sobbing. Their mom appears, messy-haired and a little embarrassed, and says, "I didn't want to bring them to the service because they're all crazy! But when I heard you were having food at the park, I went home and got them. I figured they'd be okay here."

"Yes!" you exclaim and thank her. The job was your average babysitting gig, or worse—low pay, not enough food in the house, missed college exams when the parents failed to appear—but now you feel like you and your sisters babysat just for this moment, a deus ex machina of joy.

The firstborn runs over to her mother and trots back smiling shyly, holding out a photo in a grimy magnetic sleeve. You've seen that photo on that family's refrigerator on Huntington visits, next to spaghetti-stained child drawings, a photo of the mom's former cat, and several quotes from the pope. Taken six years ago, the photo shows you, Jennifer, Rebecca, and Joshua on the family's saggy brown couch, each of you holding the child that corresponds to your birth order. You with the oldest girl, Joshua with the stinky-diapered baby. A celebration of four and four: three girls and a boy holding three boys and a girl.

Your stomach lurches when you see the picture. You wonder for a second if the parents no longer want the picture now that the sibling symmetry is gone, now that the picture is a visual reminder that children can grow up and die. But then you look at that intact set of four as they bounce along to the boom box, and you smile and thank the girl and mother sincerely. In the photo, Joshua has shoulder-length brown hair, a sunburned nose, and a genuine smile. He was the kind of teenager you could trust with your six-month-old.

The kids want to go outside, so you hand off the picture to your mother—she'll keep it on her refrigerator for years—and you follow them out to the playground behind the lodge. The kids jitter with happiness at the sight of the playground, at the feeling of afternoon sunshine. Their joy is contagious. You smile and wave at a friend who set up the tables that morning, now pushing his red-haired baby in a swing. He waves back, clearly befuddled by your ability to smile.

The second-born kid yells, "Let's roll down the hill!" A favorite West Virginia kid pastime, something you and your sisters and toddler brother used to do for hours in your backyard, gaining grass stains, pink leg welts, and tiny black slugs with each roll. You laugh and shake your head, but Rebecca—the sister who babysat those kids the longest, the sister who intends to throw her blouse and skirt in the trash can, the sister who is your family's new youngest child—is up for the challenge.

Rebecca and the kids roll like logs down the gentle slope behind the swing set, and you feel the presence of your sibling ghosts. Ten-year-old Joshua tears open a fresh package of concession-stand gummy worms. Your fourteen-year-old future great-aunt climbs out of the pool and shakes out her short blond hair. Eight-year-old Mark stands in the field, a worn-out rug draped over his head for safety, waiting for a rocket to fall from the sky.

Eventually the children get tired and hot, and you all head back in for Cheetos and cups of pop. The boom box is now playing "Safety Dance" by Men Without Hats. A song Joshua loved since he was little, the song he wanted you to play at your wedding so he could dance with you. Without Gideon, you're fairly certain you'll never get married, and your brother won't be there if you do. Instead of crying, you find yourself wanting to dance. You find yourself singing out loud, sloshing Dr. Pepper, tapping your sandals and waving your arms like the nerdiest kid at the prom. The St. Cloud Commons Lodge is a place meant for dancing, a wedding reception venue, after all. The four children follow your lead, wriggling and jumping. Your two sisters join you, and you feel the presence of a fourth Childers dancer, twenty-two and smelling of cigarettes, so solid you feel like you could knock him down. Your brother's torso is leaned forward, both arms outstretched, his head zigzagging, knees kicking, oblivious to the beat.

You know your brother's there. You have a biblical precedent. You aren't feeling good right now about sermons or church, but the Bible is embedded in your bones. You think about a story you learned in Sunday school when you were little: Shadrach, Meshach, and Abednego in the fiery furnace. On your teacher's flannelgraph, three bearded, robed men stood in the middle of the blue square while an evil king in an upper corner sentenced them to death. The teacher added a tall grate beside the men, put red paper flames under their feet, and she said, "Wait!" when her class of four-year-olds started screaming. She pulled out paper Jesus, nearly everyone's favorite, and placed Him with the men in the flames. Then the king moseyed down from his corner and peered in the grate, excited to see his convicts sizzling. He was so aghast, your teacher held him in the air while he spoke: "Did not we cast three men bound into the midst of the fire? . . . I see four men loose, walking in the midst of the fire, and they have no hurt; and the form of the fourth is like the Son of God."

Your brother's no Son of God, but he's the son you want most. You close your eyes and dance harder, slamming into a table, a sister, a folding chair. Tomorrow two old female relatives will call your mother to complain about you and your sisters. Such dancing and rolling downhill, they were ashamed to look at you. On Monday you'll grip the metal chalk rest under the chalkboard while you're teaching, reminding yourself not to slide down onto the floor. Tonight you'll realize part of your brain believed if you survived the funeral, your brother would be waiting alive at home.

Unlike Shadrach, Meshach, and Abednego, you and your sisters can't emerge unharmed, thanking God on your knees in the Babylonian streets. Tonight, and in moments for the rest of your lives, your hair will be singed, your bodies scarred, your clothing saturated in the smoke smell of grief. But right now, your brother is with you, all four siblings dancing in the flames.

Things Sad People Shouldn't Have

Guns, knives, scissors, razor blades, letter openers, shards of light bulb, anything sharp. Access to roofs, bridges, high-up windows that open, cliffs.

Cars, garages. Gas furnaces, gas stoves. Rubbing alcohol, real alcohol, rat poison, bleach. Pills that don't make sad people vomit or pass out partway through the orange bottle. Bathtubs, toasters, hair dryers, clock radios. Closet bars, jump ropes, dog leashes, belts. Bedroom doors that close.

I'd say bedroom doors that *lock*, but my brother didn't lock it. He just pushed his door shut.

Dogs that need walked. Cats that shit in litter boxes. Plants that need watered, even cactuses. Dads with new fishing poles and a plan to go to the pay lake. Moms who drag sad people out of bed and drive them an hour to an out-of-state college. (Sad people are much too sad to get up or drive, and they flunked out of the university twenty minutes away.)

Sisters who are already going through horrible breakups. Sisters who are trying to finish school. Online Christmas lists that get emailed to sisters after August 30, 2012, has passed and the sisters never want to see a Christmas again. Grandmothers who get held by their granddaughters in pink wingback chairs when they hear their grandsons are dead.

Bodies that have to be buried or burned up.

Chariot's Comin'

Good news! Chariot's comin'! Good news! Chariot's comin'!

For twelve years after my mother heard my high school choir belt out this spiritual, she crooned the chorus whenever her news was good. My dad got a bonus of a thousand dollars. The firefighters were selling five-buck plates of spaghetti. Joshua's high school English teacher granted him an extension on his *Romeo and Juliet* paper. Joshua's extensions weren't unusual: he rarely finished a paper without them, preferring to stuff his backpack with unfinished assignments until a teacher sent his mother an email. But the news was nevertheless songworthy. My mom burst through the back door, hurled her heavy leather purse onto a kitchen chair, and started to sing.

Good news! Chariot's comin'! And I don't want it to leave me behind!

When my mother sang about those coming chariots, I didn't picture Black slaves stamping the dirt floor at a midnight cabin prayer meeting, dreaming of an escape to heaven or, better, the North. And I didn't imagine my mostly white high school choir, standing motionless except for our mouths, eyebrows, and swelling chests, sweating through our black polyester uniforms. Instead I felt a ray of June sunlight. When my mother put her head down, tapped across the unswept Pergo flooring, and kept time with her swaying arms, she transformed. She was no longer a middle-aged woman in a stained blouse with long brown curls in need of a trim. She was pure and radiant joy.

My mother saw heaven's pearly gates on a Styrofoam plate of pasta. When our family found the money to make the mortgage payment and order a pizza to boot, she strode down streets of gold and waved at Apostles through their mansion windows.

Then my parents ran out of money again, and my mom had to wait for her husband's payday to buy cereal. Joshua missed another assignment deadline, and his teacher threatened he'd fail his junior year. My mom and brother trudged through the dust like sad Old Testament prophets, a modern-day Elijah and Elisha. Suddenly the teacher's mercy arrived like a chariot of fire: a twenty-four-hour extension! The chariot carried Elijah, my lazy brother, up by a whirlwind into heaven.

So for the next twenty-four hours, my mother, my sisters, and I assembled into a paper-writing army. Two hundred miles away, I sat on the phone with my sighing brother, skimming *Romeo and Juliet* on my laptop screen, pitching possible writing angles. Rebecca stretched out next to his scrawny body on his bunk, begging him to scrawl something into a notebook. Jennifer microwaved him a hot dog.

My mother sat in a scuffed wooden chair at the family computer, ready to type up anything he scrawled.

"Good news!" my mother hummed as she waited. The chariot was coming again.

❦

The chariot actually took Joshua.

It didn't bring us money or spaghetti. It didn't give us twenty-four frantic hours to ghostwrite a paper under the name Joshua David Childers. It snatched Joshua's spirit through his closet ceiling, leaving his parents and sisters to stare at the sky.

When the chariot took Elijah, his younger prophet friend stared after that fiery cart and screamed. "My father, my father, the chariot of Israel, and the horsemen thereof!" Elisha tore hairs from his bald head. He took his clothes off and ripped them in two.

I didn't see Joshua's chariot. I heard about it on the phone, so maybe that's why I didn't bother screaming. I ran barefoot down the street and collapsed on my friend's front porch.

Elijah left behind a cloak with the power to part water, letting a man cross a river on dry land. Elisha screamed again when he picked the cloak up. "Where is the Lord God of Elijah?" But he slapped the Jordan River with the cloak and walked across, and he wore that damp thing home.

Joshua left behind textbooks, comic books, pretentious DVDs, animal puppets, grandpa puppets, ventriloquist dummies, a broken CD player, a laptop choked with viruses, twenty laundry loads' worth of hipster clothes.

Most of that crap is still where Joshua left it. Like he might come home tomorrow and toss out the boxes and furniture my parents have stored on the bed and empty carpet. He could change into plaid pajama pants, dust off his puppets, download a pirated film onto his laptop.

Maybe if Joshua's hoodies had Elijah's water-parting power, my family would feel ready to clean out his room.

❦

The firefighters still sell five-dollar plates of spaghetti, but when they do, my mother doesn't sing about it. She says, "Why don't we get some of that spaghetti for dinner?" And she hands one of her daughters a twenty-dollar bill.

When my dad gets a bonus, she yells, "Thank God!" She heaves giant sighs of relief at the kitchen table when she sits down and pays the bills. But she no longer imagines herself riding to heaven in a chariot, planning a four-page grocery list while she strolls the golden streets. Her explosions of joy flew away with her son's spirit.

Now that he's gone, my mother doesn't take the chariot lightly. It's not a vehicle that shows up when the spaghetti is cheap.

The chariot will take her to see her son.

The Prodigal drags himself home, his sandals long gone, sand caking into the dried pig shit on his legs. Still on the road, he imagines himself creeping up to his father's shut-up house, slouching outside the servants' entrance until someone invites him inside.

Meanwhile, the Prodigal's father has been standing at the edge of his property, straining his vision in the direction his son disappeared. Maybe the father expected his son to blow through that money. The father sees his filthy son "a great way off" and starts running.

On October 2, 1848, about a week after Branwell's September 24 death, Charlotte described Patrick Brontë's grief in a letter to W. S. Williams, her friend and publisher: "My poor Father naturally thought more of his *only* son than of his daughters, and much and long as he had suffered on his account–he cried out for his loss like David for that of Absalom. My Son! My Son! And refused at first to be comforted."

In that letter, Charlotte cast Patrick as David–King Saul's former harpist turned king of Israel–and Branwell as David's worse-than-useless son. In the second book of Samuel, Absalom rapes his elderly father's concubines and briefly deposes him, crowning himself king. Then King Absalom rides his horse under a "great oak," and his luxuriant hair catches in the branches. He dangles–like Joshua in his last minutes in the closet–"between the heaven and the earth."

David instructs his captains to "deal gently" with Absalom, but one of them won't listen. That captain finds Absalom, alive, his gorgeous body swinging from the tree, and "thrusts" three darts through his heart. With Absalom dead, a major source of David's troubles is gone forever. No more insurrection, no more whining for laudanum in a red-curtained bed, no more angry footsteps on a laminate floor. But David cries, "O my son Absalom, my son, my son Absalom! Would God I had died for thee, O Absalom, my son, my son!"

My parents didn't wail like King David, like Patrick. They never screamed, "My son, my son." My mom still holds it as a point of pride that she "teared up, but never completely broke down." I didn't cry; neither did my sisters.

Here's how my whole family avoided screaming: God the Father saw Joshua coming a great way off. Perhaps as he removed a body-sized section of shirts and pants from his closet and piled them on his bed. Or perhaps as he slumped in a classroom chair on August 29, 2012, or as he squeezed out of my mother's body and wailed the first breath of his life. When Joshua looped his belt around his closet bar, the Father got off His throne and started running. The Father opened heaven's gates, and when Joshua appeared, He clasped my brother's spirit to His heart.

Outwardly, at least, during those first few months of shock, we all coped with the death like the far younger King David, six chapters earlier in II Samuel. He fasts, weeps, and prays while his infant son ails, but after he finds out his son is dead, he gets off the palace floor and washes his face and hair. "Can I bring him back again?" David asks when his servants raise their eyebrows. "I shall go to him, but he shall not return to me."

Absalom's death doesn't kill King David. He finishes weeping, takes back his throne, wins battles, selects fresh concubines. Patrick got out of bed, preached his sermons, lived twelve more years. I can only assume both men remembered what I feel sure they believed: their sons were dead on earth, but alive and loved in heaven, or something like it. Hell doctrines be damned, they'd see their crappy sons when they died.

A few months after Joshua's suicide, a kind atheist friend told me the afterlife is a made-up coping mechanism. Leaning back on my loveseat, he pointed at the mold-black carpet in my Morgantown apartment. "This is it," he said, his voice sad.

I knew, though I was too sad to notice, that my friend was in love with me. I could have accepted that love and freed myself from, or at least lessened, the Gideon half of my grieving. But my friend couldn't seem to understand to what extent I'd staked my calm, my sanity, my choice to continue living on my mental image of my brother as the Bible Storybook's Prodigal. Feet wrapped in rags, Caucasian-pink legs shaded pig-shit brown, Joshua lowered his head, crumpled his body, while the Father ran closer, extending his arms.

I couldn't accommodate my friend's "This is it" in my life, or even in my living room. I opened the door, pushed his six-foot, scrawny body into the night with my fingers and forearms, set the deadbolt and switched off the lights, trembled in the dark until I was sure he was gone.

"Bring forth the best robe," the Prodigal's father shouts to his hired servants. He says, "Put a ring on his hand, and shoes on his feet. . . . Bring hither the fatted calf, and kill it; and let us eat and be merry: for this my son was dead, and is alive again; he was lost, and is found."

My family never screamed for Joshua, but we absorbed the blow in our minds and bodies. I moved alone to Indiana, lost twenty-five pounds, sobbed at Gideon on the phone. My sisters abandoned career plans, took years to claw back to their lives. My dad stared at walls after work, forgetting to turn on the TV. He'd lived, unaware for decades, with early signs of Parkinson's, but now the disease sped up, folding his shoulders and hobbling his feet. My mom researched prophecies for Jesus's world-ending return, for the continent-cracking earthquakes coming to judge America's sins. "Soon!" she said from her laptop, real hope in her voice.

I shall go to him, but he shall not return to me.

There's a photograph of Patrick Brontë in clerical garb from 1860, five years after he buried Charlotte, his last remaining child, and one year before he died. A high white collar covers his chin, and black robes render his body invisible, leaving a disembodied face, surprisingly capable-looking hands. Age-hooded eyes peer through tiny spectacles. Patrick looks like he's peering forward to the day he'll clasp his family in the throne room of God.

PART 6
FEAST

"And they began to be merry." The hired servants kill the calf, roast and carve it, pile veal on the tables. The father laughs and cries as his son soaks away dried blood and pig filth. Someone plucks a tune on a harp.

My family slumped in our metal folding chairs at Joshua's after-funeral meal, elbows on paper tablecloths, eyes unfocused, half-eating our Cheetos and turkey on white.

When Juliet Barker read Charlotte's whiny October 2, 1848, letter to W. S. Williams about her father's wailing—"My Son! My Son!"—Barker thought of Jesus's parable. In her Brontë biography, Barker said Charlotte witnessed Patrick's grief "with all the jealousy of the well-behaved sibling seeing a father's love of the prodigal son." As if death were a kind of homecoming, and sorrow were a kind of party.

I chewed my turkey sandwich, sipped my Coke, sleepwalked through the next few years. A faint echo of the celebration in the sky.

What Happens When You Drown

A month after your suicide, when I've quit fearing a return to routine would mean I never loved you, I restart my daily swims at WVU's aquatic facility.

The facility has two pools. *Fitness*, eleven feet deep, where recent high school swim stars flash down cool-water lanes, chlorine-bleached hair tucked under bright swim caps. *Leisure*, four feet deep at most, where professors emeriti freestyle with saggy arms, buzzed nineteen-year-olds aim an inflatable ball at a hoop, and soft-bellied mothers soak with swim-diapered infants in water near the temperature of a womb.

Before you died, I chose fitness and swam for forty minutes without stopping. Today I choose leisure, slow-motion stroking down a lane roped off next to the hoop. I can put my feet down mid-lane when I start crying, and the warmth eases grief pains in my chest.

I use the breaststroke, the stroke you taught me, your teenage sister, fifteen years ago, after you took swimming lessons at age seven. In the pool, I think about the way my body mimics yours that day in a West Virginia lake, your suntanned hands parting brown water, your bitten-off toenails seeking purchase in the mud. I breaststroke with my head up, snapping turtle style, since no one taught you to plunge your head underwater.

After twenty minutes I give up. I paddle to the edge and cling to the pool deck, knees between my torso and the concrete wall. You never saw this pool, but I see you in water. In the lake at seven, in our grandparents' wood-framed aboveground pool at ten, your legs pockmarked from mosquitoes. In the Marshall University pool, the first time you tried to go to college, when you watched movies from an inner tube with a can of Coke. In the Atlantic Ocean, two years ago at Myrtle

Beach, when you defied the shaggy-haired guy in the lifeguard chair and floated toward Portugal on a bodyboard.

When I climb out, I find myself standing in front of a chart taped to the shiny tile wall, warning swimmers about a way they can drown. I've read it before, idly curious, but now I study the steps: *hyperventilation, O_2 drops, unconsciousness, drowning.* Each panel features a dark-haired Caucasian man, drawn thin enough and young enough to resemble you at twenty-two. I imagine your black hipster glasses onto the young man, even though you didn't swim in glasses, and your glasses were on your nightstand when you died.

In the first panel, the young man stands openmouthed on the pool deck and "overbreathes," from exhaustion or on purpose, gasping in O_2, forcing out CO_2, throwing off the balance in his bloodstream. In the second panel, he cavorts under blue water as his O_2 drops, legs kicking and arms outstretched. If he hadn't overbreathed, his rising CO_2 levels would have triggered an automatic breath, sending him choking to the surface. Since he did overbreathe, his CO_2 levels can't climb high enough to signal danger while he's awake. Third, his CO_2 rises higher, and unconsciousness sets in suddenly. His limbs droop, his head points toward the bottom. In the final illustration, the young man is underwater, belly up, lungs full of water from a breath he took while unconscious, and I can tell from his face that he's dead.

Dripping onto the pool deck, goose-pimpled arms squeezed across my chest, I feel closer to you than I have since you died. I know you didn't drown, and unlike that clueless cartoon man, you knew what you were doing, or at least understood the orders your brain gave you in a post-manic moment of despair. But still, you died from a lack of oxygen, and this chart gives me a window into the last moments of your life.

One reason your death hurts so much is I feel shut out. You can't tell me about it under a buggy porch light on our parents' deck, or even call me, storytelling between loud puffs on a Marlboro. And now here it is in front of me. *Hyperventilation, O_2 drops, unconsciousness, drowning.* The cartoon young man squats in his closet, leather belt looped around the closet bar and his neck. O_2 drops, CO_2 rises. I watch you in the chart until my hair stops dripping and my swimsuit is nearly dry.

Missing: Orange Longhaired Cat

Two weeks before Joshua's suicide, Jennifer's beloved orange cat darted across my ten bald feet of yard, shimmied under a neighbor's tall wooden fence, and disappeared. It was kind of my fault. Jennifer and her two longhaired cats were spending the night in the apartment I shared with Rebecca in Morgantown, en route to Jennifer's new life as a veterinary technology student in Fairmont.

The night of the disappearance, Jennifer offered to stay alone in her as-yet-unfurnished apartment with her cats. "Fred's a wild man," she said to Rebecca and me from the backseat of Rebecca's Subaru, surrounded by her cat carriers, scruffy backpacks, and boxes of brand-new dishes. "Lizzie'll just stare at us like a little owl, but I'm afraid he'll be really annoying, and I can take it." Jennifer was petting Fred gingerly through the top of his carrier, whipping her hand back before he bit her, pushing back her long dark-blond hair so he wouldn't tear it out.

"Nope, you're not sleeping in that apartment with no bed!" Rebecca called back from the driver's seat, and I emphatically agreed from the seat beside her.

"You're staying with us for a couple days till we get you set up," I said. I insisted Fred and Lizzie would be happier in a place with beds, homemade curtains, and a loveseat. I said the three of us sisters would have fun.

In truth, I was afraid Fred might keep me awake all night, causing me to be exhausted at the next day's pre-semester meetings for ill-paid writing instructors, and the 450-square-foot apartment was cramped already with Rebecca and me and our own two cats. But I pictured Jennifer lying on her new bedspread on an unswept wood floor, in an unfamiliar apartment without TV, Wi-Fi, or air conditioning on a mid-August night. We could stop at Walmart for an air mattress and fans, but the place still sounded desolate.

During the last two years, since Jennifer had graduated out of a bustling girls-only Marshall dorm, she had occupied a bedroom that shared a hallway with our orchestrally snoring parents and Joshua. Even at that late time in his life, our brother was a companion of sorts: often after two in the morning, he'd would pop his head into the bedrooms of any available sisters and say hello. I knew it would be an adjustment for Jennifer to be alone in a building full of strangers, free from familiar greetings and snores. Still, I was excited to have both my sisters so close, and I had no idea that during the following summer, all three of us would flee northern West Virginia like it was burning. I wanted Jennifer's first night in her first apartment to be comfortable and happy. I wanted her to want to stay.

When we got to Morgantown, Rebecca and I made a bed for Jennifer on the loveseat, placed an extra litter box under the kitchen table, and poured cat food and water into cereal bowls. Lizzie was fine, like Jennifer had predicted, and Fred was frightened but adorable for the first hour. He found a several-inch gap between the cabinets and the stove, and he squeezed himself in and crouched, fluffy orange body concealed, orange chin on the dingy yellow linoleum. "Look at him!" Jennifer squealed, and we all gathered around. He was less adorable after I got into bed and he began to yowl.

Fred's cries were incessant, a feverish newborn in a crib, a loon on the lakeshore, many decibels louder than the white noise from my bedroom's window unit. I slept with my bedroom door open since that air conditioner served the entire apartment, but after half an hour I apologized to my wide-awake sisters and closed my bedroom door, leaving them to sweat.

The closed door didn't help. The walls were cardboard thin, the apartments constructed as cheaply as possible inside a former car repair shop that'd had its heyday in the 1950s. Rebecca had heard the delicate sounds of a male tenant's romances through her bedroom wall. Kinder than me, or perhaps used to worse noises, Rebecca stayed in bed through the cat concert, but I couldn't take it. I got up after midnight and confronted Jennifer, my T-shirt wrinkled and hair wild. My cat, Arwen, was nuzzling my heels, hoping for early breakfast. I hissed, "Jennifer, can't you do *anything* to calm him down?"

"I'm trying," she said. Fred puffed up his fur by the apartment door, glaring at the doorknob and then into our eyes. She sat down next to him and petted his back and tail. Fred spat and she backed away. He'd always been a handful, but never like this. At our parents' house, he'd spent half his time lounging on Jennifer's lap while she crocheted, the other half in the backyard, dismembering voles. Clearly he'd hated that four-hour ride in a plastic box, and perhaps this damp little apartment was even worse. Fred pressed his body against the door and promised us land and money. He promised, like a first grader wishing to be chosen next for kickball, that he'd be our best friend for life.

"I can drive to my apartment in Fairmont," Jennifer said.

"No," I told her, "you don't need to do that." I knew she'd use backroads, since the interstate made her anxious, and I knew a confident, competent Morgantown driver who'd driven those eighteen rural, winding backroad miles to Fairmont after midnight. He'd lost his car to a deer.

"I'm okay. I bet he'll calm down," I said. I went back to bed.

Fred didn't calm down. I lay in the dark behind my thin, closed door, and I pictured myself yawning through the next day's seminars. Pictured myself running into Gideon in the cramped, hot space by the photocopier, seeing his curly ponytail and gray eyes for the first time since our May breakup. Illuminated by yowling, the meetings and that first-meeting looked unbearable.

I hadn't seen Gideon since May, but I'd talked to him plenty. We'd spent the summer rehashing our breakup fight over texts, six-hour phone calls, and three thousand-word emails. Two weeks before, he'd told me on the phone, his tone determined and ominous, that he was going to Florida "with a friend." We hadn't spoken since. I didn't want Gideon back, had no interest in luring him with my first-day-of-work charms, but I could feel my stress increasing about seeing him with every minute that Fred kept me awake.

So I got back up, walked back to the living room where Jennifer sat next to her pleading cat, and I told her something I hope I fully believed, that Fred would come back if she let him out. I told her our apartment's door was on the back of the building, facing a fence, not our neighborhood's quiet street. I told her Rebecca's cat often slipped under that fence to play with a pair of angelic red-haired children, and my cat catnapped daily on the porch swing outside our door. I left out a story

Jennifer knew already: Arwen had been partially blinded in a nocturnal scuffle with an unneutered tomcat named Tom.

"Fred won't be able to go outside at your apartment because it's on that awful street," I said, remembering the view from Jennifer's apartment's window on the day she signed her lease. Rusty pickups and city buses whipped down a hill and around a corner. "But you can let him out while you're here."

"You think he won't be happy at my apartment?"

"No, he'll be fine! He'll get used to it quick," I said, though I wasn't sure. "He's just sad tonight about being stuck in this weird new place, and he'd be happy if we let him out."

Jennifer hesitated for another minute, then she turned the deadbolt and pulled the door open. Fred dashed through the opening, across the dirt, under the fence. His long fur caused his body to appear to skim the ground, a scurrying runaway raccoon.

The second Fred left the apartment, Jennifer ran after him. She dove at the wooden slats, and when that failed, she tried to run down the narrow walkway behind our apartment, hemmed by the fence and our concrete building, and around the block to see where Fred might have come out. But before she could start running, a tenant appeared with a towering basket of laundry, barricading the walkway and constantly stopping for dropped socks. By the time Jennifer got down the sidewalk and around the block to the house that went with the fence, Fred had disappeared. She searched every yard for two blocks, opened gates and screamed *Fred* into bushes. Rebecca got up and we searched too, my conscience guilty, our bare toes on manicured lawns, sidewalks, and street.

After fifteen minutes of searching, I felt deeply uncomfortable. We lived in the only section of downtown Morgantown where the roads, homes, and businesses didn't cling to a mountainside, and homebuilders had taken advantage. Except for our apartment building, every structure on the flattish block was a wood-sided or brick house worth several hundred thousand dollars, each concealing a sleeping lawyer or college professor and children in flame retardant pajamas. Rebecca and I babysat some of those children for extra money. I told Jennifer we couldn't yell all night for her cat. I told her he'd come back in the morning. I told her we needed to go to bed, and we did.

❦

Fred didn't come back in the morning. Fred wasn't back in the afternoon, after I survived my meetings and saw Gideon in the hallway—not the copy room. Too stressed about Fred to feel Gideon stress, I simply said, "Hi," told him my sister's orange cat was missing, and asked him to keep a lookout on his daily runs around the town.

Fred wasn't back on Monday, when Jennifer, Rebecca, and I all had to begin a new semester. Every day for two weeks, Jennifer worried through her classes in Fairmont, then she drove to Morgantown. She rounded up Rebecca and me, and the three of us spent the remaining daylight hours peering under freshly painted porches and screaming down Chemlawn-lined streets. Every day, Jennifer called the local animal shelter, a place with a 90 percent feline kill rate in 2012, and every few days she drove to the shelter and examined each cage of doomed cats.

From the night of August 16 to the morning of August 30, my sisters and I breathed and dreamed orange fur. Jennifer needed that cat, so we had to find him. While we searched, we sometimes forgot our only sibling left at home, our New York City enthusiast who felt as miserable and out of place in a house in Huntington as Fred had felt in a Morgantown apartment. Now with no nearby sisters he could bother at night, Joshua called Rebecca at all hours, and she answered nearly always. But she missed a few calls while searching for Fred, and she told me she'll never forget it.

A few days before Joshua killed himself, Gideon showed up at my apartment door during a run. Framed by the doorway, dripping sweat, Gideon held up a tom, baby-Simba-style, that was too large, too dark, too stripy. I thanked him profusely, asked where he'd found the cat, how the cat had behaved while being carried—killing a full minute before I said that cat wasn't Fred. Maybe if I waited, the cat would shrink and change color. I imagined myself calling Jennifer, then speeding to Fairmont, Fred yowling from the backseat in Arwen's carrier. Maybe Gideon would ride with me, my breakup pain and anger dissolved into gratefulness, and we'd become healthy and happy close friends.

The cat didn't shrink, and Gideon carried him back to where he'd found him, across the flat streets, down to where the yards are so steep that thirty-foot posts support smokers on their back porches. Then my mother found Joshua's body in his closet. My sisters and I boxed up our remaining cats, and Gideon drove us home.

❦

During the ten days we were in Huntington for Joshua's funeral, I looked for Fred sometimes on my parents' cracked concrete steps, on the covered deck beyond the French doors. Maybe he'd show up skinny with bloodied paws, like Bo that time my mom was in the hospital, another feline Lassie come home. If Fred could find his way, I believed he'd walk two hundred miles to nap on Jennifer's bed and terrorize his favorite population of voles.

When we got back to Morgantown, I held my breath as Rebecca and I walked around the apartment building to our door, wondering if he'd be waiting on our bare patch of lawn, meowing miserably for pre-killed cat food. We found only our Knockout rosebush and wilting geraniums that we'd never water again. I put a plastic bowl on the welcome mat, filled it periodically with cat food for beetles, opossums, raccoons, feral cats, and maybe Fred, and Rebecca and I got down to the business of grieving.

But Jennifer couldn't focus her grief on Joshua. Her brother was gone, his body incinerated, but Fred could possibly come back, curl up in her thrift-store recliner, hiss at her kitten, shred her textbooks. Jennifer tripled her calls and drives up the mountain to the animal shelter. She paid a company to call every listing in the Morgantown phone book, an electronic voice announcing the loss of an orange longhaired cat, Jennifer's phone number, and a vague reward. She printed postcards with a photo of Fred cat-smiling on our parents' couch, and she stuck a card in every mailbox for miles. Years later, I'd find one of those cards between the pages of a book, and I'd shake uncontrollably, my body remembering the months after Joshua died.

At least once a week, Jennifer despaired completely. She came over, exhausted from searching, and Rebecca and I offered her the Aldi crab cakes we were living on in those sorrow-stricken days and tried to put on a movie. Jennifer didn't want any of it. She stood by the door, grief-dazed and insomnia-eyed, on that moldy patch of carpet where her cat had yowled all night, and she relived her final hours with Fred. She looked at the hole beside the stove, the final place she saw Fred happy, and she opened the door and stared at the gap under the fence. Then she closed the door and turned to me.

"You made me throw him out!" she yelled, sobbing. "You wanted me to lose him. You didn't want me to have Fred here." She wrinkled her nose, tilted her head, and said, "Jennifer, you *have* to put your cat outside because I need sleep for my *important job*." Ostensibly, she was quoting me, but she sounded more like an eighth grader on a Disney Channel sitcom.

I snottily informed Jennifer she'd put out her own cat, I accepted all blame and tearfully apologized, I asked her how she could care about that fucking animal when we'd lost our little brother. I loved her, perhaps even more now that I was down to two siblings, and on better days our sister trio grocery shopped and watched romcoms at Jennifer's apartment. I stitched curtains for her kitchen, sunbeam yellow printed with bluebirds. But I said horrible things, and Jennifer did too, and likely both of us occasionally wished the other would crawl under a fence and disappear.

*

Maybe I could have helped Jennifer, or at least coped better myself, if I'd understood what seems obvious now. Jennifer's grief about our brother's suicide took the form of a mean orange cat.

Unbroken by Joshua's death, I'm sure she would have mourned her friend, felt the anger at me I deserved. But those daily drives to the shelter, those bouts of screaming in my apartment—I blame all of that now on our split-second shift from four siblings to three, on that image of our brother's skinny, squatting body that none of us could shake, though only our mother saw him dead. I wish I'd understood Jennifer's double heartbreak, the way grief can pile upon grief until all the griever knows for certain is she's sad. But I couldn't understand for years, not until I'd recovered from my own bout of misplaced, intensified sorrow.

During the months after the funeral, while Jennifer scoured Morgantown for Fred, I talked on the phone to Gideon nearly every day. I called to tell him about Joshua's suicide, and I couldn't stop calling him, memories of Joshua and daily life updates replacing our fights. Before my brother died, I'd understood I needed space to heal. Now, healing was a vista decades in the distance, and I couldn't bear to lose someone I loved who wasn't dead.

So I invited Gideon over, heated up an extra crab cake. I bought his favorite coffee, though I drank only tea. He wrote academic articles on my laptop at my kitchen table, like when we were dating, and we ended the evenings with a snuggle on the loveseat. We never went beyond snuggling, and I felt grateful for his sensitivity. He still loved me, but he wasn't asking for feigned passion while I was sad.

I felt particularly thankful for Gideon's sensitivity during the university's Thanksgiving and winter breaks—my first holidays without my brother—when I spent every possible day with my family. For the past five years, I'd spent days and weeks of those breaks in Tennessee, watching college football with Gideon and his parents and walking the fence lines on the family's forty-acre cattle farm. When I'd gone to Huntington, Gideon had called every evening, somehow at the exact moment my mother put on a family movie, and he'd insisted I talk to him for at least an hour.

This year, Gideon didn't ask me to visit, and he didn't call once. I didn't want to give up family time to call him myself, and he rarely responded when I texted during that holiday season, so I stopped contacting him at all. I felt that Gideon and I had the same idea: I was with my family, collectively grieving for Joshua, and Gideon could support me best with silent love. And looking back now, years later, I think I was partly right. But grief made me myopic, selfish even, and I couldn't conceive that Gideon might have his own reasons for keeping away from me during break.

In January, when I got back to Morgantown, Gideon called and told me he'd missed me. We had a free weekend before classes started, and we spent it together, taking long, snowy walks, eating Dark Chocolate Peppermint Creations at Cold Stone Creamery, a luxury he wouldn't have paid for when we were dating. I said, "I love you," and he said it back. Once, he hugged me in my kitchen, our jeans and winter flannels pressed together. He didn't kiss me, but I could smell every kiss of our relationship: in the Atlantic Ocean, under an oak in the cow pasture, on that loveseat three feet away.

A few days after that happy weekend, Gideon and I took a particularly long afternoon walk on the Deckers Creek Trail, under icicles that clung to frozen tree limbs. Feeling like I was destroying a part of my identity as I spoke, I told him the root of our breakup fight didn't matter anymore. Now that Joshua had killed himself, I didn't think my genes should be passed on, so I no longer wanted to have kids. He acted like he believed me, and I believed myself. We talked about marriage, vaguely and theoretically, in five years maybe, after Gideon figured out his career. Six months before, a far-off, childless maybe-marriage to Gideon had sounded like crippling despair, but with my brother's ashes settling underground, that possibility sounded like hope. I drew close and grabbed Gideon's arm. He jumped away like I'd burned him.

"Let go of me," he snapped.

"What's wrong with you?" I asked him, stung. "You touch me all the time."

"Yeah, when no one can see us. People will think we're together."

"So?" I could feel my body heating up under my down coat.

"Well, we're *not* together, Pokey." He took a few steps backward and held up both winter-chapped hands, as if he were blocking threatened caresses. "Pokey, you've got to give me my space."

I asked, forcing a laugh, if he wanted to date other people. In response, he resumed walking, his eyes turned toward the mud-streaked snow across the partly frozen creek, and I knew there was someone already.

"Okay. I've got to go," I muttered, pressing my hands to my scalp through my wool toboggan. I turned around and hurried, silently cursing every step I'd taken away from my apartment. I knew I had to keep moving, or I'd lie down and sob in the frozen mud beside the asphalt trail.

"Pokey!" Gideon called, sounding stricken. He caught up and walked beside me, still not touching me, but staying close, as if his proximity could support my weight. "You're mad at me," he said every few minutes, and I didn't feel physically able to open my mouth to reply.

When we got back to my apartment, I collapsed into a cat-shredded wicker chair by the door. Gideon stood in front of the chair, looking guilty and worried, and finally I spoke. "Well, if you need your space to date other people, I think we shouldn't talk or see each other anymore." Gideon said nothing, but he leaned down and hugged me goodbye. He gripped my shoulders and pressed the top of his head so firmly into my temple I feared he would crack my skull.

After he left, I stayed in that chair, eyes fixed straight ahead and body trembling. Rebecca found me there ten minutes later, still wearing my coat from the walk, my chest and arms covered in hives. After she peeled off my coat, I crawled to the bathroom and vomited. The disappointment—the humiliation, as I saw it at the time—was more than my already grieving body could take.

Over the next year, in that apartment in Morgantown and then in the house I rented in Indiana by myself, I cried in my bed for most of the hours when I wasn't working, sleeping only when sleeping pills kicked in. I went to therapy and talked only about Gideon. I wish I'd kept my word and never spoken to Gideon again, but I couldn't stop myself from making calls and writing emails. I said horrible things, things so awful I'm frightened now I said them, frightened of what I'm capable of in the throes of anger and grief. He always answered the phone because (as he alternately explained) he wanted to defend himself, because he deserved my anger, because he was strong enough to take it, because he loved me. Once, on a near-zero-degree day in West Virginia, I heard him shivering, and when I asked why, he told me he'd seen my name on his silenced phone, and he'd run out of the library without his coat. But no matter what I said, or how often he listened or snarled right back, our relationship was over.

During that year, when I met new acquaintances and went on awful first dates, I talked about my brother's suicide and Gideon. I claimed, and meant it, that my loss of Gideon—my daily companion and maybe future husband—was far worse. I was looking for validation, someone to say, "Wow, if you feel worse about that ex-boyfriend than you do about your brother hanging himself in his closet, you must be *really* sad about that ex-boyfriend!" Usually said dates or acquaintances cringed and changed the subject, or they used my over-sharing as an opening to bring up their wicked first wives. But one acquaintance told me I was full of crap. "Boyfriends are a dime a dozen," he told me one evening over Indiana craft beer, his middle-aged bald head reflecting patio lights. "You'll get another boyfriend. You'll never get another brother." I told him he didn't get it, never drank beer with him again. Now I know he was right.

But just as Jennifer wailed for Fred, I wailed for my lost love. And just as Jennifer blamed her heartbreak on me, I blamed mine on Gideon. Neither of us was able to blame Joshua. We couldn't blame the young man who reduced his hard-earned pot and cigarette fund to buy us gifts for Christmas and birthdays, the little boy who demanded we record his voice when he sang. At the time, Jennifer and I just knew we were hurting. It's nearly impossible to sort out pain.

In February 2013, when my Gideon despair was just beginning, the dark clouds over Jennifer started breaking. She kept visiting the Morgantown animal shelter, but at more reasonable intervals, and now she was looking for a male orange kitten. She told everyone she knew to look out for an orange cat in need of a home, and in March it paid off. One of her classmates asked her if she'd like a ten-month-old male. The cat had spent his early kittenhood in a back-porch feral cat colony, but he didn't want to be feral. When the woman who fed the colony opened her door, this kitten slunk inside, stretched out on the couch, and purred. This mix of wild and tame was exactly what Jennifer was looking for. She named him Erik.

For a few weeks, Erik hid in a closet or under her bed, traumatized by his lost porch, his lost cat friends. Jennifer sympathized, but she couldn't send him back: he was half starved, coated in fleas, and his orange fur had felted into three-inch-long sheets. He was in similar shape to what Fred might have been if he'd turned up after six months in a Morgantown alley.

So Jennifer shoved food and water into Erik's hiding places. He ate when she wasn't looking and urinated on a closet of clean towels. To check on him and clean up after him, Jennifer chased him into the open with a broom. One day, he realized his new life was good, and he came out and strode across the dusty wood floor, announcing his arrival with loud mews. He ate and drank from the kitchen-floor cat bowls, used the litter box, and settled down for a nap in Jennifer's recliner. Erik had taken the only chair in the apartment, so Jennifer sat on the floor, watching his fur rise and fall with his breath.

During that time, Rebecca tugged me out of bed every Wednesday evening and drove me to Fairmont. We hit the Wendy's drive-thru, then watched a movie on Jennifer's TV, lounging with our French fries on blankets and throw pillows. After Erik came out of hiding, I sat in the recliner and took him onto my lap. At first I was afraid he'd slash me like Fred, but he purred and nuzzled my hands, so I found a pair of scissors and attacked the dirty orange mats that covered his body.

My process was painstaking: I felt for the felted base, tugged the mat loose with a comb, and scissored close to pink skin. The vet suggested a lion cut, but grooming is expensive, Jennifer trusted me, and I wanted to do it myself.

When I sat in Jennifer's recliner, metal scissors in my hands, my body settled into broken springs and cigarette burns from someone else's life, I took a full-hour weekly break from grieving. If I'd imagined Gideon cuddling with his girlfriend, I might have sliced Erik open the way Fred had sliced voles, exposing his wormy mass of intestines. So I focused. I trimmed mats off a cat every Wednesday for two months. With every cut, I stitched up the hole Fred's loss had torn in my relationship with Jennifer, and I came closer to forgiving myself. I couldn't get Fred back, but I could help Erik grow a healthy orange coat. I could sit with my sisters, my hands in cat fur, while our minds and bodies began to heal.

One evening, while I was cutting Erik's mats, Jennifer scooted across the wood floor to the recliner. "I still miss Fred, but I love Erik," she said, stroking her cat's back, a patchwork of baldness and regrowth. "I know Fred would come back if he could. I bet somebody grabbed him and trapped him in their apartment. Or maybe he got eaten by a coyote."

"Like Joshua," I said. "Joshua would come back to us if he could." My sisters agreed, and for half a moment our sorrow lifted.

Party Clothes

The biblical Prodigal appears at the feast, pig-shit-brown legs washed, bloody feet bandaged, wearing the house's finest robe, ring, and shoes. The Bible Storybook shows him in a fresh yellow turban, a robe with whole sleeves and turquoise trim that matches his father's. He smiles down at his right hand, admiring his new gold ring.

I assume Joshua wore plaid flannel pajama pants and a T-shirt to his heavenly banquet. The clothes he generally wore while sitting up all night in his room. My mother told me she freed Joshua's body from his belt with a strawberry-print kitchen knife, but she never mentioned (and I never asked) what he wore.

I suspect Joshua wore the blackish-green T-shirt he showed me two months before his suicide. Rebecca also believes Joshua wore that shirt to die—or fears he did. While we were home for Joshua's funeral, she searched the laundry room, Joshua's laundry hamper, his cluttered bedroom carpet, his drawers, the six-inch-high space under his bed, his closet with its still-bent bar. The shirt was nowhere, so she could only assume it covered Joshua's bony chest.

Two months before his suicide, Joshua pointed to his chest in our parents' dining room, standing next to the oak wardrobe he'd slid underneath at one year old, after he took his first three steps and hit the floor. His shirt must have risen and fallen with his breath, but I didn't notice. He wanted me to read his shirt's screen-printed comic panel, a conversation between a frantic middle-aged white man in rumpled clothing and a tiny beady-eyed white man with a beard like a cumulus cloud.

The T-shirt's panel was the work of Robert Crumb, a pioneering underground comic whose oeuvre, according to Stephen Holden's 1994 *New York Times* article "Anger and Obsession: The Life of Robert Crumb," includes "work that is often savagely misogynistic and pornographically explicit." Holden could have added that Crumb has drawn racist caricatures of Black people, and that his work's dominant emotion—despite his most famous pop culture contribution, a poster depicting bright-suited, big-shoed men who march under the slogan "Keep on Truckin'..."—is uncomfortably humorous despair.

The white-bearded man on the T-shirt was Mr. Natural, a guru-type character beloved by my brother and other fans of Robert Crumb. His bald pate and chin-to-knees beard evoke Crumb's own cartoon depictions of God, though in this panel Mr. Natural reads more like a friendly, skin-covered version of Branwell's beckoning skeleton. The frantic man is Flakey Foont, hapless wisdom-seeker, frequently drawn with a worried forehead and beads of sweat. On the shirt he says, "Death . . . the *end* of myself . . . no more *me* . . . it's . . . it's *incomprehensible*!" Mr. Natural replies, "Work on it . . ."

I asked Joshua what his shirt meant, hoping I'd misread it, wondering if I ought to attempt to involuntarily commit my euthymic brother to the hospital psych ward because of a T-shirt he wore. Joshua peered down and read the speech bubbles out loud, giving Flakey Foont a high, whiny voice. His Mr. Natural was low-pitched, merriment tinged with darkness. When Joshua finished reading, he laughed, hollow and forced. He repeated, "Work on it," and looked into my eyes. He laughed again, louder this time.

"I don't like it," I told Joshua, looking at his green eyes, avoiding the shirt. "You don't understand it," he said. He assured me I'd find the shirt funny, profoundly meaningful, if only I could understand.

Back in the pigpen, the Prodigal came to himself. He realized his father had loved him, and he didn't want to die alone with the swine. He would give up his dreams, his beliefs, his status as son if his father would just let him come home.

Branwell came to himself on his deathbed. On October 6, four days after Charlotte complained to W. S. Williams about her father's grieving, she wrote to him again, far less angry. She said Branwell didn't believe in the "value, or even the reality," of "religion and principle" until a few days before he died, but at the end he quit whining for his lost mistress. He appreciated his father and sisters.

Charlotte heard her father's last murmurings at Branwell's bedside for his son's peace and forgiveness, and she heard her brother say, "Amen." In the October 6 letter to Williams, Charlotte wrote: "The remembrance of this strange change now comforts my father greatly."

❦

In the year before Joshua died, he used the bulk of his call center earnings to order everything Robert Crumb. Nearly every day, the mailman brought a package. Joshua stacked Crumb comic books on his dresser, hung Crumb T-shirts in his closet, tacked up a Crumb poster on the wall above his bed.

I can't remember Joshua's poster's image. I remember only that it was bleak and sexual—nothing like "Keep on Truckin'. . ."—and the characters were white.

My parents had prayed for Joshua his entire life, but they didn't have Patrick Brontë's opportunity to pray by their dying son's bed. So my dad borrowed a discount-store tapestry from Grandpa's computer room the day after Joshua died. My dad put up the tapestry in Joshua's bedroom, over the Robert Crumb poster, hammering a nail through paper and wall. One foot by three feet of nylon, embroidered with sheet music for "Amazing Grace." Behind each music note burned a tiny lightbulb, and when one of us squeezed the bottom right corner, we heard a tinny electronic version of the song.

That tapestry declared Joshua had come to himself during the sixty seconds he squatted in his closet waiting to pass out, or perhaps his spirit had come to himself after he'd killed his brain. My brother was lost, but now he's found. Blind, but now he sees. We'd see him again in heaven.

❦

My brother was right: I didn't understand his blackish-green shirt. I missed the nuance of the characters' voices, of the panel's place in a comic, of the relationship between the guru and his sweaty student. Maybe in the context of Crumb's work it was meaningful, hilarious. But all I cared about was the meaning the T-shirt took on when it covered my brother's bony chest.

On Joshua's body, I feared that shirt meant Joshua had chosen a death where his spirit would disappear with his body. Sitting at the folding table after my brother's funeral at his deli-meat feast, I feared the shirt meant my brother was nowhere, and no one above us was feasting at all.

I feared Joshua had gone home to Mr. Natural, seeking the nothingness he promised. An artfully ironic alternative to trying to become an art film director, to living with crippling mania and depression. "Work on it," Mr. Natural muttered with a white-beard-shaking chuckle, as my brother's laugh, his slouch, his shuffle, the light and darkness in his eyes all disappeared into a void.

I (mostly) didn't fear there was no heaven, that my kind atheist friend might be right, and "this" might be "it." I'd been planning/hoping/coping to go to heaven when I died since I was eight, and my mother told me PaPa had gone there. I didn't need to hear my brother's final prayer by his bedside. I didn't need my parents' "Amazing Grace" tapestry. I didn't care about any church's rotten opinion about suicide and hell. I just feared Joshua had decided not to walk through the dust to the Father, and the Father wouldn't force someone into going somewhere he didn't want to go.

Like my family, Charlotte Brontë had hoped her prodigal would return while alive. In that angry October 2 letter to Williams, she wrote, "It has been our lot to see him take a wrong bent; to hope, expect, wait his return to the right path." But her brother hadn't returned. She'd experienced the "sickness of hope deferred, the dismay of prayer baffled," and "despair at last."

Mr. Natural talks to Flakey Foont in front of the life that will go on without him: city skyline, traffic-choked street, glowering orange sky.

Strictly religiously speaking, if Joshua came to himself as he left this world through his closet, it must have been to a self from early childhood. He quit reading the Bible Storybook at eight, after he asked a Christian basketball star to sign his Christmas-new copy. Joshua kept it unread as a treasure. Our parents gifted him his KJV Bible when he started first grade, the grade level when that book appeared on our Christian school's back-to-school shopping list, but he abandoned it forever in fifth grade when he switched to the public elementary. The only leatherbound Bible I can imagine Joshua reading is Crumb's comic anthology *Bible of Filth*.

Bible of Filth: *Bible* means the book's leather cover, heft, and gilt-edged pages, crafted to resemble the kind of Bibles my parents gave all four of their first graders, and *Filth* means hypersexualized Black women with blackface lips and tribal breasts, plus the rape of passive-faced white women by goofy-faced white men. (Crumb's defenders claim his racist comics require readers to examine their own racism; Crumb says he creates rape comics because he hates women.)

I never saw *Bible of Filth* in my brother's hands or in his comic-book stacks. I discovered it in my recent Crumb research. But I'm confident Joshua knew about that book; surely he didn't own it because it was expensive. Before 2017, when an affordable version was finally published in the United States, Crumb fans had to shell out hundreds of dollars for the out-of-print 1986 European release. In Joshua's slight defense, I only witnessed him perusing Crumb's comics celebrating the rape of white women, never Crumb's overtly racist work. Still, I can't believe Joshua would pass up *Bible of Filth*, a book written by his favorite genius, designed to piss off our mother and God.

In his final year, Joshua watched and rewatched *Crumb*, Terry Zwigoff's 1994 documentary about the artist. Rebecca tried to watch it with Joshua on his bunk, the two of them staring at his laptop on his nightstand. She quit after twenty minutes, when Crumb's description of his childhood sexual attraction to Bugs Bunny inspired Joshua to make his own revelations. Joshua begged me to watch the film alone, tossed it into the back of Rebecca's Subaru one spring 2012 morning when Rebecca and I were leaving Huntington for Morgantown. The DVD haunted her trunk until I decided to watch it, eight years after Joshua died.

Now that I've seen *Crumb*, I understand why Joshua loved him. The documentary is stuffed with the sort of raunchiness my brother enjoyed: Crumb staring up the miniskirts of beautiful-thighed female twenty-somethings in a photo shoot for *Leg Show* magazine. But it also shows Crumb's slouchy walk—terrifyingly similar to Joshua's—and the way he crouches and rocks his skinny body in front of a record player, quieting his brain, King Saul–like, with music.

Another reason Joshua must have felt connected to *Crumb* and Crumb, and the reason I worry he wanted me to watch the film: the documentary drips with suicidal ideation. Robert Crumb's first lines in the film: "I get depressed and suicidal if I don't to get to draw. But sometimes when I'm drawing I get suicidal too." Robert's brother Maxon tells the audience he's only alive because he's "like Hamlet—too afraid" to kill himself. His brother Charles shares that he has personally attempted suicide several times, swallowing pills, drinking furniture polish. A few months after the interviews, the film's epilogue reveals, Charles succeeded with pills.

But there's a segment of the film that made me feel purely happy, and I hope, perhaps believe, it inspired my brother to feel the same way. Robert Crumb reveals he got his start as an artist through an imaginary company his brother Charles invented: Animal Town Comics. So similar to the little Brontës' tiny volumes. To the Sunshine Books my siblings and I crafted on our milk-stained coffee table.

Joshua quit reading the Bible Storybook at eight, but thanks to Robert Crumb, he read something almost like it as an adult.

The Book of Genesis Illustrated by R. Crumb's cover is styled in Bible Storybook spirit: primary colors, holy-looking lettering, a hand-drawn scene from the Bible. A stern-faced God, his white beard so long it grazes the ground, chases Adam and Eve from a lush-grassed Eden onto desert sand. Both humans wear the hides of animals who lived alongside them in the garden, with Eve's hide barely covering her perky, globular breasts. Since the book's title may attract Christian parents, the front cover bears a warning: "Adult supervision recommended for minors."

"All 50 chapters!" the book's cover boasts. "Nothing left out!" All the female characters' nipples protrude through their clothing. Whenever characters in Genesis copulate or die, Crumb provides an illustration. The Bible Storybook shows a man knocking on Noah's ark in the rain, while *The Book of Genesis* shows half-submerged bellies and arms.

The Bible Storybook stops the Great Flood story with earth's first rainbow and Noah's prayers of gratefulness. Crumb includes the story's real ending. Noah drinks wine unclothed in his tent, with a weary face, stooped shoulders, and tufts of hair around his penis, then he madly curses the lineage of Ham, the son who finds him. I discovered that passage as a twelve-year-old, used the text for a sermon about drunkenness I preached to my captive-audience siblings, using my wooden toybox as the church's only pew. "Noah got drunk naked!" Jennifer squealed. All three siblings listened that day.

I'm no fan of Crumb, but I'm disappointed he stopped with Genesis. I'd have been curious to read his take on Absalom, caught by his hair in tree branches; King Saul, tormented by Crumb-drawn demons; the Prodigal, loose-skinned and starving, with pigs a reader can smell on the page.

From the introduction to *The Book of Genesis*: "I, R. Crumb, the illustrator of this book, have, to the best of my ability, faithfully reproduced every word of the original text." He studied translations, read ancient historians and current feminist historians of ancient history, consulted Hebrew scholars about the book's original words. When a friend told him he was drawing characters in "modern bathrobes," tents "from a sporting goods store," Crumb studied North African indigenous architecture and clothing. The characters in *The Book of Genesis* don't have white skin, hair, or features. They look nothing like Zeffirelli's ice-blue-eyed Jesus or the lily-skinned, brown-eyed Jesus of the Bible Storybook. They're ugly as all Crumb's people, drawn with questionable accuracy, but they're not caricatures. In his endeavor to respect "a powerful text with layers of meaning that reach deep into our collective consciousness, our *historical* consciousness," Crumb produced a work that was, for him and for Bible adapters everywhere, unusually sensitive in terms of gender and race.

When Joshua tried to show me Crumb comics, I usually told him to keep that garbage away from me. When he opened *The Book of Genesis*, I sat down with him and read it on his bedroom floor. Joshua, of course, loved everything Crumb, but I could tell he enjoyed that particular book because he remembered his childhood Bible Storybook reading, those sermons he heard on my toybox pew.

"It takes a pervert," Joshua told me, flipping through *The Book of Genesis*, his voice awed, "to get the Bible right like this."

I'm no fan of Robert Crumb, but I find my feelings changing about my brother's obsession with his life and work in the years since my brother died, in the months since I've seen *Crumb*, in the hours that I've written this essay. Recently I learned the blackish-green T-shirt was designed by Crumb's son Jesse, who died in a 2018 car wreck, and I can't help but feel for a grieving father. More recently still, when I've thought of Crumb, I've found myself feeling not only sympathy but hope.

Maybe Joshua loved Crumb because Crumb, like Joshua, the creator of that video where a cigarette-chomping ventriloquist dummy rails about Adam and Eve, had an inescapable interest in the Bible. Because Crumb, like Joshua, wrote with his siblings as a child.

Maybe, deep down, Joshua wore that shirt because he planned to someday be reunited with our parents, Jennifer, Rebecca, and me. Because he planned to go fishing in a heavenly river with Mark. Because he planned, with classic Smoo irony, to transport his blackish-green-shirt-clad spirit to the Bible Storybook's Prodigal's feast, where he'd grin in front of a meat platter at the Father's table.

As the "last dread agony" turned to "marble calm," Charlotte told

Williams on October 6, she'd "felt" as she'd "never felt before that there was peace and forgiveness" for her brother "in Heaven." She realized she'd forgiven Branwell herself, and remarked, "How much more can the Eternal Being who made man, forgive his creature!"

Juliet Barker doesn't buy Branwell's deathbed conversion. She credits the desperate, heartbroken Patrick, who, she says, "knelt in prayer by his bedside and wrestled for his soul." She says that "perhaps through mere force of will" Patrick brought about that "strange change" Charlotte witnessed.

I don't think the Prodigal's older brother bought the Prodigal's conversion either. For "these many years," the brother whines, he's done nothing but serve his father. And his father never gave him a goat to roast so he could "make merry" with his friends. Then his little brother comes home, after he has devoured his father's life savings with harlots, and his father slaughters the fatted calf.

Maybe I'm wrong to wring hope from that shitty shirt. If I am, I'll stake my hope on the "Amazing Grace" tapestry. "Perhaps through mere force of will" my parents yanked their son out of Mr. Natural's void and shoved him into the throne room of God.

Lost Photographs

My parents' family room. Christmas 2012. Three sisters huddle on the futon with drooping smiles, trying to care enough to unwrap the presents in our hands. We aren't looking at the Christmas tree: we'd see Joshua's red stocking, that "Baby's First Christmas" ornament with a bald plastic boy, and something dumb Joshua crafted from a milkweed pod. Joshua has been dead almost four months, but there he sits in our Christmas morning photo. He crouches, plaid flannel knees pulled to his chest, in the empty space on the futon. The space we leave empty without thinking because our brother sits there. Joshua has a present in his hands, but he tore it right open. He tossed the red and green wrapping onto the rug, topping the rumpled mountain at his feet. He reads the back of his new Werner Herzog DVD with his lips in a half-smile, eyebrows raised. He knows the camera is on him. Later he'll look back at this picture and chuckle at himself. Such paltry excitement on his face when he's about to watch the best film of his life.

Jerry's Pay Lake in South Point, OH. May 2013. Jennifer and I stand next to our father on the shore of a small bulldozer-made lake, trying to remember how to fish. My dad holds a bamboo pole like it's part of his right arm, but his daughters look ready to drop their metal poles into the water. So much fishing line, a dismembered worm, a sharp hook: a disgusting and dangerous puzzle. But it's a perfect spring day, a day my dad and Joshua would have gone fishing, so we rooted under the house for tackle. It had to be a pay lake—my fishing license has been expired for a decade—and Joshua preferred pay lakes anyway. Long ago, my dad fished for calm with his brothers: three young men on a riverbank at sunrise. It didn't matter if any fish showed up. But Joshua liked to dip his line in the water and pull out a fat farm-raised catfish, so my dad joined the sweaty pay-lake crowd. In the picture, Jennifer looks uncertain, eyes squinted in the sun, but her line has floated to the middle of the lake. Her red and white bobber dances on the water. Something in her tanned, muscular hands remembers when she fished as a tiny girl, chattering on the riverbank next to her daddy. My hands can't remember, so I've given up casting and unrolled enough silvery thread to dangle my bait above the water. Maybe low enough that a fish can jump and grab it. Across the lake, an elderly man laughs in his wheelchair at that silly girl with her ponytail and shorts. The lake's so small I can hear him snorting. There's Joshua in the photo. He stands beside me, guffawing with the old man. Then my brother stops laughing and touches my arm. "Sarbef, let's go get a hot dog."

JCPenney in Barboursville, WV. Late December 2012. Three sisters on the strip of linoleum in the JCPenney Guys department. We have to make it through the Guys department to get to everything else, and the picture is blurry because we're running. We feel chased by the jeans and hoodies, the T-shirts stamped with video-game villains and soft drink logos from the 1970s, the posters of male models in their early twenties, aggressively stylish and alive. An hour ago, Jennifer expressed curiosity about the mall's post-Christmas clearance, and we piled into the car. Clearance racks sounded like a mission. We felt trapped in the space between our first Christmas without Joshua and the first New Year he wouldn't see. But now there's twenty-five feet of hoodies and conversation-starter T-shirts between us and the rest of the store. Joshua lurks in the Guys department, inspecting the pattern on a dressy-looking shirt. He needs clothes that fit his life as a call center worker and future director. A precise combination of the ultimate hipster and the khakis and button-downs our mother bought him when he was six.

The Twilight Saga: Breaking Dawn—Part 2 premiere in Fairmont, WV. November 2012. Three sisters beam in our hand-painted T-shirts, our hands gripping each other's shoulders. Our T-shirts are pink, purple, red, the most feminine colors at Joann Fabrics, and we've coated them furiously with glitter. Since sometime after midnight on August 30, this has been a family of three sisters, not three sisters and a brother. Sisters can have fun without a boy. But in the top right corner, Joshua hovers with a smirk. A smirk that means our movie is crap.

Arby's in Morgantown, WV. October 2012. My parents, Jennifer, Rebecca, and I sit at a fast-food table, squeezing brown sauce out of little packets. My parents have driven across West Virginia to visit their daughters. They considered that drive too far when there were six living people in our family, but now they do it once a month. No one felt hungry when they got here, but we remembered people eat, so we decided on Arby's. Five roast beef sandwiches, three Dr. Peppers and two Sierra Mists, five orders of curly fries. The table has a sixth chair. We've buried it like a body: five coats, three purses, two novels. But Joshua shows up anyway. He dumps our pile on the floor and sits down with a Pepsi and a sandwich. I know he can't be happy. He can't handle confining spaces: cars, classrooms, tables at restaurants. His idea of a meal out is a stroll through a city, a hot dog in one hand and a cigarette in the other. For a minute Joshua chews his roast beef, and then we all start annoying him. The way Rebecca hums between sentences. The way Jennifer slouches in her seat. The way I mention Gideon again or shake quietly about my dead little brother. A tangible stress cloud forms around the table, and my brother's eyes don't look like my brother's eyes. Desperate to recall Joshua from wherever he goes when he's angry, my sisters and I try telling jokes. We remind him of when he was little, what he said whenever we drove past an Arby's. "Oh," he moaned, "it gives me gas."

My house in Richmond, IN. March 2015. Peggotty, my two-year-old Boston terrier, sleeps on my bed, curled on the largest quilt I've ever finished. I outlined plum and red triangles in a bright white muslin, even though I knew Peggotty would stain the white strips with her paws. Joshua didn't like most dogs, but I know he'd like her, this quivery girl who speaks with her eyes. I stroke the empty space in the picture next to my dog's back and long legs. My brother has stretched out just there. Joshua drove up to visit me, and after we talked a while, he needed a nap.

When Scruffy escaped for the last time, he apparently ran as far and as fast as he could. But after some other escapes, he stayed in the neighborhood. He dashed from house to house, collecting doormats. Head turned to the left, Scruffy dragged the mats alongside him, trotting back down the dead-end road, up our gravel driveway, up the concrete sidewalk and two steps to our front porch.

Years after Scruffy disappeared, my dad told me, "Those mats were the only sign that dog thought he lived here."

Joshua had the works of Robert Crumb shipped to our family's home address. He typed *Twin View Lane* after his name. I know Joshua had the books shipped to that house out of convenience; it wasn't an emotional decision. He likely meant it, or thought he did, when he told my mother, "I hate this house. I live here because I have to." But still, he sent those books, that poster, the blackish-green shirt to the place he most associated with himself. And the deliveryman drove down our street, walked up the driveway, up the sidewalk, up those front steps, and piled Joshua's packages where Scruffy piled his doormats.

Welcome. Wipe Your Paws. God Bless This House.

PART 7
THE ELDER SIBLING OUTSIDE

The Prodigal's brother is "in the field" when his brother comes home. No one remembers to fetch him. That evening, as he walks back to the house, hoping to wash his feet and rest, make notes about newborn sheep, he hears "musick and dancing." Nothing's going unusually well that he knows of. It's not a day for a religious feast. He finds a hired servant outside and demands an explanation.

The servant says, "Thy brother is come; and thy father hath killed the fatted calf, because he hath received him safe and sound."

The Prodigal's not just safe. He's sound. He's come to himself. If that's true, the scheming, dreaming drunkard the elder brother grew up with is gone forever.

The Prodigal's brother grinds his teeth. Surely he finds something to smoke. He mopes outside the door while his little brother feasts inside, a reversal of the Prodigal's fears.

The Bible Storybook writers devote the final four panels–a full third of the story–to the elder brother's anger. First, he glares through a window in his mustard robe and lemon turban. The stone walls, the window, the silver goblets at the Prodigal's party look like they're copied from the earlier panel, when the broke Prodigal stares in longingly at riotous living. Without the captions, a reader could confuse the scenes, except for the elder brother's angry eyes, his sparkling clean turban and robe, and the wholesome smiles of the people at the feast.

In the second elder-brother-anger panel, the father goes outside the stone walls, leaning his gray and white beard over his son's shoulder. He pleads while his son glares at the ground. Third, the elder brother steps back from that beard, points an accusing finger at his father.

Finally, as the father finishes his explanation–"He was lost and is found"–the elder son lets the old man wrap an arm around him. The elder brother looks chastened. Surely he's seconds from joining the feast.

The Bible Storybook writers must have feared to leave children without resolution. To leave them with the possibility that everyone might not be equally thrilled when a sinner changes his identity and comes home.

But Jesus doesn't mind leaving us in doubt. He stops the story with the father's words, moves on to another parable, leaving the father and his elder son forever standing outside the Prodigal's party. One pleading, one stewing in fury and grief.

Found

After the funeral, my phone conversations with my parents, Joshua's bedroom, and all the air in my parents' house were inhabited by my found little brother.

To make room for found Joshua, my mother tore posters from the walls, filled thirteen-gallon trash bags with comic books and DVDs, bagged up Joshua's outdoor ashtray and swept the ashes from the deck.

To make room for found Branwell, the housekeeper together with tubercular Emily and already weakening Anne threw out gin flasks and opium empties. They burned shit-stained nightgowns, urine-stiff bedsheets, wadded poetry, bloody spit rags. Charlotte didn't help them. She lay in her bed for a week after Branwell's death, later writing to her lifelong friend Ellen Nussey, "It was my fate to sink at the crisis when I should have collected my strength."

My mother heard found Joshua speak to her once as she threw out his Crumb collection, again as she bagged up his movies. Perhaps she really heard him. I won't say she didn't. "Good job, Mama," he said.

Joshua's voice comforted my mother, but I winced when she told me that story. My mother hadn't heard the Joshua I remembered. My brother was not given to encouragement of others. Certainly not for comic book or film collection destruction, but not even for real accomplishment. "Good job" was not a phrase he said.

⁂

A few months after Joshua's suicide, when my sisters and I were visiting our parents, gathered on the living room couches for the Sunday morning Service, my mother tugged her record player from a closet. She set it up in the center of the room, on an organ bench that exuded the phantom aroma of Granny's cigarettes five years after she died.

My mom set the needle on "I Have Returned," a song Marijohn Wilkin wrote and recorded in 1974. The year Wilkin had recently gotten her alcoholism under control and stopped trying to kill herself. Wilkin smiles with middle-aged placidity on the record jacket, wearing white linen embroidered with flowers.

Wilkin sang the first line in her storyteller's alto, and the effect was immediate. My mom shed a few quiet tears—she still never has "completely broke down"—and my dad, my sisters, and I started bawling. We heard Wilkin compare herself to the Prodigal Son, proudly narrating her homecoming to the God she loved in her youth.

I know my mother meant to comfort us all, to take us on a Sunday morning visit to our heaven-dwelling brother, but none of us could handle the journey. After a few more lines, Rebecca and I fled the room.

Listening to "I Have Returned" now, years later, makes me cry all over again, and I wonder at the song's lasting power. The way it preserved my months-old grief like the nicotine in Granny's organ bench.

I cried, in my parents' living room and today in my Oklahoma house, because the song is powerfully emotional. An altar call song. Designed, like the parable itself, to convey one prodigal's journey and invite other prodigals to go home.

Surely I also cried because of the contrast. Joshua would never experience Wilkin's middle-aged wisdom. He stopped attempting suicide, not because of a return to faith, but because he succeeded. We had more room on the couches for Service because Joshua wasn't taking up a whole loveseat to sleep.

And alongside that difference between dead Joshua and live Marijohn Wilkin was an equally sob-inducing contrast: the repentant Joshua my parents pictured in heaven and the Robert Crumb collector. A young man they could wholeheartedly miss and my actual little brother.

I missed my brother's smoke sessions on the deck. I almost missed his angry footsteps. I missed the brother I'd had.

❧

Charlotte's irritation at her father's mourning—"My Son! My Son!"—seems more complicated to me than Barker's characterization, "the jealousy of the well-behaved sibling." Perhaps especially when I consider Charlotte's anger alongside her weeklong collapse while her father wailed. That son Patrick wept for was a heavenly, found Branwell. A Branwell who'd just said "Amen" on his deathbed. He was not the Branwell she knew.

Found Branwell wasn't the brother Charlotte wrote about to Ellen Nussey on January 11, 1848, nine months before he died. "Branwell has contrived by some means to get some more money . . . and has led us a sad life with his absurd and often intolerable conduct—Papa is harassed day and night—we have little peace . . . what will be the ultimate end God knows."

Found Joshua wasn't the brother I once tried to talk to about my failing relationship with Gideon, trapped in a car with Joshua's music on an hour-long drive. When I finished speaking, Joshua poked my shoulder and said, "Huh, well, that's a nice coat you've got on there, Sarbef."

Found Branwell wasn't the brother who wrote with Charlotte about Verdopolis, the brother who shared the infernal regions of her mind. He wasn't the brother who, fourteen years old, walked twenty miles through the craggy, sheep-covered Pennines to visit her at school. After he walked back home, Charlotte didn't write a letter *about* him, like she would have in the years before he died. On May 17, 1832, right after his journey, she wrote *to* him. "As usual I address my weekly letter to you—because to you I find the most to say."

My found brother returned to his six-year-old self, who declared his faith to a large-built, blond assistant pastor in front of our church's thousand-member congregation. "Warm water!" Joshua said, after he plopped himself into the Plexiglas immersion baptistry. He paddled and said, "I'm swimming!" playing to the laughing crowd.

Found Branwell returned to his infant self, his downy head gleaming with baptism water in a mossy stone church.

Found Joshua returned to the day my mother clutched his tiny milk-scented body, her perineum still flaming from his exit, and declared, "This boy's going to be an evangelist."

Found Branwell would never have that love affair with his tutee's mother, or never meet her at all, because he would hold on to that railway clerk job, keeping immaculate records, or support himself with portrait painting, capturing idealized versions of bourgeois children clutching their dogs. He'd pay his landlord and tailor, drink only ale, and only at meals. Maybe he'd be a world-famous poet, known for himself and not for his sisters.

Found Joshua would live with gratitude in our parents' home, or in a vacuumed apartment across town. He'd sleep in his bed at night, smooth his sheets in the morning, drive himself to his college classes. Or he'd maturely decide a college degree wasn't for him, land a job somewhere better than a call center or Camden Park. Instead of commandeering his parents' flip-phone to sell marijuana, found Joshua would pay for his own plan, use his phone to speak with family and friends.

If found Joshua waited to see our family in heaven, then the Joshua who killed himself was as gone as if his entire existence had been burned with his body. Almost as if "this" were "it." Almost as if the brother I last saw outside the Huntington library had disappeared into Mr. Natural's void.

I respected my parents' grieving too much to say it aloud, but I felt angry. I felt like my father's "Amazing Grace" tapestry, my mother's encounters with Joshua's "good job"-saying spirit, their sad celebrations of his post-death homecoming had caused me to lose him a second time.

Found Joshua and found Branwell have returned. They kneel without irony in the throne room of God.

Low

Three years now since my brother killed himself. Sometimes my grief is still obvious. I brew iced green tea, then forget the pitcher on the counter until gray mold floats across the surface.

I sleep on a towel for a week after Peggotty vomits in my bed.

I drive to the store for canned soup, but by the time I get home, I've lost the will to carry groceries further than the doorway. I kick the soup can into a corner when I hear the pizza girl at the door.

Thank God, most days aren't like that. I throw the soiled sheets in the washing machine and steam-mop my kitchen floor.

I stash the soup in the back of the cabinet because I hate canned soup, and I stuff pasta rolls with ricotta, spinach, and prosciutto. I melt dark chocolate with cream and marmalade and cool the mixture into truffles. I set my table with cloth napkins and a vase of sunflowers, and I pour my friends fresh glasses of green tea.

I drive to the quilt shop for calicoes and batiks, and I cover my carpet with cut pieces of fabric. I make nine-patch quilts, twin sisters quilts, quilts with appliquéd tulips and paper-pieced stars, stitching the bright triangles of my life back together.

But then comes that day.

I sleep till one p.m., then skulk down the alley behind my house, an alley lined with mosquito-larva-infested kiddie pools and empty cases of Natural Light. Peggotty needs a walk, but really she's my excuse to be out in pajama pants and a torn T-shirt. She lifts both hind legs, performing a handstand as she pees on a neighbor's storage shed, and I imagine myself crawling inside, nestling among the tools and long-forgotten boxes of winter clothing.

A passing dachshund puppy strains in his collar to greet Peggotty, broad chest hurled forward, short legs nearly flat against the ground. I try not to look at the dachshund's owner, this person hurrying down the street because he doesn't want his dog to speak to my dog. I live blocks from Oklahoma State University, so I know he'll be around twenty-two, a kid with everything my brother couldn't have. An apartment with friends, a jaunty confidence to his Nikes, the courage to outlive his twenty-third birthday.

When the dachshund disappears, I walk to the site of yet another new apartment complex, where men with dirty jeans, plastic hats, and backhoes have dug fifty feet into the red earth. So much deeper than the unmarked, hand-dug hole that holds my brother's ashes, one thousand miles away in West Virginia. While Peggotty sniffs the Chem-Can toilets, I stand, eyes dull, and breathe in the iron-rich dust, the pale orange cloud that surrounds me. I want to climb the chicken wire barrier. I want to hand Peggotty's leash to one of the guys at the top and slide down the hole, digging my fingernails and toes into the vivid dirt, so I can lie at the bottom. Fifty feet closer to the earth's blazing core.

After a few minutes I tell Peggotty it's time to go home. I need to lie on my kitchen floor, though I know the linoleum won't feel low enough.

An Infestation

Three years after Joshua killed himself, and a month after I moved to Stillwater, Oklahoma, for a teaching job I could keep, a snake dropped into my bed. The coal-black snake was coiled tight when it fell from the ceiling, but the coil loosened on the way down, as if the creature were feeling for solid ground with its tail. When the snake hit my turquoise sheets and the quilt I sewed myself, it burrowed under the covers the way Peggotty burrows so she can sleep next to my bare leg. The snake settled in beside her.

I'd like to say I stayed in the bed and defended my dog, hurling my bedside pile of books, the glass of water I keep next to me when I sleep, but I jumped up and ran across the room. Arwen clawed my quilt and meowed a complaint against me, not the snake under the covers, and Peggotty poked her head out and blinked at me. I trembled in the bedroom doorway, waiting for the snake to die or disappear.

I'd been to Oklahoma once before I moved there, far too long ago to check my rental for a three-inch gap at the base of the back door, mushy flooring around the toilet, or snake ghosts that visit in the night. At seventeen, before I decided on Virginia Tech, I flew from Huntington to Tulsa to check out Oral Roberts University, a school founded by a world-famous faith healer.

The Oklahoma terrain was brown and flat, chapel services were plentiful, and the winter air was so warm I had to borrow lighter clothing from the university students. But it didn't matter whether I liked or hated any of those things. At that point, I was just visiting the university for the plane ride. I knew I couldn't move so far from home.

Before I left, I'd told nine-year-old Joshua about my plans to go to college in Oklahoma, and I'd shown him an ORU promotional VHS tape with neon lighting, tasteful miniskirts, and music from 1990s Christian rock bands. On the video, a college-aged guy with gelled hair says, "I'm going to apply to Oral Roberts University." Another college-aged guy with gelled hair pops up and quips, "Oh, are you?" Bouncing on the little trampoline in front of the living room TV as he watched the video over and over, Joshua memorized all the dialogue and said the lines along with the actors. After a few afternoons of continuous watching, Joshua lost some of his cool-college-student entrancement and noticed something horrifying: one of those girls in a tasteful mini was showing off her impossibly clean dorm room. Joshua stopped the tape and yelled my name.

I found my brother lying on his belly on the trampoline, the screen frozen at the treacherous image. "Sarbef," he said, his voice choked with fear, "are you going to sleep the night?" He'd realized my twin bed would be made and empty, that I wouldn't be there to take dictation when he wrote a play. I told him yes and let him sob. I flew to Oklahoma, then moved to Virginia, but I came back. I spent my college years at Marshall, sleeping the nights under the same roof as my family.

❦

Shortly after the ceiling snake, I went to a party one evening in the flat expanse of an art professor's backyard. I'd landed a tenure-track job by expanding my search to the entire United States, praying aloud as I sent the application to Oklahoma: "Lord, I'll go *anywhere*." The professor with the party had made a similar move twenty years before, and I felt inspired by the outbuildings and yard art she'd amassed. I followed the other guests into her studio/woodshop, where I avoided and wondered at the electric saws as I filled my plate with shrimp dip and crackers. Then I claimed an Adirondack chair near an empty fire pit.

The woodworker sulked in a chair beside me, glaring into the missing fire. A solid-looking woman, she wore the overalls and cowboy boots of a male Oklahoma farmer, but she didn't think like one. She complained about the state's fracking-induced earthquakes, her students who carved quality blocks of wood into Oklahoma State University's mustachioed, gun-wielding mascot, Pistol Pete. Then she stood up and interrupted a guest midsentence.

"Look at us," she said, "sitting around without a fire. I'm going to go get some firewood."

"Isn't it too hot?" I protested meekly. I was sweating in a sundress and slip-on shoes, still used to the cool September evenings in West Virginia and Indiana. Nearby guests agreed, and the woodworker plopped back down, angry at Oklahoma, not at me. Two decades and she didn't feel at home. After a minute she sprang back up and headed to the woodshop.

"I'm an artist!" she yelled as she walked. "I ought to be able to think of something."

The woodworker came back with three Yankee Candles. She lit them and spaced the tiny flames around the fire pit. Then she cozied up to that fruit-scented fire, crossed one cowboy boot over the other, and told a story.

A few years before, a young woman had moved to Stillwater for a job in the art department, and she'd found an unbelievable deal on a rental house.

"Four hundred a month!" the woodworker crowed, and I gasped. I paid $825 for my little rental with the soggy linoleum and holey back door.

The day the young woman moved in, she saw a scorpion on her kitchen floor. At first she screamed and ran, but she'd moved to Oklahoma alone and she wanted to live alone well, so she summoned her courage and squashed it. The next day, she squashed a scorpion in her bathroom sink. The next week, she squashed scorpions on the living room rug, the kitchen counter, her bed.

After a few months the young woman stopped by the woodworker's office to chat. "There sure are a lot of scorpions around here," she commented in passing, maybe admiring the woodworker's carvings lined up on her handmade shelves.

"Sure are. Found one crawling around my woodpile." The woodworker might have let the subject drop, but she was intrigued by something in the young woman's tone. "A lot? How many scorpions are you talking?" The young woman explained, and the woodworker howled with laughter and shock.

The woodworker laughed again as she told her guests the story. "I asked her where she was living, and I'd heard of that place. What a crappy landlord. That girl was right on top of a scorpion mound! She hadn't told anybody because she was new to the state, and she thought everybody in Oklahoma had a house full of scorpions."

I smiled and chuckled and scooted closer to the candles, hoping scorpions feared flickering light. I suppose the point of the story was that houses with scorpion hordes are unusual in Oklahoma, but that's not what I took away. I thought, *Oh God, there are scorpions here*, those evil-looking things I'd admired at the zoo. With plate glass to protect me, I'd put my nose inches from a scorpion's pincers as the creature skittered across its patch of sand. In Oklahoma, scorpions lived outside the glass, and they mustered in mounds. I felt like I could hear scorpions in the yard, marching with pincers pointed toward me.

When I got home that night, I searched the couch cushions and corners, and I shook out my sheets before I went to bed.

Until Joshua reached his mid-teens and I moved to Morgantown, my family traveled to the zoo once a year. The Columbus Zoo, Cincinnati Zoo, and Louisville Zoo lay within a two-hundred-mile radius of Huntington. My dad took us into the walk-through bird enclosures, glass-roofed rooms where red, blue, and green feathers flitted past our faces. My mother sat us down by the lions and told stories about her childhood cats. Rebecca petted the baby pigs in the petting zoo, and Jennifer petted anything available: pygmy goats, dogfish sharks, boa constrictors. Joshua slid down an elephant-nose slide and whined for slushies and rides on the zoo train. I lingered in the sandy kangaroo and koala exhibit called the Australian Outback, pretending I was actually in Australia. Once, on the way home from one of our zoos, we stopped at a Shoney's Restaurant in Kentucky.

As we walked into Shoney's, Joshua, about six, grinned and stared at the familiar salad bar with its chocolate pudding from a can and the same faded red drapes that blocked the sunlight in our Shoney's back home. The magic of the franchise: we'd never been there before, and yet we had. There was that basket of sticky Saf-T-Pops on the counter, the stack of coloring sheets with Shoney Bear in a not-yet-red shirt and hat. Even the people looked the same, like God had picked up the Huntington Shoney's, servers and customers included, and planted it in rural Kentucky. Busty, frizzy-haired women wore red aprons over white blouses and dark skirts. An elderly couple sat by a red-draped window, sipping their weak potato soup, and a haggard young woman stood near the salad bar, begging her children to eat their oily green beans before they filled fresh plates with pudding.

But God hadn't moved the Shoney's. My family had moved, and Joshua found that idea exciting. Everyone else in the restaurant had likely driven five minutes, half an hour at the most, to eat, cook, or serve that greasy food. We were outsiders, people who had escaped the magnetic force of our hometown for one glorious day, and those Kentucky people needed to know.

Joshua pushed away his burger and fries on his white ceramic plate and stood up in front of his chair. He coughed a little, like a speechifying person on TV, then made his announcement: "We're *real* far from home." My dad sat him back down and shushed him, pushing the plate back onto his son's paper placemat. "Joshua," he whispered, "those people don't want to know about us. Please just eat."

Joshua smiled, undaunted, as he finished his fries. He'd said what he needed to say before our dad could stop him, and it didn't matter if no strangers had cared. Joshua was at Shoney's with his parents and sisters, and we were real far from home.

A few days after the woodworker's party, I walked Peggotty near my house after a long rain. Soon I'd go to a picnic at one of Oklahoma's many orange-tinted man-made lakes, where I'd meet Robert, a redbearded Oklahoma native. On a sailboat, he'd tell me what his Oklahoma grandfather used to say, before he lost his family maxims to dementia: "You won't get really hot again after the first soaking rain in September."

But I hadn't met Robert yet, and I was lonely. Once every few blocks, I picked up my rain-damp Boston terrier partway through a good sniff, and I hugged her to my chest and kissed her ears. My dog and cat were the only beings in a thousand miles who knew the living members of my family.

Harnessing Peggotty for her walk, I'd worried the rain had driven scorpions out of hiding, but we encountered only earthworms. Each time I found a worm wriggling forlornly on the drying sidewalk, I stopped and moved it to the nearest front yard. I had to work quickly, before Peggotty bit the worms or rolled on them. I tried to hook each worm with a twig, and when that failed, I gritted my teeth and used my fingers. I pitied those worms, displaced from their homes in tomato patches and under dumpsters, but mostly I missed Rebecca, a lifelong earthworm Good Samaritan. While I walked Peggotty in flat downtown Stillwater, Rebecca was probably walking her own dog and saving earthworms in Huntington's Spring Hill Cemetery, pausing to speak to our brother's ashes.

That night it rained again, and Peggotty and I crawled under my covers for a hard sleep. Arwen snuggled around my head on my pillow. Partway through the night I woke—or I thought I woke—to a wriggling. I sat up in bed and peeled back my quilt, revealing a pile of nightcrawlers that jostled each other for prime space, like too many siblings in a bed. Those grateful worms had slimed up my back steps and through that hole at the bottom of the door, following their hero home.

The ceiling snake had caused me to leap from my bed, too terrified to make a sound, but this time I was more disgusted than frightened. I stayed in the bed and let out a small, choked scream. After I warbled for a few seconds, Peggotty emerged from underneath the quilt and sniffed the place I'd uncovered. She curled up on the worms, empty bedsheets to her eyes and nose, and the worms disappeared under her belly and feet. Arwen shifted her body to my pillow's center, enjoying the warm space I'd left behind.

After the worms and the ceiling snake and after I met Robert, Arwen woke me for a middle-of-the-night meal. When I turned on the kitchen light, I saw roaches. Roaches on the countertops, roaches on the stovetop, roaches on the burlap bulletin board where I kept a red paint chip the shade of a T-shirt my brother wore when he was small. I froze and watched them crawl over my life. Arwen swatted a roach by her food bowl and meowed a reminder, waking me from what felt like a trance. I dumped food into the bowl, flipped off the light, and dove back into my bed. That night only, my bed was a refuge from creatures that creep in the dark.

In Huntington, I'd occasionally found a stray wood roach in the house, an inch-and-a-quarter specimen of an outdoor-dwelling species that had likely ridden inside on someone's coat. These Oklahoma roaches were tinier, but scarier. They were legion, like the demons Jesus cast from the Gerasene tomb-dweller into the pigs, and I could tell they wouldn't want me to carry them outside in a paper towel. If there'd been a seaside cliff in my kitchen, maybe the roaches would have thundered downhill and choked in the sea, but I had no cliff, and the roaches meant to stay.

The next day I called or texted everyone—Robert, my parents and sisters, a friend from back home—and I told them cheerfully about my latest hallucination. Roaches this time. And in the kitchen! I'd thought I only saw things in my bed! What a relief that I saw things in the night, that my house was infested with dreams. Otherwise I'd have real roaches in my house, living off unswept dinner crumbs and pet food.

Nobody bought my story. Robert said, "Sounds like you've got roaches." My mother said, "That house is full of demons, and you need to move out, but you need some poison for those roaches." By daylight, I peeled back a British tea towel I'd hung on the wall—a souvenir from a time I really had been far from home—and there they were. Yellowy-brown roaches huddled in the towel's rectangle shape, fighting for space like my earthworms. I lifted the burlap bulletin board from its nail and found more. Live roaches clinging to the bulletin board's wooden back, and dead roaches stuck in the old Command strip I'd once used to attach the bulletin board to the wall.

My landlord was too crappy to care—not like the scorpion mound landlord, but crappy in the holey door and soggy linoleum kind of way—so Robert hired an exterminator when I went to Huntington for Christmas. In my parents' house, I slept in my old twin bed next to Rebecca's; she was home from her nearby apartment because I was there. I saw a spider in the shower and a few kitchen-dwelling black ants, but nothing came to visit me in my sleep.

When I got back to Oklahoma, the roaches were gone, but I still felt a presence. After a week of fitful, unvisited sleep, I sat up in the night and saw huge, black, leathery maggots haloing the indentation in my pillow. Arwen had slept that night on the empty pillow beside me, and the creatures had curled around my head in her usual place. The eyeless, rat-sized animals had small, sharp, un-maggot-like teeth, but I could tell they were maggots by their writhing. This time I jumped up AND screamed, but I stood by the bed instead of running to the doorway. I wanted those rat-maggots to hear me screaming. Peggotty was sleeping on the other side of the house, but Arwen heard me, and she woke me by rubbing her damp nose on my arm.

I called my family and Robert again, but this time I knew the difference between real roaches and the vermin of dreams, creatures that existed only in that liminal space between my waking and sleeping. I wished the rat-maggots were actually demons, so I could channel the long-gone seventeen-year-old version of me who had wanted to attend Oral Roberts University. I would cast them out in the name of Jesus, and they'd disappear in a puff of smoke. And I almost wished the rat-maggots were real, so I could poison them like roaches. I imagined the creatures back in my bed, bodies doused in white boric acid. I imagined the sharp-toothed mouths gasping as the writhing slowed and then stopped.

Robert divides his time between a house in downtown Stillwater and a wind-shaken farmhouse within the borders of the Pawnee Nation. In the Stillwater house, Robert sleeps in the room next to his grandfather who used to talk about rain. Every morning, Robert tiptoes into his grandfather's room, wondering if the old man's spirit departed during the night. At the farmhouse, Robert sits up in bed and looks out at bluebirds and prairie.

The Pawnee land belongs to Robert's grandfather, a mostly white man with no Pawnee affiliation, and the house doesn't have an address. If Robert ever had to call an ambulance—if his mother's fears came upon her like Job's in the Bible and her son got trapped under a cow—he'd tell the EMTs to come to the Maggart Place. The Maggarts were the first white pioneers to build a life on the land, and the family kept it until the 1980s, long enough for their name to stick. Robert's grandfather bought the land in the early 2000s from the owner directly after the Maggarts.

That Pawnee-Maggart land—now a place for Angus cattle and goats, oil wells, and reedy man-made lakes where cows cool their bellies—bears a story of human displacement. The Osage hunted bison on that prairie until 1825, when a treaty gave that land to the U.S. government. The United States needed a place to put the Cherokee Nation, soon to arrive via the Trail of Tears from a homeland that included the southern Appalachian Mountains. In the 1870s the Pawnees moved to that same region of Oklahoma after a bitter choice, giving up their life and lands in Kansas and Nebraska to escape encroachment from white settlers.

Then white settlers took a look at that Oklahoma land, that mild-wintered expanse of prairie dotted with scrubby cedars and ponds. What a waste to call that land Indian Territory, letting those Indians keep it for themselves. What a great place that land would be for white farms, white churches, white towns. Around that same time, the Dawes Act–empowered Cherokee Commission divided up the Pawnee land into allotments, giving individual Pawnees land of their own. The Pawnees were poor, smallpox-ravaged, homesick, and grieving, and many of them sold their oil-rich land tracts to white people for next to nothing. If the Pawnees wouldn't sell, land and oil speculators often got them drunk, handed them something to sign, and told them the next morning that they'd sold their land.

I like to bring Peggotty out to the Maggart place, the biggest chunk of flat, open land she's ever seen. She runs until she collapses, then sleeps for days. While she romps—climbing six-foot hay bales, breaking rats' necks with her teeth, bouncing her front paws at the bull like she's asking him for a fight—I think about the host of people who stood on that land before me, longing for faraway places they'd always consider their homes. Women like me with dead little brothers, lost to disease, hunger, a cold trail. Or brothers lost, like mine, to despair. I know my sorrow doesn't compare; most of those Pawnee-Maggart residents had a right to be so sad and lonely it puts my grief to shame. But still, my little brother is dead, and I'm real far from home.

Robert tells me I'm afraid of scorpions because a scorpion has never stung me. "You've been stung by a wasp," he says, "so you know it's not that bad. Scorpions are just the same."

But I don't think he gets it. It's not so much the pain that scares me: I figure a scorpion sting would sting but wouldn't kill me. I just can't get used to the idea of seeing scorpions in the wild, or the fact that the scorpion's wild is my backyard. For me, for my family, for any West Virginia native, scorpions aren't pests we squash under cowboy-boot heels. They're creatures of the mythical Wild West, or creatures that have been captured and controlled, like Komodo dragons on lamp-warmed patches of dirt in an Ohio zoo. Wasps live in backyard storage buildings, in dead driveway Chevys, in unwashed Styrofoam coolers on porches. They're the venomous, winged villains in our family stories.

When I was ten, a cloud of yellowjackets chased my dad down our backyard hill while I watched through the sliding glass door. One moment he was mowing, and the next moment the wasps surrounded his lanky body, a real-life cartoon. "Open the door!" my dad yelled. "I hit a nest!" My mom slid open the door just wide enough for him to slip inside. His face and arms were covered with welts. Wasps pinged against the glass. After I fetched a bottle of hydrogen peroxide, I stood at the door and watched the wasps hum back up the yard, gleeful about my exciting day.

Another summer day, MaMa swam for hours with my siblings and me in her backyard pool, then she marched us inside, blue and dripping. We all changed in the bathroom at once: MaMa by the sink, all four kids behind the curtain that hid the toilet. It was my job to strip off squirmy toddler Joshua's blue cotton swim trunks and clothe him in a T-shirt, Underoos, and shorts. I'd just started sorting through the kids' pile of clothes when MaMa started screaming. "There's a wasp in my brassiere!" I pulled back the curtain to help, and she screamed again, "Keep away from here! You want stung too?" MaMa flung the bra on the ground and stomped on it, a whirl of damp curls and skin. My dad put on Grandpa's winter coat and went hunting outside with a can of Raid.

Years later, my parents' apple tree got infested with insects that two-inch cicada killer wasps like to eat. Teenagers then, Jennifer and I sat under the buzzing tree, tossing insect-browned apples to Kassie, who caught and ate them. A few smaller wasps joined the party, and I got an idea: I wanted to see a big wasp fight a little wasp. A heavyweight against a featherweight. A cockfight or dogfight without the guilt. Jennifer ran into the house for a jar, and I plunged the jar over a wasp-covered apple on the lawn. After a few plunges, I trapped a cicada killer and a red wasp inside. The wasps didn't fight, just bruised their bodies against the glass, so I finally let them out. The red wasp escaped into the woods behind our yard, but the cicada killer was angry. It attached itself to my white sock and stung me until I managed to smash it. The half inch of skin around the sting turned black and rotted, leaving a sore like a wormhole in an apple.

Sometimes when I'm homesick, I look at my scar.

❦

Both sides of Robert's family use the Maggart place as a dumping ground for artifacts, near-useless items I find comforting because I miss my own family's generations of beloved garbage in West Virginia. His dad's childhood dresser. His dad's uncle's Shriner cap and navy photo from WWII. His maternal grandmother's shotgun and Agatha Christie collection. His mom's sister's childhood sheets. The sheets look like patchwork from the times Robert's grandmother cut them apart and stitched them back together, moving threadbare fabric to the edges.

One night at the Maggart place, a year before Robert met me, he was asleep on those sheets in a bed some family member had dropped off. He awoke in the dark to a gentle sound: a scorpion crawling across his pillowcase, by his ear.

Robert told me this story from the safety of my living room a few months after we met. He sat cuddled on the loveseat with Arwen and me, cowboy boots and sweat socks by the door, American Spirits and semiautomatic pistol on the bookshelf. For a second I thought we had something in common, ghost creatures that appeared in the night. But then I realized Robert had woken up.

On that scorpion night, Robert was tired—he'd spent the day moving hay bales or fixing fence—and he didn't feel like getting out of bed. He folded his pillow in half with the scorpion inside, squeezed the pillow tight with his hands and face, and went back to sleep. An hour later, Robert woke to fire in his cheek. The scorpion had maneuvered around the pillow and into the case, and it had plunged its tail through the decades-old fabric.

Robert couldn't sleep with a scorpion after a sting, and now he was angry. He reached into the pillowcase, grabbed the scorpion by the tail under the stinger, and hurled it into an empty water glass on his nightstand. He upturned the glass and watched the scorpion scrabble against the walls. "That's what you get for stinging me," he crowed.

In my living room, Robert told me: "It took that thing *weeks* to die." He sounded embarrassed but proud, and I wondered if I should dump him. I pushed his legs off my legs and got up from the loveseat. I wanted to grab my cat and hug her, protect her from this torturer of scorpions.

❦

When Robert told me his story, I'd seen a scorpion outside a zoo only once, three years before my brother died, when I was working for a month in San Antonio. The scorpion was dead, confectioned inside a green lollipop.

I lived in Morgantown at that time, and I made the four-hour drive so often I barely felt like I lived away from my family. I couldn't drive home from San Antonio for the weekend, so I'd been there for the whole month. The city's front yards, with their sandy soil and succulents, reminded me of the Australian Outback exhibits at my family's favorite zoos. I felt like I'd gone on a real journey, long and far enough that I had to buy everyone in my family a present. I found my mom a mug at a River Walk tourist shop, and I got my nineteen-year-old brother that sucker at the Alamo.

When I got back to Huntington, I found my brother where I'd left him: on his bed watching art films on his laptop. I wondered if he'd cared that I'd been away, but he greeted me with "It's great to see you, Sarbef!" and I could tell he meant it. Joshua told me about a film, maybe *Dead Man* or *Blue Velvet*, then I handed him the scorpion sucker. Joshua loved candy, green, and disturbing images: I felt proud of my gift-buying savvy. Joshua took the lollipop for a second, thinking I'd brought him a treat, then he flung the sugared creature like it had stung him.

"That's gross, Sarbef." I agreed.

❦

Robert's scorpion story bothered me for several reasons. For one, I'd known him as a devoted grandson, as a guy who liked to play with my dog and cat, as the owner of a tame, undersized beef cow. He'd bottle-fed Ticia as a sickly calf, and he hadn't had the heart to sell her when it was time. Now I knew this cow saver was capable of casual cruelty.

For two, I'd seen Robert's collection of pinned insects and spiders, and I knew he humanely killed arthropods. If he'd felt the scorpion deserved death, he could have stuck a rubbing alcohol-soaked cotton ball under the glass or popped the creature into the freezer in a jar.

For three—and here's the biggie—the story reminded me too much of my brother. The summer before Joshua died, a tiny worm somehow crawled into his ear. During one of his daytime sleeps, his ear started throbbing. He stood up and yelled, "Mama," calling her to his room.

Even though Joshua disagreed with our mother about everything, though he was desperate to leave her, though he stayed up nights and slept days so he could pretend he lived anywhere else, he generally went to her when he had a problem. "My ear hurts, Mama," he told her, his hand in the short brown hair over his ear. "I think something's in there." She had him lie on his bed, sore ear up, and she rooted in the hall closet for a flashlight.

"Hold still," my mom said, directing the light. When she saw a wriggle, she ran to the bathroom for her tweezers. Slowly, surgically, my mom pulled out the worm and dropped it into a jar. Rebecca cringed behind her.

My mom held up the jar to the lamplight and said, "Well, Joshua, look at that." She started to carry the worm out to the yard, but Joshua tore the jar from her hand and screwed the lid on tight. That pain he had suffered had a tiny face, a target for his fury.

Joshua put one eye up to the jar and talked to his prisoner. "You think you can hurt me? You're just going to stay in there until you suffocate!"

Rebecca, the worm saver, begged Joshua to calm down. She begged him to release the worm outside or quickly kill it. She cared about the worm, but more about her brother. She didn't want him to be the kind of guy who could willfully torture a living being.

Joshua refused, insisting, "He hurt me, so he doesn't get to breathe."

❦

After the scorpion story, after I jumped up from the loveseat, Robert saw the look on my face and stood up and put his arms around me. I stiffened and kept my arms at my sides. "I'm sorry," he whispered. "I thought I should tell you. It's probably the cruelest thing I've done."

I remembered the wasps I'd trapped in a jar, the frog I'd put in a barrel when I was little—my new pet. I forgot him until he was dried up and dead. And Rebecca had recently told me a long-held secret: she saved earthworms as penance for Johnny, a worm she'd buried on the elementary school playground. She'd halved Johnny with a rock, believing both ends would scoot away.

And then there was Joshua and his worm. I already loved Robert despite the fact—and even because—he smoked like my brother, lung cancer risk and all. What was wrong with one more similarity? I hugged Robert back and told him it was okay.

⁂

My night visitors arrived only after my brother's death and my move to Oklahoma, but I've never been fantastic at sleeping. When I was in elementary school, my mother informed me one morning that I'd spent the night wandering around the house. Fast asleep, I'd yelled that my friend Carrie had put a drawer of her belongings under my bed, and I wanted that crap gone. I tried to believe my mom was lying, but I knew she wasn't.

As a teenager, I sleepwalked into the room where all three siblings slept and gave a speech about nobody knows what. It wasn't their laughter that woke me up. It was Jennifer's face, her wide-eyed glee.

In college, in my childhood bedroom where I still slept the night, I dreamed an electric-blue poison arrow frog hopped across my stomach. I sat up, screamed, tried to knock it away, and found a real live centipede in its place.

"One of those flat brown ones?" Robert asked when I told him the story.

"Yes! It was like three inches long."

"Oh, centipedes are way worse here. Ten inches at least, with yellow-orange legs and mahogany bodies. Wait till you see one!" I couldn't wait, so I googled and found a picture of the giant desert centipede, only eight inches long but leggy as he'd promised. I was afraid to sleep for a week, afraid an Oklahoma centipede would drop into my bed from my dreams.

The centipedes have stayed away so far, but the scorpions haven't. A few days after Robert told his story, Rebecca came to visit, and she slept beside me in my bed. One morning, she told me I'd sat up in the night, screaming, "A scorpion, a scorpion." She'd hugged me until I'd calmed and lain back down. I had no memory of a scorpion dream, but I knew Rebecca was telling the truth.

I blamed Robert for the nightmare, but I felt closer to him too, almost like I belonged in Oklahoma. I'd battled a scorpion in the night.

⁂

Google tells me my ghostly nighttime visitors are hypnopompic hallucinations. *Hypno* from the Greek word for *sleep*, and *pompic* from the Greek word for *sending away*. Hypnopompic hallucinations happen when a person begins to wake up but can't manage to send sleep away completely. A fellow sufferer wrote that he's come to enjoy his hallucinations. "If I blink, the ants on my wall disappear, so I hold still and watch them as long as possible." My rat-maggots and bed-snakes seem unusually creepy, but at least I'm not alone.

Hypnopompic hallucinations come to people who struggle with insomnia—since my brother died, that's me—and they're often triggered by stress or exhaustion, or by an attempt to sleep in a new place.

By "new place" I'm guessing the Internet writers mean a one-night stay in a cheap motel near a zoo. Two parents and a baby boy in one bed, two girls in the other, and the future insomniac on a cot by the bathroom door. Or a night in Kentucky in the future insomniac's short-lived apartment, when four siblings make a bed of blankets, sweatshirts, and towels.

I'm guessing the Internet writers wouldn't call a bedroom a "new place" if the insomniac has tried to sleep there for two years and the night creatures keep coming. But I wonder if they'd make an exception for a bedroom a thousand miles from the insomniac's parents, her sisters, and her brother's ashes. And mostly I wonder if that bedroom counts as a new place if the insomniac has done something that is, for her, revolutionary: if she's moved a thousand miles from her parents, her sisters, and her brother's ashes and dared to stay.

Joshua wanted me to sleep my college nights at home, but he wanted to go away to school himself. His New York dreams were already forming, but I thought WVU might be a good first step: two hundred miles from home, and I could get to him in minutes. Our parents were afraid to let him go.

"Let him live in the dorms at Marshall," my dad said. "If he flunks out, we'll just drive over there and pick him up." Of course, Joshua did flunk out, and his parents did pick him up, and so Joshua was twenty-two, still living at home, taking classes at a community college.

Joshua talked to Rebecca on the phone the night he died, one room over from me in our Morgantown apartment. In the same time zone as

Joshua, Rebecca was getting ready for bed, but his day was beginning. He told her about movies he planned to watch, his classes in electronic media. Then he moved to his favorite topic, New York. "You know, Rebecca?" he said. "Someday, somebody's going to find me hanging in an apartment in New York City."

The suicide threat bothered Rebecca, but Joshua sounded hopeful. Not like a person who planned to hang himself in three hours. He sounded like he planned to live another year at least, long enough to finish school and move real far from home.

But late that night, while Joshua was lounging on his bed as usual, watching movies and chatting online with friends, terrors visited him. Maybe something like a pile of rat-maggots, but nastier: horrible words in his mind. *You'll never direct a film. You'll never get out of Huntington. You'll never live in New York.* I wonder if Joshua decided to punish those terrors by taking away their air.

A year after my Oklahoma move, a thigh-thick snake slithered onto my bed, but I didn't bother getting up or screaming. I lifted the covers and invited the red-and-black serpent into my bed, let it snuggle under my quilt with Peggotty and me.

I thought I had the answer. Coexist with my terrors. Maybe I couldn't enjoy them like the guy with his wall ants, but I was determined to put up with a few creatures that weren't there. My brother had died because he couldn't handle the brain waves that go bump in the night.

And in a way, I was proud of my hallucinations. I thought maybe they meant I hadn't gotten over my brother's suicide, that I still had the proper amount of grief. I no longer cried in my bed for hours a day, but my brain remembered I was sad.

But a few months later, I had a new kind of night terror and couldn't feel proud or unafraid. Fortunately, I wasn't alone; both sisters were at my house for a Thanksgiving visit. When first-time flyer, Huntington-dwelling Jennifer got off the plane in Tulsa, that same airport I'd flown into when I was seventeen years old, she said, "I'm really far from home! It feels good!" And I realized it did feel good to be far from the house where my brother died, from the hills he'd seen every day through the windows instead of New York City concrete. I felt thankful I lived in Oklahoma.

Partway through the visit, I partway woke to a moth on my sheets. A solitary moth seems harmless enough—something I might actually see if I turned on a light at three in the morning—but somehow I knew I was that moth. A moth who'd been a member of a whisper of moths, but now the rest of my whisper was dead. Rebecca heard me screaming from the room she was sharing with Jennifer and came into my room and wrapped me in her arms. After several minutes I realized I was wailing like a person getting murdered, and my heart was beating so loudly I could hear it between screams. As I calmed, I closed my mouth and felt my moth-sized body grow to fill my nightgown.

Rebecca went back to bed, and I lay awake watching my sheets. If anything showed up, I was going to be ready. I was going to take the glass on my nightstand and trap those creatures until they were dead.

Mansions

During our second summer together, Robert and I flew to London and drove a tiny blue rental to Haworth, a place I visit like a faraway second home. I visited that first time alone, then once with Rebecca, and now Robert and I stood on the steep cobbled street between the Black Bull and the Brontës' church.

Before our trip, we watched *To Walk Invisible*, a months-old Brontë biopic. In that film, on a convincing replica of that cobbled street, flame-red-haired, alcohol-rumpled Branwell stumbles uphill toward his father's parsonage, and Emily and Anne walk together discussing Emily's (likely) real-life inspiration for Heathcliff. "All that anger," film-Emily gasps. "So rich!"

I turned my hiking sandal sideways, pressed my bare skin onto the July-warm stones where Emily imagined and Branwell staggered home. I told Robert, "This is my favorite place in the world."

We happened to be in Haworth in 2017, the year the Brontë Parsonage Museum docents called "Branwell's bicentenary." Two hundred years since he was born. To celebrate, Simon Armitage, the UK's not-quite-yet poet laureate, curated an exhibition called *Mansions in the Sky—The Rise and Fall of Branwell Brontë*. Armitage chose pieces from Branwell's letters, poetry, paintings, and possessions: a faded leather wallet, a goshawk in watercolors, a Masonic apron, a notebook that ought to detail his tasks at the Manchester and Leeds Railway. The pages are filled instead with poems and sketches. Armitage composed a poem for each object, pairing the poems and inspirations under glass.

In the exhibition's guidebook, Armitage writes that he'd wondered if, "behind the bad-boy caricature, there was a neglected and misunderstood genius waiting to be revealed." Armitage answers his own question with amusing terseness: "There wasn't." But he says he nevertheless admires this "young man of fierce ambition and hyperactive creativity" from Armitage's own native moors.

Armitage took the phrase "mansions in the sky" from "The Struggles of Flesh with Spirit," a lengthy poem Branwell sent to William Wordsworth at nineteen along with a request for writing advice in a tone-deaf, self-important letter. After calling Wordsworth "a divinity of the mind," Branwell boasts, "Surely in this day when there is not a *writing* poet worth a sixpence the feild must be open if a better man can step forward." For the exhibition, Armitage paired the letter and poem with his own poem, "William, It Was Really Nothing," where Branwell imagines Wordsworth reading:

> mid-breakfast, letter in hand,
> eyes on stalks and jaw hanging loose.

Wordsworth kept Branwell's poem and letter but didn't reply.

Wordsworth's silence is key to the exhibition, that showcase of a life Armitage says can be summed up by the word "disappointment." For Armitage, the exhibit title, like Branwell's original line of poetry, evokes unattainable love, unattainable glory. Dreams that lead to ruin. He writes of Branwell, "After dreaming of heaven and building his mansions in the sky, planet earth was never really going to be good enough."

I found "The Struggles of Flesh with Spirit" among Armitage's chosen pieces in the museum's exhibition room, a part of the house someone added after all the Brontës had died. Reading Armitage's guidebook, I'd taken "mansions in the sky" as straightforward metaphor, so I was surprised to find a poem so overtly religious, so full of longing for the "many mansions" in heaven Jesus promised believers in the Gospel of John.

I remembered Charlotte's opinion of her brother's spirituality: he didn't believe in the "value, or even the reality," of religious principles and beliefs until the final days of his life. So I wondered if Branwell's pious fervor in this poem shared the sincerity of the frightful Christian pop songs my brother composed at twelve on his bottom bunk, devoid of his creativity and voice. Joshua appeared to be hoping to produce a work of genius without effort, and to impress his Jesus-loving parents and sisters, and he failed on both counts. I cringed and advised him to stick to writing plays.

But as I peered at Branwell's Victorian scrawl, scanning the poem for the exhibition's title, I saw—or wanted to see—a truly tender portrayal of Branwell's mother, who died of cancer when he was a little boy. And, given the facts of Branwell's severe depression and early death, some lines, if not impressive as poetry, were at least far more haunting at Branwell's bicentenary celebration than they could have been when he mailed them to Wordsworth at nineteen. I read:

And often has my mother said,
While on her lap I laid my head,
She feared for time I was not made,
But for Eternity.
So I can read my title clear,
To mansions in the skies,
And let me bid farewell to fear,
And wipe my weeping eyes.

❦

Every room of the house portion of the Brontë Parsonage Museum contains period items and realistic replicas along with Brontë originals. The very table where the sisters kneaded their bread, that black horsehair sofa where Emily—after weeks of forcing her weakening body out of bed to write, to bake, to comb the carpet—lay down to rest on her last day.

But there are no ultra-stale breadcrumbs, and to see splatters of tubercular Brontë blood, visitors must enter the museum's exhibit area, leaving the bedrooms and work rooms behind. The effect is a scrubbed-clean, life-sized Victorian dollhouse, protected by velvet ropes and docents from chaos-making hands. In that dollhouse, I looked into a room messy as my brother's, nearly as messy as Mark's apartment when I saw it days before he died.

After I bought my ticket, before I entered the house, I stood among the rain-worn gravestones and read Armitage's guidebook, learning about the installation of Branwell's bedroom-studio from the stage-prop house of *To Walk Invisible* into the room Branwell actually used. Still, that room startled me. Someone must have lain on that narrow bed to create those head-dents in the pillows, to crumple the blanket and sheets. In the film, Branwell slides out of that bed to crouch on the ink-stained rug, weeping and clutching a half-written poem and a half-drunk bottle of gin. The wrinkled poems were there, and the gin empties. All that was missing was Branwell himself and the damp, human odor of despair.

As I leaned my torso over the velvet rope, examining Branwell's sketched self-portrait tacked over the fireplace, the careless orange blanket on a cracked leather chair, I listened to the chatter of viewers who peered around me. A young female docent explained to a group, "It's supposed to represent the disorder in his mind." A few minutes later, two middle-aged British women crowded behind me. One remarked, "Those brilliant people, can't be bothered to tidy up." The other one corrected her: "He was drinking himself to death." The first woman breathed, "Oh," and they stood for a minute in silent reverence. I felt certain they believed they were looking at Branwell's actual filthy sheets, his real ink-stained rug, liquor bottles he purchased 169 years ago, somewhere down the cobblestone road.

Their reaction took me to New Year's Day in 2016, the first time Robert visited my parents' house in West Virginia. In the two months we'd been dating, I'd told Robert about Joshua. His sense of humor, his mental illness, the way he died. After Robert greeted my parents and sisters, he walked over to an eye-level eleven-by-fourteen of high school senior Joshua, on the wall facing the Christmas tree. "Your brother," he whispered.

Later I gave Robert a tour of the house: an excuse to show him Joshua's bedroom. At Thanksgiving I'd seen Robert's somewhat preserved bedroom from his teen years in his parents' home: his *Field and Stream* wallpaper border, a phrase he'd found lovely in high school Latin and tacked up in 30-point font on the wall. I wanted to show him the room where I read and slept in my own childhood and teens, but I also felt an urge to show him the site of the suicide. Perhaps I wanted to welcome him into my grief. Perhaps I meant to test him.

"Here it is!" I sang, trying to hide my nerves with forced cheerfulness as I pushed open that stuck door. "Joshua's room. This was *my* bedroom from when I was eighteen months old through college. Look!"

I stepped around Joshua's puppets, the end table my mom stashed in there to make room for the Christmas tree, and creaked open the closet's wooden folding door. "Some old stories I wrote are up there on that shelf, and I still have Barbies in the closet!"

I turned my head, saw that Robert hadn't followed me. He stood stiffly in the doorway, horror-struck at that open closet. I closed the wooden door, stepped back over the chairs. Perhaps I'd lost him. "Hey, that wasn't the original closet bar," I said, in case that helped, as we walked back down the hall. "My dad replaced it, after, you know." Robert squeezed my arm.

Standing in front of Branwell's art-installation-bedroom, hearing those women's reactions, I felt a similar impulse. To comfort, or at least to clarify. "Hey," I wanted to say. "This stuff isn't real. And Branwell died in his father's room, down the hall."

❦

On our drive to Haworth, Robert and I stopped off in Little Ouseburn: the physical location of Branwell's most deadly mansion in the sky. Around the Parsonage Museum, the narrow roads are often bordered by stone sheep fencing. Little Ouseburn is hedgerow country. At that point in our journey, Robert was adjusting to British driving, so the left side mirror scraped against living green walls.

Twenty-eight-year-old Branwell began his tutoring position with the Robinson family at Thorp Green Hall in January 1843. In May he described his situation, and his student's forty-three-year-old mother, in a letter to a friend. Whipping between references to himself in first and third person, Branwell wrote: "He is living in a palace, with a delightful pupil, —I curl my hair & scent my handkerchief like a Squire . . . but my mistress is DAMNABLY TOO FOND OF ME He asks his friend seriously to advise him what to do. . . . She is a pretty woman, about 37, with a darkish skin & bright glancing eyes."

I wanted to see that "palace," but it burned down near the end of the 1800s. The owners rebuilt, and the new structure became part of a private boarding school. Before we visited Little Ouseburn, I'd read a blog by a Brontë enthusiast detailing a lovely day he'd spent in the town. The school, he assured readers, cherishes its connection to the Brontës. He easily found a friendly person at the school who told him the building's story over tea. Robert and I drove through the school's open gates and parked next to a bed of rain-shimmering red tulips at the height of bloom. I felt a flash of Branwell's squire-like pride when I noticed the flowers matched my red boots.

We walked for a few minutes between flowerbeds and twentieth-century buildings, built to look older. We passed a sign directing parents who were dropping off children at an equestrian camp, then the campers themselves. Twelve-year-old girls in jodhpurs, flicking each other with riding crops. At last we spotted a woman at a desk through an open glass door. Perhaps the tea person from the blog. We poked our heads in, and I asked about the Brontës. The woman looked alarmed, eyeing me and then the bearded man with me. "Well, I know nothing at all about *that*, but there are children here! You'll have to go!" I'm sure I would have felt embarrassed if my situation hadn't rhymed so well with Branwell's in 1845, after Lydia's husband learned of the affair. Turned from the grounds, headed north to the parsonage in Haworth.

Before Robert and I left Little Ouseburn, we stopped our car between hedgerows on a quiet street. My map told me our road ran alongside the River Ouse. A year after his dismissal, Branwell titled a poem "Lydia Gisborne," after his love's maiden name. He wrote:

> On Ouse's grassy banks—last Whitsuntide,
> I sat, with fears and pleasures, in my soul
> commingled.

As the speaker sits, the sun goes down, taking his hopes with it:

> The sky though blue was soon to change to grey.

I knew the poem described Branwell's addiction-triggering disappointment. A sorrow that disappeared and then intensified later that year. When Branwell learned of Mr. Robinson's death, according to Barker, the so-recently despondent Branwell was "unable to conceal his glee." He believed he'd marry Lydia, smell like a squire, write his poems in the palace, never have to work—or get sacked—again. But days later he received further news: Mr. Robinson's will decreed that his widow would forfeit every cent of his money if she married Branwell, or even contacted him. In *To Walk Invisible*, a servant from Thorp Green Hall gives Branwell the bad news at the Black Bull. Branwell glares sardonically at the servant, refusing to believe him, but in the next scene, he sobs drunkenly on the ale-spattered floor. Branwell never again held a job, never again saw Lydia, and two years later he was dead. Still, when I read that poem, I found myself imagining away the impending grey skies, picturing only the riverbank and the palace-dreaming young man.

Peering over the hedgerow, I could see the river but not the grassy banks, so Robert climbed on top of the car. His knees dented the thin metal roof, and he had to hurry because a car appeared behind us, but he got the picture. On the ride to Haworth, I stared at that riverbank. I saw Branwell lounging in the grass, experiencing a moment that—within the context of his short, sad life—must have felt something like joy.

❦

At the Parsonage Museum, Robert and I discovered we'd missed Charlotte's bicentenary by one year, a celebration that the novelist and American expat Tracy Chevalier titled *Charlotte Great and Small*. If I'd chosen a bicentenary deliberately, I would have chosen Branwell's. It felt like a memorial for all sad, creative, short-lived men. Still, I felt wistful about missing Charlotte. Fortunately, there's a video tour with Chevalier on the Parsonage Museum website.

In the video, Chevalier shows off *A Correspondence*, a series of black-and-white collages by New Mexico–based artist Ligia Bouton, inspired by one of Charlotte's love letters to Constantin Héger. Charlotte met Héger in Brussels in February 1842, when she and Emily began their studies in language and literature at a school run by his wife. Two of the collages include a portrait of Héger, whose image would pass for the romantic male heroes of *Jane Eyre* and *Villette*: heavy-browed, sharply intelligent, easily angered, unavailable.

Charlotte described Héger to Ellen Nussey in a letter that May, apparently too breathless to separate thoughts into sentences: "a man of power as to mind but very choleric & irritable in temperament—a little, black, ugly being with 'a face' that varies in expression, sometimes he borrows the lineaments of an insane Tom-cat—sometimes those of a delirious Hyena—occasionally—but very seldom he discards these perilous attractions and assumes an air not above an hundred degrees removed from what you would call mild & gentleman-like he is very angry with me just at present." Later in the letter, Charlotte wrote that he and Emily didn't "draw together at all," but Charlotte managed his anger well herself by crying.

Over the next year and a half, Héger taught Charlotte how to focus her French prose, lessons that, according to Barker, transformed the future novelist's English writing. Héger noticed Charlotte's brilliance and gave her extra lessons. She fell rather violently in love, but, biographers believe, had no sexual affair. She grew more and more miserable.

At the end of 1843, twenty-seven-year-old Charlotte returned to Haworth and began writing her love letters. In the letter Bouton chose, dated 8 January 1845, Charlotte wrote, in French: "Day and night I find neither rest nor peace. . . . How can I bear my life unless I make an effort to alleviate its sufferings?" Madame Héger wrote to Charlotte, limiting her to one letter every six months, and Monsieur Héger himself rarely replied.

Seventy-six days before Charlotte wrote Bouton's chosen letter, she sent a note to Brussels in her friend's father's pocket. She wrote, "Monsieur, I am full of joy this morning—something which has rarely happened to me these last two years . . . because a gentleman of my acquaintance . . . has offered to take charge of a letter to you." In the note, she complained of "six months of waiting," response-free, after her previous letter, but hoped this time—"the thought delights me"—to get a response quickly via her acquaintance. Monsieur tore that note up, threw it in the garbage. One of Bouton's collages contains seventy-six Post-it-sized pieces of paper—Héger's cut-up portrait among them—representing those seventy-six days that Charlotte languished before she ignored Madame's rule and wrote Bouton's letter, pleading for a response yet again.

Gaskell left Charlotte's passion for Héger out of her biography, painting Branwell as the only Brontë who burned for someone who was married. The extent of Charlotte's obsession might have gone unrecorded if Madame Héger hadn't fished the letters out of the trash and stitched them back together. Seventy years later, the Hégers' children gave the four remaining letters to the British Library, which loaned Bouton's favorite to the Parsonage Museum for Charlotte's bicentenary. Two of Bouton's collages feature Charlotte's reproaches from that letter: white letters on thick black paper. First, Bouton played the role of Monsieur Héger, tearing the phrases in half, then she became Madame, stitching them loosely with black thread. One collage reads *Ni lettre ni message* (Neither letter nor message), the other *Non, rien* (No, nothing), the words separated by the tear.

My favorite part of the video shows a knitted version of the bed fire scene from *Jane Eyre*. Chevalier came up with the idea and commissioned Welsh artist Denise Salway, the Knitting Witch. The rather magical result is a heavy-browed knitted man, his eyes shut in a red-curtained bed. Red, gold, and white gauzy knots of flame creep up a bedpost by his feet. Jane stands at the front in a gray dress, pouring blue threads of water from a cream-colored pitcher. The oh-so-problematic West Indian attic-wife lurks behind the bed, all wild black hair and white nightgown, a lit candle in her hands.

"I particularly like Bertha," Chevalier says on the video. "She's looking suitably mad." I like Bertha the most too, the way she stands behind cold-water-bearing Jane, holding her flaming heart. I've always identified with Jane, teacher and mediocre pianist, fond of disappearing with books into window seats. But looking at these woolen women, I see myself far more in Bertha. I see myself lying under my dining room table in Indiana, keening with grief over Gideon and Joshua. I remember the emails I wrote to Gideon, sad and angry enough to light a bedstead on fire, and I'm thankful they never existed in paper form, held and sewn by another woman's hands.

❧

From the video evidence, Charlotte's bicentenary exhibit seems to have ignored her brief time with Arthur Bell Nicholls, her quieter love. Both in our mid-thirties, Robert and I held hands in the grassy lane where Charlotte, thirty-seven years old, often walked with Arthur in 1854. Patrick didn't approve at first of his brilliant, only-remaining daughter's courtship with his impoverished curate, so the couple chose a place to walk that Patrick couldn't see from his windows. In 2017, we strolled past a neighbor's brown chickens and a pheasant.

As Charlotte wrote to friend after friend, announcing her engagement, she hardly seemed the same person who described Héger as an "insane Tom-cat" and begged him for a reply. To Ellen she wrote, "I am still very calm—*very*—inexpectant. What I taste of happiness is of the soberest order. I trust to love my husband—I am grateful for his tender love to me—I believe him to be an affectionate—a conscientious—a high-principled man." With such a lackluster description, I'd suspect Charlotte married someone she couldn't love, if it weren't for her fond references to her "dear husband" after her marriage. And for the heartbreaking words that, according to Gaskell's biography, she whispered when she heard Arthur praying by her bed: "Oh! I am not going to die, am I? He will not separate us, we have been so happy."

Although Charlotte's tone is "very calm" in those engagement announcements, her hopes for happiness with Arthur lurk, predator-like, under the surface. Writing to one friend, she nearly echoed her lovesick brother's feelings on the grassy riverbank: "Care and Fear stand so close to Hope—I sometimes scarcely can see her for the Shadow they cast." And to Ellen: "Fears come mixed inextricably with hopes." She'd survived the disaster of Héger, buried her mother, four sisters, and an infuriating brother. Except for her novels, hope had gone badly for Charlotte. I can understand why she would distrust joy.

After our walk in the lane, Robert and I returned to the parsonage. A docent caught us in the doorway, asked us if we'd like to help them prepare for Emily's upcoming bicentenary. The original manuscript of *Wuthering Heights* was lost to the ages, and they were asking visitors to re-create it, each writing a line. Of course we wanted to help. The docent led us into an office in the museum part of the building and handed each of us a sharpened, never-used pencil. I sat first at a twentieth-century desk and looked down at an oldish-looking copy of *Wuthering Heights*, a brass ruler marking the next line. As instructed, I wrote in a paper-bound, acid-free notebook: *"Now am I old enough to go to Penistone Craggs?" was.* Robert sat down next and finished the thought: *the constant question in her mouth.*

Robert and I snapped pictures of each other as we sat at the desk, then I photographed my round printed letters shifting into his tiny script. "We have to stay together now," I said, half joking. "I was thinking the same thing!" he replied. Something about our handwriting together on one Brontë sentence, destined for preservation in an archivist's vault, felt more permanent, and far more romantic, than a marriage license.

During my first year with Gideon, I kept everything that related to him in a box in a high shelf of my closet. To add or remove items, I stood on a chair. Gideon rarely gave me gifts, but I amassed relationship paraphernalia: his forgotten flannel shirt, a souvenir cup from a Pittsburgh Pirates game, a long-sleeved T-shirt I bought at a gift shop when I was cold and coatless at Blackwater Falls. I'd seen TV girls boxing up their relationships after a breakup, and during that first year we were broken up nearly as often as we were together. During the course of a month, a week, a day, a minute, I vacillated between believing that we'd spend our old age isolated together in a spartan trailer in the woods and that our current conversation would be our last. As long as I kept everything Gideon in that box, I held on to a shred of my dignity. Or at least I saved myself the minutes it would have taken each time we broke up to sort him out of my life.

Looking at Robert's and my side-by-side writing in that re-created manuscript, I thought I understood a hint of Charlotte's mingled terror and hope. I was allowing my life to entangle with Robert's, and it was already impossible to sort him out and box him away.

Robert and I had another shared thought: we had to look for Penistone Craggs, the site of the fairy cave in *Wuthering Heights*. We both had a feeling it was real. I turned again to Brontë-loving bloggers: one said Penistone Craggs bears the real-life name of Ponden Kirk and provided a Google Maps pin. We drove our little blue car until the wheels spun on a steep, wet dirt road, then we climbed the rest of the way on foot. Every tenth step startled insect-hunting magpies from the moors into the sky. At last we reached the top of the hill, and we edged up to a precipice. I held my breath, looking behind me at someone's sheep, then thousands of feet down to lime-green lichened rocks and violet heather. I didn't see any sort of cave, let alone a home for fairies. I consulted the blogger's directions again: we had to creep over the edge, down into a crack in the rock.

Robert spent his youth up high in the American West, gripping wobbling construction ladders and scaling the Rocky Mountains. He stomped on the Pennine precipice, checking for loose dirt and stones. When he found the path, he lowered himself down ahead of me and stretched up his hand.

While on her honeymoon trip to Ireland, Charlotte wrote to a friend, saying she'd worried about marrying Arthur because he was "not a poet or poetical man." She wrote, "One of my grand doubts before marriage was about 'congenial tastes' and so on." I have to smile at the self-mockery in the quote marks around "congenial tastes": that phrase describes a reason I clung so hard to Gideon. We loaned each other our copies of *My Ántonia* and *To the Lighthouse*, calling each other when we discovered pencil marks under our own favorite lines. During my suicide-breakup madness, Gideon told me on the phone, "I'll never be able to talk about books to anyone like I can with you," and I sobbed all the harder under my dining room table.

It took me years to remember that my best moments with Gideon had held the possibility of happiness, but not the substance. A lurch of hope, then a crash, something akin to what Charlotte felt when she sent a note to Héger in her friend's father's pocket. At Blackwater Falls, Gideon and I watched a couple in their sixties dance on a wooden deck built onto an Appalachian mountainside, knees brushing knees, cheeks brushing cheeks, inches from the cascade of amber-black water. "I'd like to dance like that, Pokey," Gideon said. "Me too," I said shyly, imagining the two of us shuffling in the mist, our souls thrilling together. But Gideon walked away from the falls as I shivered, as my stomach dropped. Perhaps I wasn't the right dance partner. Perhaps it wasn't the time. Back home, the evening before Robert and I left on our trip, we two-stepped barefoot on my living room floor.

In that same letter, Charlotte described her trip with Arthur to the Atlantic coast. She seemed to take it for granted he couldn't see the beauty she saw, and she worried he'd try to talk to her, disturb her poetical enjoyment. But she happily reported: "Covered with a rug to keep off the spray I was allowed to sit where I chose—and he only interrupted me when he thought I crept too near the edge of the cliff."

At the cliff in Yorkshire, Robert helped me climb into the fairy cave, to settle next to him in a tiny room of rock. We sat in silence for several minutes. He let me imagine myself into *Wuthering Heights*, a book he'd never thought of reading, though he'd begin it as soon as we got home. Then he reached into his shirt pocket, pulled out an American Spirit. I grimaced, thinking he was going to smoke. But he tore the cigarette open, emptied the leaves onto the cave floor. "For the fairies," he said, and I realized I was mansion-building. I hoped life would let me stay with him until I died.

After their Ireland honeymoon, Charlotte and Arthur remodeled the parsonage, adding on Arthur's study, turning the house into a place they could live happily with Patrick until the end of Patrick's life.

But before long Charlotte was pregnant. As Gaskell put it in her biography, Charlotte was "attacked" soon after Christmas "by new sensations of perpetual nausea and ever-recurring faintness." In late February, Charlotte wrote to Amelia Walker, an old school friend: "Let me speak the plain truth—my sufferings are very great—my nights indescribable—sickness with scarce a reprieve—I strain until what I vomit is mixed with blood."

I've experienced such a night only once in my life: at the height of my grief, in Indiana. I was trying on alcoholism like a coat, and I mixed too many Salty Dog cocktails with deep-fried catfish. I vomited for eighteen hours. At first the exiting gin and grapefruit tasted stale and sour, and then they corroded my throat. After my stomach emptied, I dry-heaved, my body thrashing around the cold porcelain toilet, my mouth flapping open like a dying snake's. When I finally spat blood, I felt relief for a moment, just to have something to puke.

Gaskell says a doctor diagnosed Charlotte with a "natural cause" and prescribed "patience," implying she'd find relief and happiness after a few bad months. She didn't. I found Charlotte's death under glass at the Parsonage Museum: white embroidered baby bonnet paired with one of the last letters Charlotte wrote. "I am much reduced and very weak." The words were so faint I could picture her trembling hand.

Barker says she wonders if Charlotte, her husband, or father thought of abortion, which was illegal, dangerous, and taboo, but common in Victorian England. I wonder too. I wonder if the only option anyone proposed was patience. It's possible—she lived with two male pastors in a tiny town—but she wasn't isolated. She was a famous writer, separated by a train ride or telegraph from progressive-thinking friends, even from Gaskell herself, who wrote in a letter that if she'd known about Charlotte's last illness, she would have insisted Charlotte "do what was so absolutely necessary, for her very life." I know I'm projecting my own years of despair, my hopes of becoming a mother, my inability to imagine living as the last sibling alive, but I wonder if keeping a pregnancy that killed her was Charlotte's unconscious—or perhaps even deliberate—decision.

I did need patience to recover from my night of vomiting, along with rest, Popsicles, tall glasses of water, and the watchful eye of a friend. But to recover from the reckless, suicidal state I'd fallen into—the heavy drinking, plus swimming alone in unfamiliar lakes, going days without eating, checking my century-old garage for holes that might prevent carbon monoxide poisoning—I needed something more. I needed a major depressive disorder diagnosis. I needed to be the first person in my line of siblings, parents, great-grandparents, and family on back through the ages to seek help beyond, and along with, our pride, vitamins, and prayer.

To heal to the point that I could love Robert, live well without Joshua and Gideon, support my remaining siblings, build my dream mansion not in the sky but on earth, I needed—and I accepted—therapy and pills.

In 1846, back when Charlotte was writing *Jane Eyre* in the parsonage, giving Jane a happily-ever-after with a heavy-browed married man, Branwell still slept alone in the room I saw full of empty bottles and crumpled paper. One evening he fell deeply, drunkenly asleep in his bed, with a lit candle in igniting distance of his sheets. Barker writes that Anne "fortunately" walked by. She fetched the much larger and stronger Emily, who "dragged her brother out of his bed, flung him into the corner and the blazing bedclothes into the middle of the room, dashed to the kitchen for a large can of water and doused the flames." I like to think Charlotte imagined herself as an avenging Bertha, burning Héger's bedstead when no letters came, but Branwell may have given her the idea.

To Walk Invisible doesn't show the blaze. A dreaming Branwell climbs out of his bed, his woolen socks almost touching a candlestick he's left lit on the floor. In the dream, Branwell finds his beloved lying on a chaise with a red lace gown covering some of her aging skin. Her legs are wrapped around a thrusting young footman. Branwell yelps, "Lydia!" His sisters and father and Lydia's husband watch in chairs, arranged in rows like they're attending a concert, cackling at Branwell's misery. The scene cuts to Branwell, closed-eyed and shaking on the painted wood floor of his room, as Emily pours water over his face and tries to shout him awake.

In the next scene, Branwell's bedroom has been dismantled. The ink-stained rug is missing, the mattress is gone from the crooked iron bedframe, most of the drawings have been torn from the walls. Anne takes a rag to the baseboards, Emily fills a basket with her brother's laundry, and Charlotte sorts through books and papers on the floor.

When Patrick walks in, they all stop and look at him with frustrated eyes. "I think," he says, "rather than come back in here, he should stay in my bedroom. For the time being."

I felt oddly elated to see the bicentenary version of Branwell's room: his again for the first time since the fire. Since I'd seen film-Branwell in this room, with that exact slant to that stack of papers, that same stain on that rug, I felt as if real-life Patrick had received what he was hoping for, a return to normalcy after that miserable "time being" of harboring his son in his bed.

I thought then, and I think now, in Oklahoma, of my brother's bedroom, of his belongings gradually diluted by stored furniture, out-of-season wreaths, and fur from napping cats. I wish it could be useful, remotely sane, for my family to reconstruct that room as it was, instead of finally, someday, arming ourselves with rags and baskets, determining what to wash and donate, what to throw away. I'd like Robert to see that room. I'd like to visit it myself, like a shrine.

I wouldn't re-create the room as Joshua left it. Body-dented closet bar. Suicide note on his pillow: "I'm sorry, Mama and Daddy, I'm just too stressed about the things I have to do." Marijuana pipe out on his nightstand for once, since he didn't care if his mother saw it after he died. The room could look the way it did in January 2011, when my brother started a fire of his own.

In January 2011 my parents knew Joshua smoked, but they hadn't mentioned it since that awful day my mom found him puffing on a university bench. To better avoid the subject, Joshua hid his cigarettes and smoked in secret. Down the road, concealed by a low hill from my parents' front windows. Or, behind the storage building, on the flat several-foot crest between the downslope to our house and the downslope into a thicket of maple and locust, under the thirty-foot white pines my dad planted when I was a little girl.

At four o'clock one morning, Joshua chose the flat spot behind the storage building. Surely he found his tennis shoes on the unvacuumed blue carpet next to his bed, put them on with his plaid pajama pants and our dad's nineties-era Members Only jacket he'd taken to wearing that year. He grabbed his lighter and Marlboro Reds from a drawer of the white dresser I left in that room, and he shivered up the hill.

Behind the storage building, dead conifers lay under the live: our family's Christmas trees, ranging from that year's mangy green needles to sepia skeletons. He finished his cigarette, dropped the butt, and walked toward the house. Then, behind him, a crackle. He turned and screamed: the backyard was lit orange. It looked like the whole woods were on fire, and the garden hose, plugged into the spigot on the back of house, was way too short.

Joshua sprinted inside, called the nearby volunteer fire department, woke our parents. The fire truck was on the scene before our parents could lug sloshing buckets up the hill a second time. As the truck pulled away, Joshua called Rebecca, asked her to put his voice on speakerphone so she and I could hear his story together in our apartment. I don't remember what he said, but I remember his excitement. Akin to what I felt when viewing the gauzy flames on the Knitting Witch's wool bed, when reading that same scene in *Jane Eyre*, when reading Barker's description of Branwell's fire. The light, the crackle, the haze.

The next day, my mom bought Joshua a melamine ashtray, told him to smoke his Marlboros on the deck. He happily complied. "I hate it," my mom told me on the phone, "but he's got to put out those cigarette butts. Someday he'll quit smoking, and I'll get rid of that awful thing."

Like nearly every moment I know about in my brother's last few years, that fire seems to me like a beginning of the end. *Someday. For the time being.* All downhill from there. But still, I'd choose that era of Joshua's bedroom for my re-creation.

On that January night, Joshua sounded as happy as I felt in the fairy cave, happy as Charlotte in Ireland, far happier than Branwell on the grassy banks of the River Ouse. Perhaps anything felt possible that night. A career in directing, a New York apartment, a happy relationship, successful mental health treatment that he chose himself, emotions stable enough to allow him to become an old man. Sure, the fire was his fault, but he'd gotten it put out like a responsible person. He saw Christmas trees burning in the dark.

Smoo Cave

At eight o'clock in the evening Robert and I made our final turn, onto fifty-five miles of one-lane mountain road. Just after the turn, we spotted a truck tire propped upright on the grass shoulder, with *SLOW* painted in white across the top arc and *LAMBS* across the bottom. We would have driven slowly without the lamb cliques and loner lambs moseying across the asphalt like it wasn't there, in search of unbitten grass and fresh clover. Robert yelled, "It's the golden hour!" The hour of reddish-gold light just before sunset, when Oklahoma's sun-fried prairies and cows look lovely. But in the northwest corner of Scotland, that golden light set aglow lochs, limestone cliffs, spring-green treeless mountains, fuzzy lambs and full-grown meat sheep with ratty ropes of never-trimmed wool. Rain rinsed our little blue rental car, then moved away, leaving us with shimmering gray clouds in a golden-blue sky.

During our drive we'd been listening to Neil Gaiman's *Norse Mythology*, a somewhat novelistic retelling of the few remaining Norse myths. In the stories, Thor feasts on his goats, then reanimates them to pull his chariot, male Loki becomes a mare and births a foal, and a suicide by hanging turns out well. Gaiman says Odin, all-father of living beings, "sacrificed himself to himself," hanging by the neck from the world-tree. At the end of nine days, Odin knew he'd gained great wisdom. He "fell, screaming, from the tree" and walked away.

Robert chose *Norse Mythology* because we were driving into land Vikings settled. We'd be staying in Durness, which may take the second half of its name from the Old Norse place suffix *-nes*, and the name of our ultimate destination, Smoo Cave, derives from the Old Norse word *smuga*, meaning "hiding place," "narrow cleft to creep through," or, more simply, "hole." I discovered this alternative meaning for Smoo, and alternative word origin, the year after Smoo died. I was googling my brother's nickname, missing him and wondering if that name meant anything to anyone else.

As it turned out, that name means a Viking boat dock. A place of murder and trickery by Highland clans. A cave formed by both river and ocean, with a subterranean chamber no one has yet reached. A home to prehistoric cave dwellers and an ancient entrance to the underworld. I was intrigued. I wanted to visit Smoo Cave with Rebecca on that trip when we visited Haworth, but the public transportation route looked as difficult and time consuming as the tasks the Norse gods, dwarves, and giants assigned each other. Change trains and buses eight times, ride for fifteen hours, quaff the ocean from a drinking horn until you change the tides. But on this trip I had the rental car, a hefty roadmap, a great audiobook, and Robert to brave the left-side and one-lane driving. On this trip, getting to Smoo Cave felt possible. But Robert wanted to stop instead of drive.

Robert pulled over into a gravel patch signed "Passing Place" and took out his camera, laughing gleefully at the beauty. Then he got back into the car, drove to the next Passing Place and stopped and snapped again. When we came across a saltwater cove, a narrow doorway to the ocean, Robert stopped and snapped in the middle of the road. Rarely, we met a southbound car, and Robert volunteered to be the car that backed up to the previous Passing Place, letting the other driver go ahead. I was sun-dazzled too, but when I discovered we'd moved ten miles in an hour, impatience rose in my throat. There was no cell service on that road, so we couldn't call our hotel about our late arrival. I feared we'd lose our lodging, and I feared that one-lane road in the dark.

But when I was about to dampen Robert's joy with *just hurry please*, he exclaimed again. "Would you look at that sunlight! It hasn't changed a bit! This is like Alaska! We're just a few weeks past the solstice—how close are we to the Arctic Circle?"

I consulted our roadmap for latitude lines. "I'm not sure, but a lot closer than home!" We'd driven into our audiobook: "It was the summer, when the sun barely sets in the north lands, and the day lasts forever, so it was late in the night that still felt like day."

Three hours later, when we reached the smooth stucco siding of the Smoo Cave Hotel, where the owner did let us in, the golden hour had only faded to twilight. In the four years I'd wished to visit this place, I'd been spinning metaphor: Smoo Cave as hole, hiding place, underworld entrance. As the three-foot-square space under my Indiana dining room table. As my Indiana garage. As Branwell's father's bed, Mark's apartment, Joshua's closet. If I'd visited Durness in what Gaiman calls "the bitter days of midwinter, when the darkness is broken for only a handful of hours and the sun is cold and distant, like the pale eye of a corpse," maybe I could have continued associating Smoo Cave with terrible sadness. But I was there in midsummer, when the darkest hour is soft purple light.

❦

In the morning, Robert and I walked over to Smoo Cave. At the ground level of our hotel, we could stroll over the grassy top of the cave, creep to the middle of a wooden bridge and peer down through a hole in the rock. The cave's mouth is down between white limestone cliffs, accessible by a long, steep gravel trail, then a set of perpetually rain-damp concrete stairs.

I put off our descent for a few minutes, suddenly shy of the moment I'd been waiting for. I read the shellacked environmental interpretation at the top, the laminated brochures in rain-safe wooden boxes. Here again were some of the stories I'd read at home, now illustrated with maps and a photograph of a grumpy-looking badger, with text in Gaelic along with English.

One story: Donald McKay sent his dog into the cave under cover of night to see if the devil was present. The devil was there, so the dog skedaddled outside. At sunrise the man and dog still kept out of the devil's way, and the returning light took away the devil's power. "In a temper," the devil blasted through the cave roof, leaving the very hole by our feet.

Another story: Donald MacMurachie murdered nineteen people and hurled their corpses down that hole, "safe in the knowledge" that no one would check for bodies in the devil's lair. I felt my metaphors coming back as I stood on the wooden bridge, looking down through the hole, wondering if the devil was in there.

Perhaps the devil was there, perhaps he wasn't. Devil or not, I felt haunted. Reading those brochures, signs, and plaques, I felt struck again and again by my brother's nickname. "Smoo is a large sea cave," "The waterfall here at Smoo," "Smoo is part of this geopark." It felt weird to be in a place where everyone knew the word *Smoo*, and it didn't mean a particular West Virginia young man. I felt closer to Joshua than usual and more hopelessly far away.

After a few minutes we descended the stairs with a wooden handrail, directly across from a mountainside where sheep seemed to cling to a vertical face of rock. At the bottom, we walked directly into the dry, bright first chamber—a giant room, its entrance facing the North Sea—then crossed a covered wooden bridge into the smaller second chamber, lit by the devil's hole we'd peered through at the top. The second chamber holds the cave's waterfall, fed by a river called Alt Smoo, but the weather had been dry lately by Scotland's standards, and the rush had become a trickle. The dry weather was lucky for us, since the third chamber, illuminated by electric lighting, is accessible only under dry conditions, and only by a small boat. We bought tickets in the first chamber at a folding table, put on white hard hats, and boarded.

We were also lucky to board a boat piloted by Colin Coventry, a white-bearded spelunker who called himself Colin the Caveman on the cave's safety signs. Two years after our trip, he died. Colin was, he said, "obsessed with the idea" that there's a gigantic cave system under Durness, a human habitation during Neolithic times, when the water level was lower, when Scotland was dry and warm. The easy ways into further subterranean halls are now filled with water and the peat that developed four thousand years ago, after Scotland dampened and cooled. The few pounds tourists pay for summer boat trips fund winter explorations into what Colin believed, along with his colleagues, to be the difficult entrance. Wielding pickaxes and hand shovels, they tunneled through along the fault line in the first chamber, into dirt and rock.

After I settled into the boat along with Robert and the other tourists, I pointed up at the ceiling hole in the second chamber. I asked Colin, "Is that the blowhole the devil left?" I was hoping for the story with Scottish details, in a Scottish accent.

"Yes," Colin said with an air of finality, then he got right to science. The fault line, ice melt, carbonic acid in the rain. Colin was a comic: he grated together two loose pieces of chert, said, "This is how Fred and Barney made fire. Yabba dabba doo!" But on this tour, and in his cave exploration journal on the Smoo Cave website, he wasted no time on the supernatural possibilities of this cave.

Except: in the third chamber, Colin directed our steps out of the boat onto the cave floor. He pointed at a pool of water, said, "Don't fall in there, or we'll never see you again! You'll go down forever!" He'd warned us about this already. The hole of unknown depth, a likely former entrance into the undiscovered cave system. "Oh no," a woman responded, chuckling with an American accent. "I can see the ground!" But she scooted away.

Forever. I knew Colin was joking. Still, I couldn't help but think of the bridge across the Gjaller River, "across which," in Gaiman's words, "all who die must travel." Battle-dead feast and battle in Valhalla, and everyone else goes to Hel.

I'd like to punch anyone who says my brother's in hell, the Christian place of torment, which borrowed its English name from the Norse realm of the dead. I think my brother could be happy in Hel, where the dead are punished only if they were nothing like my brother: truly evil on earth. He'd hate the feats of manly courage on daily display in Valhalla, and Hel's ruler—also named Hel—has a piercing green eye and red hair on one side of her face, grayed corpse on the other. A creepy-comic-book lover's dream.

After we climbed out of the boat, we found a scraggly brown border terrier—he looked so much like Scruffy—chained to a leg of the first-chamber table. Some tourists had left him behind. The people manning the table were putting up with the dog but ignoring him, and he was wailing like the devil was in the chamber and he couldn't flee because of the chain. When I sat down next to him, he jumped up on my raincoat, begging for release. Finally he gave up, settled down on my feet for a scratch. Robert explained to a guy at the table: "She doesn't like dogs to be sad."

The next tour ended twenty minutes later, and Colin Coventry walked out for a smoke break. "You're a patient bastard, aren't ya?" he said. I scooted over so Colin could scratch him. "Hi Spot!" he said. "You're Spot, aren't ya! Poor Spot! Your owner tied you to a lamppost and left you somewhere!"

Colin left, and Robert took a turn at scratching. When the dog fell asleep, we tiptoed off like parents leaving their baby in a crib, and we watched from outside the cave until we saw his family take him: a middle-aged couple and a preteen in matching fleece.

As Robert and I walked on toward the North Sea, I smiled to myself. I'd managed to alleviate a tiny bit of the suffering in the world.

❦

The next morning, Robert and I boarded a small ferry across the Kyle of Durness, bound for the lighthouse at the northwesternmost point of mainland Scotland, Cape Wrath. Except for Robert and me, the passengers were all approaching elderly: the tourists, the ferryman, the man who jolted the minibus over the mountains to the lighthouse. Even a pair of Weimaraners were marked with the tumors and sags of canine old age. We seemed to have boarded a Scottish version of those West Virginia buses that shuttle active seniors to Amish country.

When we reached dry land, a man set off on a bicycle, a couple readied the Weimaraners for a walk, and the rest of us took the minibus up the hill. The driver told us the eleven-mile ride would take close to an hour: he drove fifteen miles per hour for his riders' safety and comfort, and, like Robert, he liked to stop for a view. A glimpse of the North Sea, so many species of gulls, clover blossoms like the ones at home.

The road felt like home too: I felt the carsickness I experienced on elementary school field trips to the Huntington Museum of Art, when I wondered if the bus would need to bend in half to navigate a pin-tight curve up the mountain. Back then, I dozed to survive the nausea, and I tried that on the minibus, wadding my raincoat as a pillow against the window. The next day, the side of my head would be bruised and tender from my skull's echo of the bumps in the road.

The mountains felt like the mountains at home because they are those mountains. During the Smoo Cave boat tour, Colin told us that fifty million years ago, Scotland broke off from North America. I know where the land fractured: Appalachia. In 2010 the very area of Scotland we were riding through was declared part of the International Appalachian Trail.

My brother was no hiker, but this land was in his blood, passed down from Scots and Scots-Irish who put down roots in Appalachia because they felt at home. When my parents mailed their saliva to Ancestry.com, they both received charts with a dotted arc labeled Central Appalachia Settlers. The line roughly traces the route eighteenth- and nineteenth-century immigrants followed from Scotland and the

Ulster region of Northern Ireland—where Scots had settled in the 1600s, displacing Irish people—finally stopping in West Virginia. A fierce, hurt, defensive pride seems to have traveled to Appalachia with those settlers, those seekers of religious freedom and enough to eat. Or maybe that attitude has developed in both places by complex historical coincidence, perhaps tied to absentee exploiters of pasture and coal or the rugged, isolating shape of the land. Whatever the reason, I felt the connection on our drive to Durness, when Robert and I stopped in a petrol station just over the Scottish border and we told the cashier we were headed for the Highlands. "Scotland's a beautiful country, people underestimate her," the man said, and in his tone I heard my own voice defending West Virginia after an American friend scoffed at Appalachian beauty in comparison to the Rockies.

After a few minutes the mountain road shook me upright, and I heard the guide telling a story. Unlike Colin Coventry, this guide was all about Scottish tall tales in a Scottish accent. He said we'd probably heard—and I had—of Bonnie Prince Charlie's flight from Scotland to France after his failed attempt in 1745 to take back his family's throne. To escape, the prince dressed for days in a woman's gown and petticoats. The guide cared nothing for historical documentation, the woman who designed and sewed the disguise, the scraps of dress fabric Bonnie Prince Charlie left behind. "It simply can't be true," he said. "No true Scotsman" would wear a woman's clothing. A true Scotsman would rather die.

I nearly chuckled—for years, I taught fallacies in first-year rhetoric and composition, and I never dreamed of hearing such a perfect "no true Scotsman" in real life. But then nausea took over. I knew it was the motion sickness, but surely it was also the deadly masculinity, exacerbated by that fierce, defensive pride. A similar toxic mix surely factored into the deaths of Joshua, Branwell, and Mark. I hoped the guide was joking, but in his tone I heard an ancient cultural attitude that made me feel like I'd slipped into the Valhalla side of the underworld.

As we approached our destination, the guide talked about Cape Wrath's use as a military training facility—more deadly masculinity—and Robert got so excited I couldn't attempt to sleep. He said, "I think my dad dropped bombs here!" He was right. Robert was born in the United States but conceived in England, when his father, a U.S. Air Force fighter pilot, was stationed in the Cotswolds. While his young wife shivered in the converted servant quarters of a seventeenth-century manor house, Robert's father flew north to Cape Wrath, practiced flying low over rough terrain, enduring G-forces, blowing things up with precision. When we exited the bus at the Cape Wrath Lighthouse, signs warned us in giant letters to keep away from unexploded shells.

The lighthouse has a café. An elderly Scotswoman sampled the wares, reported back to the group about her purchase. "The sandwich is very nice. The coffee is not nice." We decided to skip the not-nice coffee and walked over to the cliffs to watch the birds.

Cape Wrath contains the Ministry of Defence Bombardment Range and a Special Protected Birds Area. On the same piece of land. As we read on a sign, attached to a stone fence: "Whilst it may at first seem incongruous that a military firing range is such an important natural habitat, it is worth noting that the use of the land in this way preserves it in its natural state better than some types of farming, forestry and other commercial activity found in rural areas on the UK mainland."

It doesn't just "seem incongruous." It *is* incongruous to mix nest-exploding bombs with a seabird breeding area. But at Cape Wrath, the flowers and grasses grow wild, the sheep fences are crumbling into piles of rock, and the only regular disturbance is an active-senior minibus. From our overlook, Robert and I shared one pair of binoculars. Long-legged sandpipers and redshanks hunted mollusks in the sand, penguin-plumed razorbills flitted on and off their nests in the side of six-hundred-foot cliffs, and tube-nosed fulmars plunged from sky to ocean, spotting fish and shrimp beneath the waves.

❧

After the ferry trip, I took the Smoo Cave boat tour again, without Robert this time. This time, the waterfall was mighty. I remembered the cliffs along the Monongahela River in Morgantown after a heavy rain. During the boat tour, Colin pointed out the waterfall. He said, "People don't believe me when I say this place is dangerous, but now you see. The water can come in that quickly." He said it would be "much too embarrassing" if he had to be rescued with his tour boat since he's on the Scottish Cave Rescues crew. The water would continue filling the cave overnight, so he planned to cancel the tours the next day.

When I rejoined Robert after my tour, I felt both thankful and unsatisfied. Thankful because we ended up at Smoo Cave when the boat tours were open, and unsatisfied because we were leaving the next morning and I still felt no closer to my Smoo. Then I thought of that third chamber, that peaty hole of unknown depth, and I knew what I wanted to do.

The last time I swam in a cave, I was nine, on a school field trip to a park in Kentucky, and Joshua was ten months old. I thought if I paddled around in that third-chamber pool, I might trigger a visceral flash of memory. My body might remember how I felt when my brother was a bald, two-toothed baby with a guttural giggle, who crawled to me across the living room floor.

I was pretty sure I knew what Colin would have thought about me taking a night plunge into that pool, about me climbing over the safety rails, stepping through the second chamber's tied-off boat, swimming past the waterfall and on into the third chamber's depth-dark water. But after the tours closed for the day, there would be no one in the cave to warn me against it. I knew Robert would walk in as far as he could and follow me with his pocket flashlight, even jump in and try to save me if I sputtered or disappeared, but he wasn't the sort of boyfriend to tell me no.

After dinner I used the hotel Wi-Fi and found that pool on wild swimming message boards. One guy took a dip on a summer night, lived to proudly ill-spell the tale. Another guy said he'd thought about rappelling down through the devil's blowhole, but decided against it. He'd found too many stories of drownings in Smoo Cave. I dug deeper online, but the only drowning stories I could find were the centuries-old yarns on the shellacked signs. Under the tale of the dog and the devil, the sign tells of eighteenth-century murder, concealing the local killers with passive voice. "Excise Officers tried to find an illegal still in the chamber, but the boat they were being taken in was deliberately rowed beneath the waterfall and the two men drowned."

My main takeaways from this story: the cave is particularly dangerous when the waterfall is flowing, and people who are new to the cave are far more likely to die than people who are at home here. The waterfall was truly impressive during that day's boat tour: enough water to drown a battalion of excise men. I wasn't sure what that extra water meant for the third-chamber pool, but I decided not to swim. My life meant too much to my sisters, to my parents, to my friends, to my dog and cat, to Robert. I still missed my brother horribly, but I realized I no longer had any desire to join him. My life meant too much to myself.

I was moping around outside the cave in the golden evening when I noticed something: words spelled in limestone on the sheep-covered, grassy cliff face, directly across from the concrete stairs into the cove. Rock graffiti. *Jack. Lex + Max. Sorry, Amy.* I'd ignored the words for days, but they were calling me now. I turned to Robert. "Will you help me write something?" He started ahead of me on the gravel track up that mountain, looking for suitable rocks.

At the top, we found the best rocks had been piled into cairns, an ancient practice with a name borrowed whole from Scottish Gaelic. I wondered if any of the rock piles were built to honor a dead child, mother, friend, romantic partner, or brother, or if they just meant *I was here.* One shorter stack of rocks looked suspiciously like a cairn someone had robbed for letters, but we wouldn't finish the destruction. "Let's fix that cairn for my Smoo!" I said, and we tried, creeping behind the sheep on the mountain, picking up the few remaining limestone chunks, but we quickly realized the task was beyond us, given our limited time. We went back to the letters idea, tried *Sarbef* + *Smoo*. When we struggled to find rocks, and the golden hour faded, we decided to leave my name off the mountain. "Just the cave's name," Robert said. "Maybe it will stay a long time."

He meant: perhaps no one will erase the word, repurpose the rocks for their own letters, a limestone version of children's alphabet blocks. Now that we stood among the words, each one surrounded by half-formed letters, we realized that's what everyone does. This hill likely ran out of unused loose limestone long ago.

We wouldn't disturb the cairns, but we decided to continue the letter repurposing tradition. We left *Sorry, Amy* intact—perhaps someone was still pleading for Amy's forgiveness—but we took apart *Lex* + *Jack*. They'd had their chance to declare their love to the cove.

We started out forming the letters thin but large, two rocks wide, then we added layers, robbing more names around us. Soon—or hours later; as we piled rocks, time seemed to slow with the sun—*Smoo* was the biggest, boldest rock word on the cliff. Finally, Robert squeezed my hand, and we walked back to the hotel in the midnight twilight.

❦

On our final morning in Durness, Robert and I rose early, hoping to see our handiwork by the light of the sunrise. But we walked out of the hotel into pouring rain. Still, *Smoo* gleamed at us as we stood on the cave roof, next to the devil's blowhole, peering down at the cove. "Look!" Robert yelled, laughing. "Look what someone has done in the night!"

"Those silly people," I said. "Couldn't think of anything. Just wrote the name of the cave." We walked on, admired our work from all angles. From the concrete stairs. From the shelter of the cave's first chamber. From the place where pebbles melt into sea.

I felt like I wanted to stay forever at Smoo Cave, hearing the rain-fed rush of the Alt Smoo, looking up at my brother's name. But we had to head back. We had plane tickets purchased, an expensive rental car to return. We had a long day's drive ahead of us, beginning with fifty-five miles of one-lane road.

Robert walked back up the rain-slippery steps, reached for my hand, but I hesitated. I saw something beside him on the concrete. I saw *someone*, and Robert was bending down, helping her up the stairs. Surely it was my imagination, or a waking dream, though after our trip, when I told my mother, she was certain it was a holy vision. A glimpse of a far-off place or future time, granted to prophets, apostles, and ordinary people in the Bible. All I know is that somehow, on those stairs, I saw the back of a toddler girl with hair I'd heard about in our audiobook. Living, growing curls a god tasked a dwarf to spin from gold to cure a goddess's baldness. The curls my brother had as a tiny boy. It was still raining, but I saw her hair in sunlight.

After a moment, the girl and her curls disappeared. I followed her and Robert into the rest of my life.

For Joshua's obituary, my mother chose a photo I came to consider the visual representation of my found brother. A photo fit to illustrate an obituary that began "Joshua David Childers, 22, went to be with his Lord Jesus Christ." An accidental photo of found Joshua's ghost, captured three years before my brother's suicide.

The obituary photo was from Joshua's senior picture shoot at a professional studio. He wears maroon plaid in front of a beige pull-down background. He sports a fresh, nearly Baptist haircut. He's taken off his hipster glasses, and the photo's focal point is his pair of striking green eyes.

Those eyes are earnest. The eyes of a proud high school graduate and a happy, thankful son. The photo captured my living brother's often-sweet humor, but it missed his mean sarcasm, his unlaundered laziness, his frequent weariness over taking his next breath. It shows a young man who might soon work fifty-hour weeks, marry a woman with a Bible in a quilted cover, drive his children to church in a beat-up minivan. Who might even become an evangelist.

I hated that obituary photo, but I let it go, just indulged in a little Prodigal's oldest sibling seething. I conceded that it's a mother's right—especially a mother as present and caring as Joshua's and mine—to pick the obituary photo for her child.

A photo of my real end-of-life brother would have been no improvement, with sunken cheeks and pig-slop-sad eyes. Such a photo would have newspaper-published the moment before the Prodigal came to himself. Before he decided to use his closet to go home.

Choosing that photo, my mom acted on the same principle she'd used when choosing the photo for her mother's obituary: gorgeous in her twenties in her nursing cap, before her cheeks were ravaged by age and cigarettes. And her father's: taken in his fifties for a church directory, before heart disease shrank him to bones. She wanted a photo of Joshua healthier, younger. When he might live until lung cancer took him. When his cheeks still held a bit of baby fat and fluffy hair still covered his forehead.

A few months after Joshua died, I walked the steep Morgantown streets to the university library, hefted home Charlotte Brontë's collected letters, seeking the company of a fellow grieving older sister. I remembered the Branwell-Joshua connection I'd felt during my visit to the Parsonage Museum at twenty-eight, and Charlotte's love of the Pennines I'd sensed as I walked her moors, so similar to my love of West Virginia.

When I found that October 2, 1848, letter to W. S. Williams–"My Son! My Son!"–I felt angry at Charlotte. I hated that implied comparison to treacherous Absalom. I called her a liar when I read another sentence in that letter, self-consciously beautiful in its coldness: "I do not weep from a sense of bereavement–there is no prop withdrawn, no consolation torn away, no dear companion lost–but for the wreck of talent, the ruin of promise, the untimely, dreary extinction of what might have been a burning and a shining light."

I still carried that week of funeral planning in my bones, and I sneered at Charlotte's admission that she'd collapsed in her bed after Branwell's death, leaving the grief-labor to her sisters. I wondered if she might have found the strength I'd managed if she'd been born first like me, a *real* oldest sibling. If brilliant Maria and steady Elizabeth had never lived, only to die as children from an illness they caught at school. But now, the Prodigal's angry older brother reminds me that we oldest-born siblings shouldn't think so well of ourselves.

Charlotte claimed she didn't miss Branwell. Maybe she didn't. Maybe her love for her difficult brother died more completely than mine. But if I'm brutally honest with myself, that claim that she didn't miss Branwell, and even her weariness at her brother's continued moaning, drunken failure of a life, doesn't mean I didn't see myself in her letters. On the morning of August 30, when Joshua still dangled undiscovered from his closet bar, I allowed myself this brief thought: *My life would be so much easier if my brother died.*

If my brother died, I could drive to my parents' house and have a predictably good or okay time, beset only by normal family complications. I could take a road trip with my siblings. I could have a relationship where my boyfriend or husband wouldn't worry about my safety on my visits home. I could go to sleep without fearing that Joshua would call Rebecca and sob over the phone that he'd gotten angry and accidentally killed our parents. I could go to sleep without fearing I'd wake up in the morning to learn my brother was dead.

While Joshua lived, I'd framed old photographs of him in childhood: four children on a red backyard swing, pool-wet hair soaking white terrycloth robes. I'd memorialized that already-broken happy foursome on the walls of my Morgantown apartment. I'd already grieved so hard I was shocked when my spirit collapsed on that sunny August afternoon.

If my parents' method of grieving my brother's suicide caused me to re-lose my brother–something I no longer believe–I lost him not for a second time but a third.

Charlotte wrote in that October 2 letter to Williams of her "long ago" grief: "I had aspirations and ambitions for him once–long ago–they have perished mournfully–nothing remains of him but a memory of errors and sufferings."

If it had been my choice–and if obituary readers wouldn't have gasped at the tragedy of a dead child, then scoffed at his adulthood–I would have chosen the photo of six-year-old Joshua, runny-nosed in his winter coat. Or one-year-old Joshua in a diaper and white undershirt, his head poking out of the clothes dryer. The brother I could most easily grieve. The brother I wanted most to remember.

It's taken me years, but I've entered my parents' grieving party. I've realized my parents and I were doing the same thing, with my childhood photographs, that "Good job, Mama," that Marijohn Wilkin album, and my dad's "Amazing Grace" tapestry. We erased the Joshua who had experienced and caused us all so much stress and pain and remade the Joshua who waited for us in heaven.

When Joshua died, I lost the emotionally closed-off, sometimes violent, twenty-two-years-two-months-two-weeks-old brother I knew, and I felt the loss again of the brother I'd adored as a child. But as I grieve more thoughtfully, after years of healing, I've found I can choose what memories I miss. That I can disconnect the trauma I carry from my brother and hold fast to my beloved Smoo.

I have returned.

Joshua is gone forever, and I have him back.

Notes

In "Smoo: An *Oxford English Dictionary* Definition," I borrowed exact phrasing from the *OED* entry "small" ("Of limited size; of comparatively restricted dimensions; not large in comparison with other things"). I also borrowed exact phrasing ("a narrow cleft to creep through" and "a hole") from the entry "smuga" in *An Icelandic-English Dictionary* by Richard Cleasby and Gudbrand Vigfusson, published in 1874 and accessed at cleasby-vigfusson-dictionary.vercel.app/word/smuga. I used the same language from *An Icelandic-English Dictionary* in the essay "Smoo Cave." "Hiding place," the alternative meaning of "smuga" that I included in both essays, came from the entry "Smoo Cave" on the website *Undiscovered Scotland*, accessed at www.undiscoveredscotland.co.uk/durness/smoocave/index.html.

In "Moonstruck" I used Emma Gurney Salter's English translation of the original Latin text, St. Bonaventure's *Vita Beati Francisci*, published as *The Life of Saint Francis of Assisi* (New York: E. P. Dutton, 1904) and accessed at www.ecatholic2000.com/bonaventure/assisi/francis.shtml.

In "Mansions" I used Margaret Smith's translation of Charlotte's letter to Constantin Héger dated 8 January 1845, from *The Letters of Charlotte Bronte*, edited by Margaret Smith, 3 vols. (Oxford: Oxford University Press, 1995–2004). Excerpts from Charlotte Brontë's letters come from these volumes. Excerpts from letters written by Branwell Brontë and Elizabeth Gaskell come from Juliet Barker's *The Brontës*, rev. ed. (New York: Pegasus, 2012).

Crux, the Georgia Series in Literary Nonfiction

Debra Monroe, *My Unsentimental Education*
Sonja Livingston, *Ladies Night at the Dreamland*
Jericho Parms, *Lost Wax: Essays*
Priscilla Long, *Fire and Stone: Where Do We Come From? What Are We? Where Are We Going?*
Sarah Gorham, *Alpine Apprentice*
Tracy Daugherty, *Let Us Build Us a City*
Brian Doyle, *Hoop: A Basketball Life in Ninety-Five Essays*
Michael Martone, *Brooding: Arias, Choruses, Lullabies, Follies, Dirges, and a Duet*
Andrew Menard, *Learning from Thoreau*
Dustin Parsons, *Exploded View: Essays on Fatherhood, with Diagrams*
Clinton Crockett Peters, *Pandora's Garden: Kudzu, Cockroaches, and Other Misfits of Ecology*
André Joseph Gallant, *A High Low Tide: The Revival of a Southern Oyster*
Justin Gardiner, *Beneath the Shadow: Legacy and Longing in the Antarctic*
Emily Arnason Casey, *Made Holy: Essays*
Sejal Shah, *This Is One Way to Dance: Essays*
Lee Gutkind, *My Last Eight Thousand Days: An American Male in His Seventies*
Cecile Pineda, *Entry without Inspection: A Writer's Life in El Norte*
Anjali Enjeti, *Southbound: Essays on Identity, Inheritance, and Social Change*

Clinton Crockett Peters, *Mountain Madness: Found and Lost in the Peaks of America and Japan*
Steve Majors, *High Yella: A Modern Family Memoir*
Julia Ridley Smith, *The Sum of Trifles*
Siân Griffiths, *The Sum of Her Parts: Essays*
Ned Stuckey-French, *One by One, the Stars: Essays*
John Griswold, *The Age of Clear Profit: Collected Essays on Home and the Narrow Road*
Joseph Geha, *Kitchen Arabic: How My Family Came to America and the Recipes We Brought with Us*
Lawrence Lenhart, *Backvalley Ferrets: A Rewilding of the Colorado Plateau*
Sarah Beth Childers, *Prodigals: A Sister's Memoir of Appalachia and Loss*